EARLY DAYS IN THE RANGE OF LIGHT

ENCOUNTERS WITH LEGENDARY MOUNTAINEERS

DANIEL ARNOLD

COUNTERPOINT
BERKELEY

All photographs are by Daniel Arnold unless otherwise noted.

The following photographs are used courtesy of The Bancroft Library, University of California, Berkeley: Page 29, Brewer, William—POR 1; Page 191, LeConte, William—POR 21; Page 264, "F.P.F. on Mount Haeckel," Photo 33, BANC PIC 1994.039—ALB v.9; Page 348, Clyde, Norman—POR 2.

Library of Congress Cataloging-in-Publication Data

Arnold, Daniel.
  Early days in the range of light : encounters with legendary mountaineers / Daniel Arnold.
      p. cm.
  Includes bibliographical references.
  ISBN 978-1-58243-519-0
  1. Mountaineers—Sierra Nevada (Calif. and Nev.)—Biography. 2. Mountaineering—Sierra Nevada (Calif. and Nev.)—History. I. Title.

  GV199.9.A76 2009
  796.522092—dc22
  [B]

                              2009024438

ISBN 978-1-58243-519-0

Cover design by David Bullen Design
Interior design by Megan Jones Design
Map by Kat Smith
Printed in the United States of America

COUNTERPOINT
2117 Fourth Street
Suite D
Berkeley, CA 94710

www.counterpointpress.com

Distributed by Publishers Group West

10 9 8 7 6 5 4 3 2 1

To Ashley

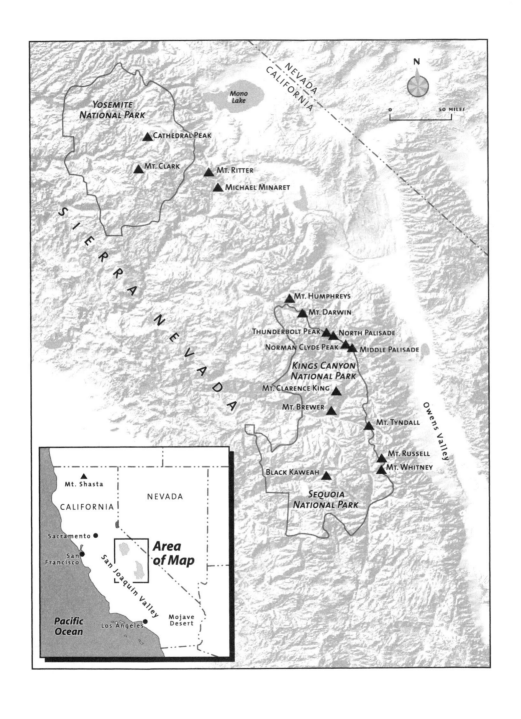

CONTENTS

LIST OF PHOTOGRAPHS

"The Range of Light"

I N THE SUMMER of 1931, a handful of the strongest and most experienced mountaineers in California gathered at Garnet Lake, near Mount Ritter, a place where deep blue pools reflect the splintered outlines of craggy black peaks. They had come to explore and climb the mountains of the Ritter Range, and to learn something new about the calling they shared.

The Californians had a visitor from the East, and it was his presence, and the knowledge he brought with him, that distinguished the occasion. Robert Underhill, a professor at Harvard and a member of the Harvard Mountaineering Club, had been invited by one of the Californians, Francis Farquhar. The two men had met the previous summer on an expedition to the Canadian Rockies during which Underhill taught Farquhar rope techniques that had not yet spread to the western half of North America.

Climbers in the Sierra Nevada had occasionally used ropes, but only to lasso projecting horns of rock, or for a follower to use as a hand-line through a difficult spot. At the Underhill Camp, as it has since been called, they learned how to tie themselves into the rope and to catch a falling climber. Before, a fall on a serious route could only end in catastrophe. Now, so long as the rope held, a falling climber had a second chance.

The Underhill Camp brought California into the modern age of climbing. Even today with vastly improved equipment, the rope systems employed by climbers from Joshua Tree to Yosemite to Castle Crags can all be traced back to the basic methods taught at Garnet Lake in the summer of 1931.

But the camp also ended a grand, too-often forgotten chapter of the mountaineering story. Men and women had been climbing the peaks of the Sierra Nevada for nearly seventy years before Underhill set foot in California. This early lot of mountaineers had no ropes or pitons or special training. They had only their fingers, their boots, and an immoderate excess of boldness. What climbers now call free-soloing was simply standard practice then. They traveled the high places without the physical and psychological armor which we now haul into the backcountry to shield ourselves from the elements and from the mountains' hard indifference to our soft bodies.

Seventy years saw many faces come and go in the high peaks: geologists, artists, historians, conservationists. Some took jobs simply to be close to the mountains: a coolheaded postman stationed in Yosemite, the cantankerous principal of the Independence High School. A few of the early mountaineers, like John Muir and Clarence King, have become part of the mythic West. Others, like Norman Clyde, are prominent only within the realm of climbing history, while the adventures of Charles Michael and James Hutchinson have been largely forgotten even by climbers.

These early climbers and their stories work a kind of gravitational magic on me, pulling me into their world. It is the directness of their approach to the mountains that I find so appealing. Lacking outdoor schools and climbing walls, no one taught Muir or Michael the "right" way to climb. They learned their lessons straight from the mountains; from the rocks, glaciers, and storms. Since they had no equipment they paid more attention to the world around them than to the objects they carried. Muir often traveled alone through the Sierra with little more than a notebook, a knife, and a pocketful of bread crusts. On their honeymoon in 1896, Bolton and Lucy Brown hiked across the width of the Sierra to climb a new route on Mount Williamson, and Bolton estimated that with their provisions for four days, his pack weighed twelve pounds and Lucy's weighed three. The "fast-and-light" mentality sweeping through today's outdoors community would be entirely familiar to the first generation of mountaineers.

Innovations in climbing gear beginning with Underhill's ropes and mutating toward the nylon and aluminum barrage of the modern gear store have allowed climbers, including myself, to visit some of the most dramatic places on earth. I have loved being high up El Capitan and Half Dome, looking wide-eyed across Yosemite; there is nothing equal to the sensation of being a microbe riding a granite wave. But I do not love the equipment that takes me there. Staring at a mess of carabiners, cams, and pitons makes me feel like a technician in a laboratory; spending days in a harness gives me the feeling of being leashed.

Over the past decade I have traveled slowly back in time. I spend more and more of each summer wandering the mountains and less time dangling from ropes. And I spend my city time in libraries reading the accounts of the early days on the thick pages of old copies of the *Sierra Club Bulletin,* and on the sheets and scraps of journals and letters. The stories I have encountered are gripping for their moments of physical courage and their stunning descriptions of the Sierra landscape. Probably the greatest pleasure for me has been to learn the ancestors' reasons for venturing into the mountains in the first place. From Brown's pursuit of the untainted wilds of his boyhood fantasies to Muir's search for a new God to replace his father's, they struggled to explain the impulses that drove them to high summits, to answer that unanswerable *Why?* that follows mountaineers up every climb.

Somewhere along the way, I decided to tell the history of this time, and it seemed most appropriate to tell it through the individual stories of mountains and mountaineers. I began to assemble a list of peaks that best represented the spirit of the era. All would have to be high and visually striking—peaks climbers would lose sleep over in the nights before an attempt and look back on afterward with pride. There could be no easy route to their summits. Many peaks in the Sierra have steep, dramatic faces on one side, but easy hiking on another. The peaks I chose are climbers' mountains, accessible only via difficult terrain from all directions.

With a list of peaks in hand, I returned to the libraries. I wanted the most adventurous climbs made by the most headstrong climbers, so I read the report of each mountain's first ascent. The best of these episodes is what you will find here: fifteen of the most difficult and notable routes along with the stories of the men who climbed them. The climbs cover the Sierra from north to south and from 1864 to 1931. Because the peaks were all difficult and coveted, the first climbers to reach their summits tended to be the most active and accomplished mountaineers of the era.

The library was my winter refuge, when snow ruled the high country and the days held more dark than light. For the past four years, in the summers, I have followed the climbing ancestors, physically retracing their routes up the mountains. I realized that in order to tell their stories, I had to climb the way they did, so I left my modern climbing paraphernalia at home. When I climbed their routes I carried no ropes, no harness, no climbing shoes. When the footsteps I followed were lightest, as with Muir, I left my sleeping bag and backpack behind, too, and spent days living out of a small canvas sack slung over my shoulder. With the nylon and aluminum advantages removed, the playing field tilted back in the mountains' favor, and several of these climbs tested both my ability and good sense.

The mountains have not changed nearly as much as we have. Flashing digits may hurry us along, but the rocks and high meadows remain apart above the bustle. The asphalt noose around the mountains has tightened, the surrounding valleys have been mined, graded, and drained, but across the pavement threshold lies a country that is quiet and still. Time does not move the same way in the mountains as in the cities. Here, a corrective step of a hundred years can be taken simply by leaving behind our encumbering gadgetry. These peaks do not seem to age.

Of course, it is the place as much as the time that is magical. There is no other mountain range on earth quite like the Sierra. The cycle of long summer days and starry nights is hypnotic. The mountains rise sheer and strong above stone-bound lakes and carpets of green, a contrast of defiance and comfort that seems lifted from a dream. With the sweet gurgle of a trout stream filling the ear and a soft meadow to rest in, thoughts that this may well be the mountaineer's heaven are inevitable.

Muir thought the Sierra Nevada—literally the Snowy Mountain Range—was poorly named. Snow may dominate the winter, but not the summer, after the spring melt reveals the granite, and sunlight sparkles again on white crystalline stone flecked with glittering blacks, greens, and reds. Every morning the alpenglow lights the eastern faces, and in the evenings his rosy sister plays her nightly farewell. So Muir proposed to call his mountains "The Range of Light," and no better name has yet been suggested.

· 1 ·

William Brewer + Mount Brewer

[JULY 1864]

Mount Brewer (13,570 feet) from Big Brewer Lake

AT THE HEAD of the canyon stood the mountain, an immense pyramid of gray and white granite studded with spires and pleated with sharp ridges. It filled the eastern sky, claiming a tremendous slice of the horizon for itself while seeming almost to shove the neighboring peaks and precipices to the side. The mountain had no name yet. Few of the hundreds of peaks in the Sierra Nevada did in 1864. But as far as William Brewer could tell, it was one of the highest—maybe *the* highest—peak in the entire range. Brewer hoped so. From the top of the Sierra he would be able to see the whole granite backbone of California. Brewer was no fan of vanity or self-indulgence, but to be the first man to stand on that summit and soak in the view would be a pleasure he had earned and would enjoy in his own quiet way.

Down on the canyon floor, miles from the mountain, creeks filled a funnel-shaped hollow with cold water, and Brewer, with his small team of scientists, made a camp there among thin pines and boulders above the lakeside. It was the first of July, still early summer in the Sierra. At ten thousand feet above sea level, the days were crisp and the nights chilling. The ground tilted so steeply downward that the creeks jumped and skipped over drops and fallen logs. The glacier responsible for carving this canyon had deeply trenched the bedrock and the scale overwhelmed the men. Cliffs, fifteen hundred feet high in places and sheer from bottom to top, lined both walls in a procession of stone faces rising up toward the mountain, while piles of rectangular boulders, levered off by frost-thrust and gravity, buried their lower buttresses. The amount of this loose debris alone was an eerie sight. Tossed onto just one of those talus fields, our greatest works—say, the Acropolis or Coliseum—could be lost amid the fragments produced during the sculpting of the canyon walls.

Brewer had been mapping and studying the geology of California since the autumn of 1860. His route crisscrossed the state, from coast to foothills, from the uncertain border with Mexico to the snows of Mount Shasta. In all he had traveled nearly fourteen thousand miles, covering half that distance on horseback and another three thousand miles on foot. As he pointed out in his letters home, the distance laid out straight would have taken him halfway around the world. Along the way he crawled through mines, collected flora, followed rivers, imagined ancient glaciers, and spoke to everyone he met: rancheros, gamblers, sawyers, migratory herdsmen (and women), politicians, prospectors, lunatics, and confidence men. The characters that wander through the pages of his notes fix names and faces to the human migration within California, the hustle of pathological optimists driven by big dreams and bigger disappointments.

Four years later, there was only one part of the state Brewer had not visited: the wall of mountains dividing the eastern deserts from the western valleys, the same barrier that forced overland pioneers from the East to choose between the Mojave Desert to the south and the Tahoe snows to the north. No wagon roads ever cut through this wilderness of peaks; even today no pavement makes the crossing and foot travel remains the only way to pass over the southern Sierra. In Brewer's time, the existence of a few Indian trails was known, but most of these paths could be followed only by rumor and guesswork when viewed through the eyes of white men. So, early in the summer of 1864, when Brewer and his fellows pushed past the foothills and up toward the deepest part of California's unexplored mountains, they traveled without maps or waymarks through a wilderness beyond the grasp, thus far, of even the most ambitious settlers, lumberjacks, and sheepmen.

The men had no tents or even sleeping mats. At night they rolled themselves into blankets atop piles of pine needles. Trees offered some protection from weather, but when it stormed or snowed they simply got wet. Brewer described the sensation: "You cannot imagine how cheerless and uncomfortable it is to lie out in the rain—how one looks up at the black sky, lets the rain patter on his face, saturate his hair and beard, as he thinks of home and its cheerful fireside and luxurious comforts." By the time they reached the lake they had all but exhausted their provisions obtained in Visalia, a foothill township they had passed through at the beginning of June, and so they ate venison three meals a day, supplemented at times by bear and once by owl (which Brewer found disagreeably "mousy"). With the daytime devoted to roaming the mountains and the nights spent fighting off subfreezing temperatures, they all acquired immense appetites and ate prodigious quantities of meat.

Besides Brewer there were four other men at camp. Clarence King and James Gardiner were ambitious young men fresh from college who had been in the state for less than a year. Charles Hoffman, a German-born surveyor and mapmaker, joined Brewer during the summer of 1861. He has been called the "progenitor of modern American topography," a stodgy-sounding honor that does little to capture the man who took so much pleasure from a song and the occasional keg of beer that the men shared when encamped closer to civilization. He and Brewer developed a close friendship during their time together in California. Dick Cotter came along as a mule packer; "a very good fellow," wrote Brewer, who "most unfortunately knows nothing about packing, so we have to learn him and I think that he will do well." Cotter turned out to be strong, tough, and capable of managing not only the animals but many other handyman tasks that helped keep the expedition pressing forward. Each man had a horse or mule and they had two additional pack animals for their scientific equipment and other supplies.

I joined their little camp, too, as best I could with 143 years between us. Those mountain pines grow slowly and live long; the big Jeffrey pine with the ruddy bark and widespread branches under which I put my blanket could well have sheltered one of Brewer's men, too. As afternoon introduced evening, gray clouds piled up in my sky and the gaps between the branches of my tree seemed to grow in proportion to the blackness above. Faithful to my purpose, I had left every scrap of water-repellent nylon and Gore-Tex behind, and I felt uncomfortably naked and exposed under that heavy sky. If it stormed I would have no tent to hide under or jacket to zip; I would simply have to lie there and do my best to channel Brewer's stoicism. I rummaged through my brain for practical advice, but all I could find was Brewer's lament of his soggy beard, so I readied myself to stare upward, let the rain soak me, and think of home.

And yet, from under a blanket there is a prickly kind of pleasure in the anticipation of an oncoming mountain storm. Our ancestors made gods out of wind and lightning for a reason: the power in those forces is awesome to behold. The only difference now is that we rarely expose ourselves to the weather. We're urged not to, as if our bodies were too soft and weak to endure the experience. Well-meaning protectors tell us these sorts of things. *Find shelter! Seek cover!* But it's hard not to stay and look when the clouds start to rub up against the mountains and the whole sky begins to crackle. Brewer may have dreamed of the fireside, but he never turned away from the mountain.

With a tent, those evening thunderheads would have been an annoyance, a reason to retreat under the rain-fly and read a book. Without the tent, those same clouds reclaimed their natural stature as elemental powers. Met forthrightly, a good storm wakes my insides and reminds me that, just like the bears and marmots, I am built for this place, built to survive and enjoy these rumbling demonstrations. The equipment and machinery we use to make travel in the wilderness more comfortable cannot help but blunt the experience. The loss is our own. At worst, we grow forgetful that the same basic potency that animates the storm animates ourselves.

On the second of July 1864, as dawn backlit the mountain and turned the sky above the canyon depths a shade of blue barely distinguishable from black, Brewer and Hoffman unwound themselves from their blankets and ate a hasty breakfast. Brewer stood on long legs, which provided him a lengthy stride; he had a long neck and face, and a dark, square beard. Hoffman was built more compactly and watched the world through penetrating eyes set in a handsome, hawkish face overrun by his own beard and flowing moustache. They set out for the mountain before the other men stirred, before that blue part of morning had even begun to retake the pines. Both wore hobnailed boots. They carried a barometer and a theodolite, the first for measurements of elevation based on air pressure, the second to measure horizontal and vertical angles between their position and the other summits of the range. These were the basic tools of the survey.

The closer their steps brought the mountain, the grander it became, swelling up and out. The canyon turned into a great stone box with no soil to soften its floor. Small hanging gardens of grasses and wildflowers still trimmed the edges of creeks, while a few remaining trees, mostly foxtail pines with thick, spiraled trunks and bluntly tapered crowns, put their roots directly down into cracks riven through the rock. The two men zigzagged steeply up through piles of raw, black-speckled boulders scattered atop old flagstones of granite left glassy by the passage of glaciers and streams. Their boot nails jangled on the stones.

The air thinned as Brewer and Hoffman climbed up out of the canyon by way of a talus field at its head. Here they entered a vast cirque made all of talus with a string of blue-black lakes in the crease at its bottom. Behind them, the canyon cut a straight furrow for miles down toward the lake camp and their companions. Above, the mountain's southern shoulder led up through a chaotic jumble of stone to the summit, a distant pinnacle pressing into the sky. And beyond the mountain? They didn't rightly know. Desert, presumably. Yes, probably they would look down into the arid Owens Valley and then out over the deserts of the Nevada Territory, with the other Sierra mountains trailing off to the north and south. But they couldn't know for sure with three-quarters of the outlook blocked and the steepest stretch of rock yet before them.

How tantalizing to be so close to that vista and still hemmed in! For days they had been confined in the canyons, able to see only the one mountain and a few of its satellites. Now, soon, above this last precarious granite stairway, the entire range might be visible below them. All of their questions would be answered then: the sources of the Kings, Kern, and Kaweah rivers located, likely routes to the east mapped, the peaks numbered, their heights measured. With their own eyes they would assemble and interpret the last broad blank spot in California.

Best of all would be the freedom gained on the summit, which the mountains gift to climbers simply for taking the last step: an unlimited horizon without the barriers and confines of the lowland world.

◆ ◆ ◆

spring flood." The river did not suffer alone; asylums had to be opened for sick and lunatic miners destroyed by their own work.

When Brewer arrived in 1860, California was already changing again. The days of plopping down next to an unnamed creek and pulling fifty dollars of gold out of a single pan had passed. Industrial sites with ore stamps and other heavy machinery replaced the romantic ideal of the lone miner with a pickaxe and a burro. Land speculation and mining scams ran wild as latecomers and residents alike tried to recapture the boom years. The history of the state, or lack thereof, added to the confusion; the political paroxysms which brought California into being happened so rapidly that the state lines had never been surveyed and existed only as numbers in California's constitution. No one, from the poorest hardscrabble miner to Governor John G. Downey himself, had any real idea what the state contained, either geographically or mineralogically.

The solution, a geological survey to assess California's holdings of natural resources while mapping the state, prompted a squabble within the young state government. Many elected officials, including the governor, had mining interests of their own at stake and wanted the survey conducted by associates who could skew results in their favor, provide inside information, and generally be kept under control. Another party, led by Stephen Field, a justice of the Supreme Court, saw the wisdom of an impartial, scientific survey. For once, the champions of science prevailed. On April 21, 1860, Downey signed into law an act which named Josiah Dwight Whitney state geologist and directed him, "With the aid of such assistants as he may appoint, to complete the geological survey of this State, and prepare a report of said survey for publication . . . Such report shall be in the form of a geological, botanical, and zoological history of the state." In a concession to the mercenary interests, a subclause instructed the state geologist (and his assistants) to employ any spare time they had in examinations of gold, silver, and copper deposits.

Whitney, a Yale graduate, had already conducted surveys in New Hampshire, Iowa, and Wisconsin, and was well regarded by the growing community of natural scientists in the East. His smooth, high forehead looked uncannily like one of the Sierra's granite domes that he spent so much time studying, and he wore a well-kept but expansive mane of silver-grizzled beard. Unfortunately for his legacy, he is probably best remembered now for having called John Muir an "ignoramus" and "mere shepherd," and for vigorously defending his own contrary (and mistaken) theory of cataclysmic formation for the Yosemite Valley. Dogmatism was Whitney's weakness as a scientist, but his strength was an unshakeable belief in the value and sanctity of pure research. If any of the legislators held lingering hopes that he would run around the countryside looking for new goldfields in order to make them all rich, Whitney was to be a considerable disappointment.

While the politicians in California wrangled over the shape of their survey, Brewer was in the middle of a teaching semester at Washington College in Pennsylvania. It was his second year in a chemistry professorship, as well as the second year of his marriage. His wife was pregnant. That summer she died from complications of childbirth, and their newborn son lasted only a few weeks. Suddenly and painfully alone, Brewer received a letter from J. D. Whitney asking him to be the field director for a survey of the state of California. A wilderness land on the other side of the continent must have seemed a far better place to heal than an empty household filled with ghosts and bittersweet memories. It hardly mattered that Whitney wanted him to leave in just a few months and be gone for an unknown duration.

In his letters from California to his brother, Brewer does not mention his wife and child by name, but they often hover just off the page. On a night near Santa Barbara in March of 1861, he spent the midnight hours in a heavy coastal rain guarding against horse thieves and wrote, "Watching such nights is by no means poetical, and it woke musings and memories of a very different fireside but a short year ago."

From New York, Brewer traveled by steamship to Panama, a colorful land to his New England eye, full of heat and moisture and riotous plants; then by rail across the Isthmus; and finally up the Pacific Coast on another steamer to the San Francisco Bay. In all, the trip took three and a half weeks. This was the standard route for passengers with means in those years before the completion of the transcontinental railroad, the only other option being a fifteen-hundred-mile overland journey by horse or wagon from the end of the tracks in Missouri. Brewer arrived in San Francisco on Wednesday, November 14, 1860. The good news—the election of President Lincoln—had arrived hours before, sent first by telegraph and then by the Pony Express, and Brewer called this eight-day transmission "an unprecedented quick trip of news."

Ten days of chaotic preparations followed Brewer's arrival. Equipment and supplies for the field party had to be purchased and checked over; they laid in stores of certain eatables and tea and coffee, as well as blankets and saddles and other riding tack. Meanwhile, the newspapers celebrated the scientists and their mission, sharing in the politicians' optimism that the work would refuel California's economy; as a result many prominent locals wanted to speak with them before they left. Governor Downey and Justice Field both swooped down on San Francisco from the capitol in Sacramento in order to meet with Whitney and Brewer, and, no doubt, to keep an eye on each other in the process. During

Brewer's work in California, Downey often pressured him directly for help with a variety of mining speculations. Brewer blamed the survey's future funding difficulties on the governor's irritation at his and Whitney's repeated refusals. He often worried that the survey would be shut down completely for this reason.

The real work began in the hills and low mountains outside of Los Angeles, which Brewer described as "a city of some 3,500 or 4,000 inhabitants, nearly a century old, a regular old Spanish-Mexican town." The houses there were "but one story, mostly built of adobe or sun-burnt brick, with very thick walls and flat roofs," constructed so low "because of earthquakes." They spent little time in the city itself, passing through only to resupply between excursions to the surrounding farms and up into the stony hills and canyons. Brewer concluded that the only thing preventing the area from being "a paradise" was the need for "*water*, more *water*."

Prominences were important from the beginning. Few accurate maps of any scale existed in California, so much of the survey's time had to be devoted to mapmaking, and mapmaking required the kind of unobstructed view that hilltops provided. None of the heights around the Los Angeles area were anything like the mountains he would find in the Sierra—they lacked both elevation and steepness. Still, the dense chaparral made the local summits plenty hard to reach. Mile after mile the men would bushwhack through manzanita brush and sharp scrub oak, emerging at last on top of some rocky knob with shredded clothes and empty canteens and bone-dry throats. Even then, in the hills, Brewer felt the pleasure of the summit and the gratifying physical strain of the upward labor to get there; he wrote expansively of the views: of deserts that looked trim as fields, mountain chains stepping down into the sea, distant islands riding the Pacific. There was still work to do, of course—once on top, after resting a moment and admiring the horizon (and, most likely, after a good laugh at the disreputable state of their trousers and the amount of chaparral debris with which they were all covered), they would unwrap the delicate instruments they had carefully protected through the struggle with the brush, and set about making their observations.

Brewer took an immediate liking to camp life as well. On a later occasion he described their nights: "and thus we sleep—such glorious sleep—sound and refreshing; no bad air, no close smell of feathers, no musty, ill-aired beds from which one rises in the morning with gummy eyes and heavy brain and mouth tasting as if half full of Glauber's salts and clay." He returned to the discomforts of indoor living throughout his letters, and pointedly noted that the only time he and his fellows caught colds were during extended periods inside. Brewer also found a bemused kind of pleasure in the artifacts of western life. "A touch of the country and times was indicated by our rig," he wrote. "I was dressed in colored woolen shirt, with heavy navy revolver (loaded) and huge 8 inch bowie knife at my belt." Their camps were always heavily armed against bandits of all kinds and Brewer practiced with his pistol until he was a sure shot, though the outward show of force proved to be deterrent enough and the guns were only ever used on animals. Despite the abrupt change from the genteel East Coast university scene, and his occasional bouts of homesickness, Brewer wore his rough clothing and big Spanish hat with comfort and traveled the frontier with the quiet ease of a born Westerner.

Whitney originally selected Brewer because of his credentials as a scientist. Brewer was raised on an upstate New York farm; he attended university to learn modern approaches to agriculture and graduated in the first class of Yale's new Sheffield Scientific School (a decade after Whitney's years at the university). After teaching for a time he went to Europe to study under some of the leading natural scientists in the old country, finding himself drawn more and more to the study of chemistry and geology without ever giving up his farmboy roots. In the summer of 1856 he trekked six hundred miles through Switzerland, botanizing and studying the mountains along the way. Brewer was so well qualified for the work in California that Whitney did not even meet with him in person until just before their departure for San Francisco, relying instead on the recommendations of mutual contacts at Yale.

What Whitney could not have known was how well Brewer would manage the operational frustrations of the fieldwork. It was a daunting task, to survey an area more than twice the size of all of New England with a small team and an uncertain funding stream in a half-lawless state, but mishaps and delays did little to throw Brewer from the work. Brewer demanded much from the men who accompanied him, but as he was usually the first to toss off his blanket, the first to the summit, and the last to return to camp each day, the men could hardly complain of ill-use. He had a soft-spoken approach to commands, a lively appreciation for a good story either told or received, and a firm grip on propriety in a state flush with gold and unchecked bribery. To those who remained in the field party for any length of time, Brewer inspired lasting respect and loyalty.

And yet, despite his poise and work ethic and physical strength, even he was occasionally staggered by California. Once, far back in a dry canyon in the Santa Susana Range north of Los Angeles, Brewer discovered a stratum thick with oysters, clams, and other seashells—the beach of a former ocean now lifted high above the water and up into the hills. "How lonely and desolate," he wrote. "Who shall tell how many centuries—how many decades of centuries have elapsed since these rocks resounded to the roar of breakers, and these animals sported in their foam? I picked up a bone, cemented in the rock with the shells. A feeling of awe came over me . . . And then I felt overwhelmed with the magnitude of the work ahead of me." But Brewer was a practical man in a state filled with pragmatic concerns; he was alone, the weather was warm, the day was ending, and he worried that grizzly bears would come out with the moon, so he made his observations and hurried back to camp.

Over the next two years, the survey moved generally northward up the coastal ranges of the state, at times returning to San Francisco to deposit specimens, write up notes, make topographical computations, and do other desk work. Toward the end of their first year, the Overland and Pacific telegraph companies completed their transcontinental line and the continent shrank accordingly. The celebrated eight-day lag of the previous year's election news was cut to fifteen minutes for messages both momentous and mundane at the price of a dollar per word. Californians eagerly paid the tariff now that the Civil War had roared to life. Newspapers were no longer just a pleasant diversion in the backcountry but benchmarks of the nation's future. Brewer read the papers with considerable anxiety; he was an ardent Unionist and, after the fall of Fort Sumter, often flew the stars and stripes above camp. Throughout the war years he sprinkled his letters with casual slaps at the Confederacy; in one he described early summer mosquitoes swarming "with not one-tenth the fear and twice the ferocity of a southern secessionist." His humor seems primarily aimed at cheering himself up—he had serious apprehensions about the fate of the Union and the possibility that California's government would slip into "secesh" hands.

In the fall of 1862, Brewer traveled north to the foggy forests and cold, green rivers about Mount Shasta. Here at last was a mountain of an entirely different order than the coastal hills Brewer had hiked thus far. Snow-clad Shasta braced its topmost pinnacle eleven thousand feet above its base and fourteen thousand feet above the sea. Its broad shoulders bore glaciers and cliff-bands marked by strange sculptures of wind-carved ice and ice-carved rock. Its slopes ran down and down, tracing out a vast conic outline, before submerging under a smothering population of dark firs, cedars, and pines which rolled away into Oregon to the north and the Sacramento Valley to the south. Mount Shasta is a dormant volcano, a great pile of ash and lava rocks built up over the years of the mountain's activity and now frosted with permanent ice and snow. Like the other Pacific Rim volcanoes, Shasta is an isolated hulk, starkly different from California's granite peaks where one high mountain merges into the next on the long miles of the Sierra crest. Mount Shasta seems peculiarly massive with its head so high above its base and with no neighbor to suggest its scale.

The mountain captivated Brewer. He had seen nothing so large and lonely in America, nor so desolate. Above the tree line the vegetation simply stopped; there were no flowers or other little alpine plants to decorate and soften the lines of barren rock and snow that piled up so high above him. The snows reflected moonbeams as well as sunshine, so whenever he woke in the night the mountain was still there, still bleak and magnificent.

Whitney roused the climbing party at 2:00 A.M.; it would be a long day and the snow would be firmest before the sun warmed it, but that meant stirring up a frigid camp under a moonlit mountain that looked even colder. There were six of them, three men from the survey including Whitney and Brewer, and three local men, one who had been to the summit before, and who acted as guide. Theirs was probably the only climbing party of the season, though the mountain had been climbed on and off for the preceding ten years. For hour after hour they trudged up steep snow in the bottom of a gulley bordered on both sides by sharp ridges. The architecture of these spiky cliffs fascinated Brewer. "The lava first wreathed into curious forms when it flowed down there, and then in later times weathered into fantastic shapes—walls, battlements, pinnacles, shooting up hundreds of feet, more forms than can be described." They emerged from the gulley through a tight space between red- and ochre-colored cliffs with two thousand feet yet to climb to the summit. The air thinned noticeably and conversation died as they panted on. When they finally reached the summit at noon, having needed close to four hours for their final push, three of the men vomited "severely" and Whitney's fingers were frost-nipped. They all had headaches and felt lethargic and dozy; the others started back down the mountain early while Whitney and Brewer finished their barometric measurements.

Brewer was elated, despite the effects of the cold and altitude. He spent the next days staring up at the mountain for hours at a time, enjoying the afterglow of their successful climb. He was alone. The others had scattered to other tasks and lower elevations with warmer temperatures, leaving him to finish a last set of observations. "How I enjoyed those hours of solitude," he wrote, "so far from men, such a picturesque spot!" It happened to be his thirty-fourth birthday, but he had the woods and the mountain for company and this apparently suited him for the occasion; perhaps he felt a certain kinship with the solitary mountain. His thoughts drifted:

Six years ago yesterday I was on the Great St. Bernard, in Savoy—how unlike that view from this, and my mind wanders to the Swiss Alps and the views I saw there. And then it wanders home and to loved ones there, and then to battlefields, and scenes of carnage and blood and sorrow in the East and to hospitals, where men are enduring the keenest physical sufferings—but all is quiet here, so quiet that no wonder thoughts and imagination wander.

Later, when they compared their data and made their calculations, he discovered, as he had hoped and expected, that Mount Shasta was the tallest known mountain in America. He was very pleased. "I feel proud," he wrote, "that I took *first* accurate barometrical observations to measure the highest point over which the stars and stripes hold jurisdiction."

The next summer, Brewer explored the Yosemite Valley, his introduction to the architecture of the Sierra—and what an overture! The crystalline granite sparkled in the sun; the waterfalls leapt over the valley rim, pulverizing themselves into rainbow-catching mists; the cliffs ran up so high and plumb that Brewer gave up on finding East Coast comparisons in his letters to his brother and resorted to measurements: this many thousands of feet of perpendicular stone here, so many hundreds of feet of free-falling water there. He paid his compliments to El Capitan and Half Dome, the two granite monarchs which stand straight and tall above the valley floor, but his favorite was that liquid thunder known as Yosemite Falls. During the peak melt the falls has the flow of a small river. It pours itself through a notch cut high up the valley rim, exploding out into free air and dropping more than a quarter-mile on its first vault before adding another thousand feet through a cloud of spray over its lower falls. It is, somehow, both shattering and lovely.

Brewer was so taken with Yosemite Falls that, as with Mount Shasta, he desired to make an accurate measurement of its height. So he and Hoffman climbed to the rim of the valley up through what is now called Indian Canyon, a tricky route gaining three thousand feet via forests divided by cliffs with narrow ledges perched above steep drops. Brewer found the experience "exciting from its danger." This was a different sort of climbing than he had practiced the previous autumn. Instead of struggling against cold, snow, and altitude, he now faced an exercise in rock gymnastics requiring the management of handholds and toeholds above airy places where a slip would have serious consequences. The round-trip to the top of the falls and back took them fourteen and a half hours. The next day, back on the valley floor, sitting at the base of the waterfall with hands so sore they trembled when he held his pen, he wrote, "I have seen some of the finest scenery of Switzerland, Tyrol and the Bavarian Alps, but I never saw any grander than this."

In July, Brewer and Hoffman continued up into the Yosemite high country— the northern end of the High Sierra. Here, too, as with the Yosemite Valley and the Shasta region, they had been preceded by other explorers, but they made some of the first topographic measurements of the land and speculated on its geologic origins while following the tracks of old glaciers and studying the course of the Tuolumne River. Meanwhile they soaked in the wild splendor of the mountains: a confusion of pinnacles, peaks, and domes all made of bare rock with flower-filled meadows between and crystal streams filling sapphire pools. Whitney accompanied them part of the way, but as usual he was overcommitted and had to rush off for an appointment after only a few days, leaving Brewer and Hoffman to carry on without him. "And what an experience!" Brewer wrote. "Two of us alone, at least 60 miles from civilization on either side, among the grandest chain of mountains in the United States."

◆ ◆ ◆

BREWER HAD BEEN in California for nearly four years. He knew the state with an intimacy that few others had—certainly he understood its geography and geology as well as anyone. He had seen its deserts, climbed its northern giant, explored the hill country up and down the long coastline, and spent his season in Yosemite studying the ways of the granite. But Yosemite was only the north end of the high part of the Sierra. There was still that wall of peaks to the south. Entire rivers poured out through the foothills below the mountains, but no one knew their exact source, only that there must be plentiful reserves of snow and enough slope to make the waters race. There were summits in there, to be sure; they could be glimpsed from the valleys on either side. The mountains had Brewer's attention now, so he made preparations.

At the end of May 1864, Brewer, Hoffman, King, Gardiner, and Cotter left San Francisco on their animals for the long march to the Sierra. It took them twelve days to ride south and then across the Central Valley to Visalia. Drought had a stranglehold on California that year. It seems that the state was determined to show Brewer her many moods. Two years earlier, California had flooded so severely that steamships cruised the waves *above* the ranchlands of the Sacramento Valley rescuing men and cows; the water even overtopped the telegraph poles. But this year no rain fell, only dust kicked up by hot, dry winds. Cattle carcasses lined their trail, starved by the lack of grass. At the end of each day's ride the men were coated in grime; the dust even infiltrated their dinner and their kettle so that a finished cup of tea revealed a deposit of sand at its bottom. One of their mules, a faithful animal who had been with the survey for four years, died on the crossing, overcome by the combination of heat, dust, alkaline water, and poor feed.

Still, the closer they came to the Sierra foothills, the higher their spirits rose. At night, around a small fire, they relaxed in the twilight temperatures and the young men of the party sang songs of home. They had all migrated to California from locations to the east, and though by now they shared Brewer's contentment with frontier living, none were ready to grow western roots or give up their previous attachments.

These nights spent talking and singing around the fire—the combination of cultured minds and flannel shirts and the comforts of bare ground—were as important to Brewer as his moments of solitude. Though he sought out lonely places during his time in California, he was not, by nature, a loner. He had enjoyed many fine camps along the way and they passed several of these old haunts on the trail to the Sierra, prompting memories of past pleasures. At one, near San Jose, they had propped a beer keg on two cow skulls and laughed and sung for a broad arc of the moon. Brewer wrote a caricature of each man present, including himself.

> That demure, modest looking individual on the ground leaning against the tree (but close to the beer keg) is the humble Botanist. His face is indistinctly seen, as it is modestly hid behind a huge stone pipe, a native "California Meerschaum" from which occasionally curls up a blue column of smoke as from the crater of a half-sleeping volcano. His last pair of pants are a little torn, and a flag of truce is displayed in the rear— emblem of peace, even if not of plenty.

At Visalia they bought a final round of provisions as well as a replacement for their dead mule. From there they traveled steeply uphill through the outer band of the foothills, arriving at a family-run sawmill, the last outpost of human industry. Here at last they had sweet, clear running streams and lush grass for their animals. The sawyers had spruces, pines, firs, and cedars to cut; they also had giant sequoias. These trees, which grow only on the western slope of the Sierra, are the largest in the world. Upright and stately, the eldest are close on to three thousand years old and three hundred feet high and weigh upwards of four and a half million pounds. Brewer visited one fallen tree that had been

High Sierra Field Party of 1864, left to right: James Gardiner, Dick Cotter, William Brewer, Clarence King (Photo courtesy of Bancroft Library)

hollowed by lightning and fire and rode through its inside passage on horseback for seventy-six feet (he measured it) without ducking his head. The sequoias are so rare and massive that for a time they were popularly dismissed as a fable or a western hoax. In the meantime loggers had their way with them. The wood was too light and fibrous to be used as lumber, but it resists disease and fire so they used it for fence rails and shingles instead. One leveled stump, still rooted in the ground after the rest was felled, was used as the dance floor for a forest jamboree. The image is disturbing: sixteen couples romping on the freshly hacked remains of a creature older than Christendom and the city of Rome. It provokes a queasy feeling for the hubris of our species.

Beyond the sawmill rose the great western tilt of the Sierra, and here I caught up with Brewer's party. I spent my first night on a bed of alpine gravel and pine needles under a hard, black sky pricked full of starlight. The sawmill is long gone, and the foothills are filled with roads and dams and other modern diggings, but the higher one goes, the less has changed, and the mountains themselves have barely blinked since Brewer's visit. I slept poorly that night, which came as no surprise. Each time I rolled over, my blanket opened and I dumped myself into the gravel, awaking with a mouthful of pebbles and sticks. So I had a lot of time to watch the stars and think of Brewer and try to keep my feet warm.

He had never seen terrain so difficult to navigate. Steep valleys creased by torrential streams and ribbed with granite outcroppings crisscrossed the way toward the peaks. Most of the time they could not see their destination, so Brewer spent hours scrambling up to high granite domes and bare knobs—vantages from which he could see the mountains in the distance and the unruly canyons in between. Then, back down in the obscuring shade of the forests and ridges, through an obstacle course of boulders, cliffs, and thickets, they would attempt to follow the passage Brewer had scouted from above. The valley sides and ridge crests were so steep and rocky that they could not ride their mules and instead had to lead them on foot. Even so, the danger that one of the animals would lose its footing and topple over backward or break a leg plagued them—and the mules, too, were perfectly aware of their own jeopardy and complained and balked in displeasure. "The region is so *very* rough," Brewer wrote, "that I am filled with anxiety." Forward gains came hard and he sometimes doubted whether they would reach the mountains. Eight miles in a day was considered good progress.

A thin lacework of footpaths now covers the area of the approach that gave Brewer so much grief, and I was my own mule, so the miles dropped by more quickly. I rarely had company when I followed the ancestors, but on Brewer's trail I was joined by a good friend. Evan descends from Brewer in more ways than one; he is finishing his chemistry PhD at Stanford, though chemistry has changed even more than mountaineering in the years since Brewer took his degree. We followed the paths when they followed Brewer's approximate route; other times we struck off through the woods and around the cliffs to stay on his line.

There are many good reasons to travel the mountains with Evan; one that I enjoy is that he calls my attention to the creeks and meadows. On my own I tend to be distracted by the bare rock above—studying the cliffs, waiting impatiently for the peaks to come into view above the intervening hills—but Evan redirects me to the gardens at boot level. He has a good eye and an acute appreciation for the shapely purple bells of the lupine or the cheerful outlook of golden buckwheat.

Sometime around the solstice, Brewer and his team left the domed granite behind and moved up into the outer band of sharp-topped peaks. They camped beside a small meadow in cold temperatures despite sunny days; in the shade the thermometer never rose much above forty degrees and at night it dropped into the teens, harsh numbers for thin blankets and no shelter. Brewer found the area bewitching. "The whole aspect of this region is peculiar," he wrote. "The impression is one of grandeur, but at the same time of desolation. The dark pines, the light granite, the sharp cones behind, the absence of all sounds except the sighing of the wind through the pines or the rippling of the streams." They had a book of sermons with them and read one aloud the next day as it was Sunday. Brewer was determined to observe the Sabbath, partly out of genuine religious feeling, but more so to have a day off. "I shall not work Sundays this year as I did last," he wrote. "The state can afford to do without it. I will not use myself up as I did last summer."

Evan and I spent a night near their meadow camp in a scattering of outsized granite boulders, which looked like the upshot of a child-mountain toppling his blocks. To make their beds the early mountaineers cut springy boughs from young pines, and lit old wood for nightlong fires, but there is too little of the wilderness left now for that kind of ill-usage. I contented myself with gathering dry pine needles and wearing a warm hat. Evan was enthusiastic about my project, but not so enthusiastic as to leave behind his own sleeping bag and air-mat, which he spread out beside another boulder.

The mosquitoes were thick that night, but so was my beard, and I put a shirt over my eyes to keep the pests off my cheeks and forehead. Though I had been cold the night before, I could already feel my appetite expanding and my inner engine ramping up to produce more heat; meanwhile, the nerves in my hips and shoulders which had kept me awake with complaints of jutting pebbles were now quiet. That the body can accomplish these transformations undirected in a few short days leaves me impressed and pleased that our genes remember our past as outdoor animals. Brewer is right. My back is happiest pressed into the ground—my nose is sharpest after breathing pine-scent all night long. Evan and I chatted aimlessly for a while over the buzz of the mosquitoes. When Evan tells a story, whether about climbing a mountain or studying metabolites or changing a tire, he produces a fantastic volume of detail, a nearly frame-by-frame account of what passed before him. This feels right in the mountains where there is space and time to hold that kind of storytelling. When it grew dark enough and late enough I slept soundly in the lee of my house-sized stone.

On Tuesday, four of Brewer's party set out to climb a local peak, the highest in the immediate area. They took the long way around to reach the easier southwestern slopes of the mountain, and, after crossing a thinly forested ridge in that direction, sighted a grizzly sow, which Brewer estimated at the size of "a small ox . . . perhaps 900 pounds or more." They shouted at her from behind cover in order to watch her run, and then proceeded to slog over weathered blocks of gray talus.

The view from the summit roused them. Brewer knew that the southern Sierra formed an imposing wall, but he had not expected any individual peaks to be over twelve or twelve-and-a-half thousand feet high. But their current summit, and it was only an outlier, was already over eleven thousand feet, and there, on the other end of a long valley, was a mountain that was much taller still, probably well over thirteen thousand feet. To discover an unknown mountain in the heart of the Sierra with that kind of elevation gave them all a thrill. And the mountain itself was a stirring sight, a clean, symmetric pyramid of steep white granite set at the top of a stone canyon.

They did not have long to look. A fast-moving snowstorm blew in and drove them down off the summit. They returned to camp wet and tired but with a pointed ambition: to reach and, if it proved possible, climb that highest mountain, that lofty pyramid of gleaming stone.

They named the peak they climbed that day Mount Silliman in honor of Benjamin Silliman, a professor who taught Brewer agricultural chemistry at Yale. Though it is not high, it is a shapely mountain. Two planes of steep orange-hued granite form the north face, joined at a sharp angle like the prow of a ship jutting from the cirques below. The opposite side of the mountain is less steep and hosts many fine trees; the highest on the mountain look dead and storm-polished but still cling to life through thin strips of bark. Evan and I followed Brewer through the broad basins and the gray talus and the golden burnished pines up to the peak top. There we gained views over the sheer north face and across to the high mountain miles to the east. It seemed almost to glow in the sunlight—no wonder that it caught and held Brewer's eye. The valleys in between spread their curves and contours below our feet; from our high post we could see all the twists and turns of the route Brewer took between the two mountains.

They descended from their meadow camp by following Sugarloaf Creek down into the long Sugarloaf Valley. Here they found sandy beds of decomposed granite and more rough travel both for themselves and their animals. Mules were a mixed blessing for the mountaineers of the era. They were a necessity for anyone who wanted to stay in the Sierra for months on end with enough supplies to remain healthy and fed. They were also stubborn, awkward animals that, though far nimbler than horses, were much less maneuverable than their human chaperones. The accounts of the early Sierra climbs are filled with lengthy passages describing mule-related shenanigans: trails built for the discerning tastes of mules, rivers through which the animals had to be forced, mules that balked, mules that kicked, mules that wandered off, usually at night. Sometimes the effort of an expedition seemed focused more on moving the mules from one camp to the next rather than on mountain climbing. And yet, the stories were often mixed with praise that bordered on worship. For all their quirks, the brutes were smart and tough and would calmly handle terrain that no other pack animal could manage. As Brewer put it, "Much as is said and written about the sagacity of horses—poets sing of it and romance writers harp on it—it is far inferior to the much abused mule."

Where Sugarloaf Creek throws itself bodily into the Roaring River, they forded the waters and began a steep passage up through ancient moraines—now clothed with pine and fir—which were pushed out from the mountain canyons during the last ice age. For half a day they cut back and forth up these forested slopes, riding their mounts wherever the dense canopy and thin soil kept the forest floor bare. By nightfall they entered the austere canyon beneath the mountain, tiny figures in that mighty, open-aired cathedral. Clarence King, the youngest member of the party, had this to say of it:

> The form of the mountain at the head of our ravine was purely Gothic. A thousand uprising spires and pinnacles pierce the sky in every direction, the cliffs and mountain-ridges are everywhere ornamented with needlelike turrets. Crowning the wall to the south of our camp were series of these jagged forms standing out against the sky like a procession of colossal statues. Whichever way we turned, we were met by some extraordinary fulness of detail.

The next morning, Brewer and Hoffman decamped in the predawn and began their attempt on the mountain. They were both eager. Hoffman had missed out on the Mount Shasta climb because he felt too ill to rise that morning, so this would be his highest summit. They had climbed peaks together in Yosemite, but nothing as imposing as this. From down in the canyon the top looked so thin and high that it might as well have been a mathematical point, an abstraction on one of Hoffman's maps. The view from the top of their Yosemite peaks had been "sublimely grand"; they hardly knew what to expect from this still higher outpost above an unknown landscape.

The two men knew each other well by then and had shared enough steep work to be familiar with each other's pace and stride. Slipping into a steady rhythm with a well-known partner comes naturally, and they had the clank of their iron shoes against the rock to mark time. Perhaps Brewer pointed out a few herbs or flowers that reminded him of Switzerland, or Hoffman exclaimed over some particularly fine rock spire, but probably they spoke little, saving their breath. They both found the upswelling granite flagstones of the canyon floor to be taxing on the muscles and slow to ascend. The angle was not yet sharp enough to require their hands be used for balance, but plenty steep to make their legs ache, and certain places required delicacy lest a slip become a tumble into the rocks below. All this time the mountain reared up before them; the front that faced them spread its cliffs and spires from one corner of the canyon to the other. They could only hope, since they could not see, that one of the other sides of the pyramid would look down upon them with a gentler expression.

When they climbed up out of the canyon by way of the hanging talus field at its head, they finally felt a sense of progress toward the summit. It was still high above them, but now at least they could see the individual rocks from which it was made so it no longer had a dishearteningly abstract quality. Having spent more than a fortnight above the foothills they were better acclimatized than they had been on Mount Shasta, but now they could feel the air thin and each breath seemed to be lighter and less substantial. One section of eight hundred feet took them three hours to ascend, a slow crawl over steep stacks of rectangular boulders. Like stairs to a giant's castle, these blocks of rough granite, knobbed with crystals and split by frost cracks, dwarfed the men. As they hauled themselves up the steps one by one, their view to the west expanded—now they could look above the canyon rim, back to Mount Silliman, and out into the foothills—but still the talus walls of the cirque prevented them from looking down into the unfamiliar country which they had traveled so far to see.

Just below the top, the neck of the mountain stiffened, jutting up at an angle close to vertical. The summit rocks rebuffed the climbers on their first attempt and they had to drop back down and then further around the southern end of the peak. Here they tried again, and were sent down once more by steep stones which they did not trust themselves to hold. They traversed further around to the east and there they found a narrow, serrated ridge that led up to the summit pinnacle.

If the view from Mount Silliman had sparked excitement, this view left Brewer stunned. It defied all his expectations. Instead of looking down into the deserts, they looked up at jagged peaks unlike anything they had ever seen. They were not on the highest mountain in the Sierra. They were not even on the Sierra crest. Mountains filled the horizon, some shaped like spires, others like sails or thunderheads or castles; all were made of sharply cut stone, all were high. Brewer was astonished. "Such a landscape," he wrote. "A hundred peaks in sight over 13,000 feet—many very sharp—deep cañons, cliffs in every direction almost rivaling Yosemite, sharp ridges almost inaccessible to man."

Brewer and Hoffman's peak, with its satellites to the north and south, had been just tall enough to block the sightlines to the highest mountains. Right up to the end, they thought they had been climbing a central, commanding summit, when in fact they were on a lower ridge parallel to the true crest. The jagged wall of the Sierra burst into view all at once the moment they first popped over the shoulder of their mountain.

Back on Mount Silliman, this view was still hidden from Evan and me. Brewer's mountain glowed with light and captured the eye, but there were hints of an upheaval hidden behind the false front. In retrospect, Brewer might have seen things differently, might have noticed the spiry summit of the Black Kaweah off to the south, might have wondered if there were enough peaks present to fully populate the crest and whether the silhouettes from the west matched up with the view from the Owens Valley (as Clarence King later claimed to have questioned). But assumptions press hard images into our brains, and the clues were slight compared to the alluring vision of that airy pyramid on the horizon.

Brewer and Hoffman spent hours on the summit, trying to make sense of the confusion of peaks that filled the east. Brewer reckoned that at least a dozen stood higher than their own, and several were tall enough to be Mount Shasta's peers, though he did not then suspect that one of the mountains in view would prove to be the highest mountain in America until the purchase of Alaska. Too soon, the falling sun drove them down off the peak. Much of the day had been spent on the climb and many hours would be needed for the descent. They left their instruments at the top, knowing they would need to return to finish their observations.

Later, thinking back on the summit, Brewer wrote, "It is not at all probable that any man was ever on the top before, or that any one will be again, for a long time at least. There is nothing but love of adventure to prompt it after we have the geography of the region described." His thought proved prophetic in unintended ways. "Love of adventure" is as apt an explanation for why people climb mountains as has ever been offered. Brewer had it. Science might have justified his travels in the mountains, but love of adventure fired his spirit when he looked up at a high peak top and quickened his long stride on the way toward it.

Up on that summit with Hoffman, in a mining state still wild with materialistic desires, it would have been difficult to imagine how many other people would share his craving for the climb and vista. He could not have guessed that his letters would soon be read as a manual describing the prototypical California mountaineer as much as for the history they contained. He could not have known how many would follow the basic outline of his mountaineering education, learning to climb snow on Mount Shasta and rock in Yosemite and then applying these lessons to the High Sierra. The impulse to visit high places proved more universal than anyone from Brewer's generation could have imagined. Brewer left a paper in a bottle on the summit with their names. When the bottle was discovered thirty-two years later, in 1896, it was a woman, not a man, who found it. Helen Gompertz, another of California's climbing forebears, was one of a generation of students at the University of California at the end of the nineteenth century who took up Professor Brewer's tools and John Muir's books and became mountaineers.

The day after climbing Mount Silliman, Evan and I descended into the sandy-bottomed Sugarloaf Valley. A chafing humidity surprised us there; the valley dropped down to a comparatively warm seven thousand feet and the moisture to fuel the evening's storm clouds was already arriving from the west and stacking up against the mountains. The sugarloaf for which the area is named is a solitary, thousand-foot-high granite dome rooted in the middle of the valley and split into several bulging pieces like a pointy-headed cake left in the oven too long.

At the crossing of the Roaring River we left trails behind for good. I led us directly up the creek spilling out of the canyon below Brewer's mountain, despite Evan's advice that the route would be unpleasant and barely passable. He thought that we would end up tunneling through steep brush for thousands of feet, pulling on shrubbery as handholds just to make headway, and that the ravine I had chosen lacked the moraines Clarence King described. And Evan was absolutely right, though he did fail to predict the logs covered with branch-spikes which threatened to dislodge and crush us along the way. In a remarkable display of his good nature he told me, when we emerged hours later in the canyon above, that he thought the ravine had been "interesting" and "untouched" and that "you don't get to go that far off the beaten track very often."

We arrived at the lake that evening worn-out and covered in debris. I made a minor effort to splash off the day's grime in a cold creek which seemed to have melted only reluctantly and prickled my skin. A springy three-inch layer of pine needle duff covered the ground beneath the trees fringing the lake; I doubt even the ancestors bothered to cut branches for their beds here. The squall came up that night and we retired early, partly in anticipation of the storm, partly because we were spent and couldn't seem to put more than a few sentences together to call a conversation.

The next morning we woke to an ugly outlook. Black, fast-moving clouds flew by above and seemed to inflate angrily as they buzzed our summit. The canyon walls allowed us only a thin slice of sky to watch so the dark shapes burst over the south rim with unsettling suddenness. But they hadn't yet dropped rain, and the sky was quiet, so we decided to go as far up the mountain as the weather would allow.

An hour later we arrived at a larger lake which reflected the white mountain in its morning gray. Tiny wildflowers grew up through cracks in the rocks all around its shore. Yellow monkey flowers hung from cliffs directly above the water, while pink and purple Jeffrey shooting stars clustered in gregarious bunches among the lakeside boulders. Most graceful of all were the cream-colored columbines, their elegant petals tapering back into long slender spurs behind the yellow cluster of their anthers.

Columbines have been Evan's favorite since he first discovered them with his wife in the Sierra. It seems all Sierra mountaineers have favorites. Mine is the purple-trumpeted meadow penstemon. John Muir's was cassiope. But it was sad to watch Evan study the columbines now. His wife was leaving him, moving her things out of their apartment while we were standing by the lake below Brewer's mountain. Evan had asked that we not talk about it much. I wonder how many of Brewer's companions in California knew of his wife and child. Few, I would think; maybe only Hoffman. Evan and Brewer strike me as similar in this way also—good storytellers when it comes to recasting events, but unlikely to share their private pain.

Seeing Evan watch the columbines showed the quiet path for what it is: hard and lonely; but his grief won't be cheapened by talk or dissolved before he is ready. Among creeks and meadows, bare rock and snow, there are places with enough beauty and potency to embody the strong things we feel. Whether Evan reserves the columbines for memories of Amanda, or gives them to another woman, or holds them apart against the frustrations of loving, they will be there under the peaks with their elegant spurs and yellow anthers waiting for him to return even while friends and women come and go.

The clouds ripping over the canyon rim crowded around the mountain and hinted at worse to come. We hurried away from the lake and up the slabs curving down from the canyon head. It became a game of chicken, the weather building and the sky thickening while we pushed our legs and lungs, and swung up the rocks toward the summit. I had no jacket, of course, and I expected to be soaked at any moment. To the south, long strands of gray rain dangled from the undersides of fleecy black masses. But their cousins above our summit still held back as if waiting for a signal. Though I felt no electricity in my beard yet, I felt sure that somewhere up there a thunderclap was building that would announce the deluge.

We left the hanging streamside gardens behind as we entered the talus cirque under the south shoulder of the mountain. A few stalwart alpine dandelions clung to shallow beds of gravel, but nothing else interrupted the tilted field of angular gray-and-white rocks. We pressed up this last stretch under our angry sky, pulling and yanking ourselves over the larger rocks, leaping over the smaller

The author below the summit and the storm (Photo by Evan Pearce)

ones, feeling the uncomfortable time warp of our fidgety brains racing forward ahead of tired muscles starved by flimsy air. When we ran out of stone to climb and found ourselves beside the summit pinnacle it still hadn't stormed, though a solid toss could have put a rock through the dark fleece. And then suddenly the clouds lifted and pulled back, knocking around shafts of sunlight and baby-blue air—as if they had been only teasing us, only laying on a playful bluff.

The mountains! North to south, they erupted from the earth, casting tangled ridges in all directions, the ridges themselves sprouting more peaks and spires. Deep canyons dropped out of sight between the summits while spider-silk waterfalls and rambunctious creeks raced down toward the tree line. No state of mind could duplicate the surprise of coming upon these mountains unprepared, as Brewer saw them, but I have to think that from my seat astride the summit pinnacle my feeling of wonder was no less. The whole scene was so stark, the lines so abstract and improbable, that it ought to belong more to the imagination than the walking world, yet there it was, before my eyes, as if bold thoughts had been polished up and scattered over the land.

◆ ◆ ◆

BREWER AND HOFFMAN returned to camp from the summit just as darkness hardened around the pines. Their fellows cooked them a celebratory pot of venison soup and listened eagerly as Brewer tried to describe what he had seen on the mountain. It was late by the time they all rolled into their blankets with images of new lands and sharp summits in their heads. The young men in camp decided on the name for the pyramid which had given them these visions: Mount Brewer. Though in his letters Brewer did not mention the christening, he did not object to it either. It suited him well: a tall, handsome peak—not the highest in the range, but placed just right to enjoy one of the grandest views in the Sierra.

· 2 ·

Clarence King + Mount Tyndall

[JULY 1864]

Mount Tyndall (14, 018 feet), north face

O F ALL THE men camped under the pines that night, it was Clarence King whose imagination was fired most by Brewer's news of the crest and the high peaks. King had traveled across the country to California hoping for exactly this sort of landscape and adventure. He was a short, stocky young man, twenty-two years old, quick-witted and very strong, with a blond beard and a bluff manner. Brewer and Hoffman both judged it impossible to cross the ridges and canyons on foot to reach the crest, and had said as much around the fire, but those wild peaks whispered in King's ear all night long and he woke the next morning with clear eyes and his heart set on the mountains.

He took Dick Cotter aside and asked their now-experienced mule packer "whether he would like to penetrate the Terra Incognita with me at the risk of our necks." King got the answer he hoped for. "In a frank, courageous tone he answered after his usual mode, 'Why not?'" Cotter had a boyish face, which he kept clean-shaven when he could, and broad shoulders that socketed long arms ending in enormous strong hands. King described him this way: "stout of limb, stronger yet in heart, of iron endurance, and a quiet, unexcited temperament, and, better yet, deeply devoted to me, I felt that Cotter was the one comrade I would choose to face death with, for I believed there was in his manhood no room for fear or shirk."

If King sounds extravagant and pompous it is because he was both of those things and more. His admirers saw in him the quintessential Renaissance man of the West. His detractors thought him arrogant and starry-eyed. One of the other members of Brewer's field team who was not along for the expedition into the southern Sierra but had worked with King on other legs of the survey called him a "confounded little 'blow hard.'"

Blowhard or not, crossing the entire width of the Sierra to climb its highest peak was a bold proposition. The team was already undermanned and ill-equipped, but at least they had their guns and mules and a relatively unobstructed route back to Visalia. King and Cotter would leave behind everything that could not be carried on their own backs and put high mountains and deep canyons between themselves and the nearest human beings—which, at least in King's mind, was precisely the point.

After securing Cotter's company, King asked permission from Brewer to divide the party and strike off for "the top of California." Brewer hesitated. King reported that his reluctance sprang from "a certain fatherly responsibility over our youth, a natural desire that we should not deposit our triturated remains in some undiscoverable hole among the feldspathic granites." Brewer in fact had other concerns. "We were short of provisions," he wrote. "This meant partial starvation to those of us who remained that they might have the necessary food." But he did also worry over their welfare. "I feared for their safety, as I knew the dangers they must face . . . scaling untried precipices and meeting unknown difficulties." As the day slipped past, Brewer yielded, as King felt sure he would. If nothing else, Brewer was as curious as anyone about what lay on the other side of his mountain; besides, he was hardly the type to deny young men with an adventure to chase.

King and Cotter planned to leave the very next morning. They would carry food (venison, bread, beans), scientific equipment (barometer, wet and dry thermometers, pocket level, compass), and notebooks. They had no such thing as backpacks, so they rolled their provisions and equipment in their sleeping blankets and tied these bundles to their backs using lengths of rope from the mule-tack. Cotter brought along a large bowie knife and King had matches and a canteen. Always interested in measurements, Brewer hoisted the bundles and reckoned their weights at thirty-five or forty pounds apiece. King expected their supplies to last them a week with careful rationing.

With their kits organized they had nothing to do but unpack them again and wait until night advanced enough to make sleep possible. They stretched out early, hoping for a long and sustaining rest, but King barely slept. Under normal circumstances his mind hummed noisily enough with thoughts and plans; with the added buzz of unexplored peaks cutting the sky just over the horizon, and the anticipatory jitters of a dicey passage to reach them, he could not compel his brain to shut off. He had not even seen the new mountains yet, but their summons was irresistible to his romantic temper.

◆ ◆ ◆

AFTER AN HOUR or so on the summit, Evan and I descended from the mountain and returned to the camp in the pines. Evan's time was up. His work had reached an important juncture and he had to hurry back to it while I followed King up and over Brewer's mountain.

Along the stretch that Brewer and King had packed their belongings on mules I brought a backpack. It seemed only fair since they had the luxury, however dubious, of a mule train. But now King would be on foot toting a lumpy sack tied to his back with bare ropes, and I aimed to follow his lead. I had found a fibrous length of manila rope at a hardware store, which seemed close in spirit to their mule-lines, and I had my blanket. While Evan packed up his gear, I experimented with King's design. I spread out the blanket and clumped my food and meager possessions in the middle. I tied the corners of the blanket together across the little pile of goods, and then girth-hitched the middle of the rope around the knotted corners, leaving two long straps. With the bundle balanced on my back, I wound the rope ends around my shoulders and waist until the sack felt relatively secure. I felt quite pleased with myself.

Evan took one look and laughed. He immediately dubbed it "the hobo sack" and tried to imagine the conversation I would have if I encountered a backpacker along my way. He imitated my voice: "Well, it's the latest thing in minimalism. Haven't you heard of fast packing?" I suggested that I just introduce myself as "Rip" and ask for the latest war news along the Potomac. But I never got the chance. During the time I followed King I saw a total of three people and all so far away that I could barely distinguish their arms and legs.

The strong light of afternoon had already passed, leaving behind budding shadows, and Evan had hopes of making ten miles or so before dark. He took a photograph of me modeling the hobo sack, then swung on his own pack and disappeared into the woods.

The sounds changed. Between two people there is always the opportunity for conversation and banter. Even in silent lulls, the potential for talk hangs in the air. Alone, the air felt thicker in my throat and lighter in my ears. The creek burbled and hummed, small black-hooded birds repeated their private notes, the hiss and sway of the breeze in the pine needles surged back and forth along the lakeshore. None had anything new to say, but now they all seemed louder and more stereophonic, as if before I had been listening through a plywood wall.

I moved myself higher up the canyon for the sake of a head start in the morning. The clouds returned. They draped Mount Brewer in a shapeless gray wrap which lacked the crackling vigor of the morning's black cruisers and settled instead into a stout-bodied sluggishness. I found a thin deposit of gravel that offered more cushion than bare rock and spread out my blanket. I enjoy both the camaraderie of a good partner and the mental space of solitude, but I find the transition in either direction jarring, leaving me either thick-tongued and word-shy or hypersensitive to the quietness. Sitting on my blanket, eating a dinner of cheese and crackers, my own voice sounded loud and false in my ears and I used it sparingly.

With the uncanny timing the clouds had shown all day, they lifted, like a curtain pulled back to begin a play, just before the setting sun began a slow-motion ignition of the mountain. For half an hour, the mountain slipped from orange to rose to red—outsized, lavish hues in this landscape of forest and rock—each moment producing a shift in shade so fine I could barely grasp the new color before it vanished. I watched the entire show, from first blush to last light, riveted. Night followed quickly after the extinction of the last glow on the summit. I lit a candle and wrote a few notes. The stars appeared, not with their usual slow magnification, but in hard, bright instants as unseen clouds swirled and dispersed overhead.

◆ ◆ ◆

THE NEXT MORNING, Brewer, Gardiner, King, and Cotter set out from camp with me as their shadow. Brewer and Gardiner carried the packs for the morning in order to give the expeditionary pair an easier start. They followed the same route up and out of the canyon, but instead of working directly up the southwest side of the mountain, they pressed forward toward a saddle in the long ridge running south from Mount Brewer. No part of the Mount Brewer "wall," as they began to call it, dropped below thirteen thousand feet, so by the time they reached the saddle they had already gained nearly as much elevation as Brewer and Hoffman had two days earlier when the two men reached their summit.

The last few steps up to the ridge crest let loose the eastward view, and King now had his first chance to see the land he had proposed to cross and the mountains he hoped to climb. The scene justified his hopes and fears in equal measure. Below his feet the stone fell away down into a canyon more than three thousand feet deep (though King credited it for five thousand), its bottom obscured by intervening ridges and cliffs and the sheer vertical distance. "Rising on the other side," King wrote, "cliff above cliff, precipice piled upon precipice, rock over rock, up against sky, towered the most gigantic mountain-wall in America, culminating in a noble pile of Gothic-finished granite and enamel-like snow." He had heard about places like this—he had talked to Brewer, and read the accounts of the Swiss mountain scientists—but he had never seen anything like it. "I looked upon it as one contemplating the purpose of his life," he wrote. And then, as if afraid to reveal too much earnestness, he added, "and for just one moment I would have rather liked to dodge that purpose."

The Mount Brewer wall ran parallel to the main crest, and the deep canyon filled the space between with empty air. To complicate matters, a five-mile-long ridge, a granite saw blade with mountains for teeth, cut across the canyon between the crest and their wall. The highest peaks on the crest stood beyond that barrier. To approach them, King and Cotter would first have to descend into the canyon, then climb up and over the serrated cross-ridge and down its far side through unknown country hidden from view—all just to reach the base of the high mountains.

King wrote a gallant and touching parting scene: "Professor Brewer asked me for my plan, and I had to own that I had but one, which was to reach the highest peak in the range . . . Our friends helped us on with our packs in silence, and as we shook hands there was not a dry eye in the party." Brewer recorded this moment with a more restrained sense of the occasion: "We carried their packs up to 13,000 feet, pointed out the way they must take, and after a hearty shake of the hand and a 'God be with you,' we saw them descend into the cañon and disappear." He and Gardiner continued back up to the summit of Mount Brewer—along a far easier slope which he and Hoffman had found during their descent—in order to finish their observations and reclaim the equipment he had left there two days before.

When I reached the saddle below Mount Brewer's summit I paused to get my bearings while I still had the advantage of elevation. King, of course, had no map since no one had ever been this way before, so I did not carry one either. The only guide of any kind that I brought was King's own description of their route, which he wrote as an adventure tale, not as a navigational aid. Sitting at home, imagining my pursuit of King, I knew that traveling mapless would alter my perspective, but I had no idea what this would mean until I sat there at the saddle trying to make sense of the confusion of granite and snow spread out before me. The mountains seemed twice as large and I felt twice as small. My position and proportion had changed. Instead of magnifying my own stature, literally towering over the mountains every time I opened the map and looked down on them, I would crawl around at ground level with the chipmunks and marmots. It was disquieting, as if I had lost one of my accustomed senses, but I also felt liberated. The mountains would keep their secrets hidden from my prying eyes until I had earned the privileged view, and I would take the cliffs and ridges as they came without the plotting and planning of map work.

King's account of his days with Cotter is one of California's classic adventure stories. They climbed tall cliffs, clinging desperately to fingerholds high above fatal drops while dodging rockfalls and enjoying many a near-miss. How much of that was exaggeration? I had no way to be sure. Everything I knew about King led me to believe there would be self-puffery in his storytelling. But now, sitting at the pass, staring at the peaks which King had lit out for with no knowledge of the terrain and little in the way of a plan, I could not help readjusting my admiration for the man while wondering what exactly I had gotten myself into.

From the saddle, King and Cotter first climbed south along the ridgeline of the Mount Brewer wall, looking for a descent to the east. Beneath them cliffs dropped away so sharply that they could poke their heads over the edge and look straight down for a hundred feet or more before the angle eased from vertical. At one point a steep chute of snow split the rock all the way to their feet. They considered leaping into it and plunging down the thousand-foot slide into the amphitheatre below, but they tested this idea by throwing a boulder into the alley and the stone flew down the snow at such a frightening speed that they gave up the idea.

They climbed further along the top of the Mount Brewer wall, weaving back and forth among rectangular blocks of solid granite which jutted up like fat fingers, some as high as fifty feet. As the ridge narrowed, the passage through these spires became more difficult and dangerous until at last they decided to force their way down the eastern wall, no matter how steep it looked, rather than continue along the ridgeline. They found a break in the cliffs and began to climb down it, hands gripping the edges of square-cut blocks and boots finding ledges, but gravity pulled at their packs and they felt unbalanced and in "constant danger of pitching headlong." So they untied their sacks and Cotter climbed down a ways, and then King lowered the sacks to him on their forty-foot lasso before climbing down himself to join Cotter at the lower stance.

Less snow covered the Sierra the year I followed King and Cotter—less snow in general falls on the Sierra now compared to 150 years ago, and warmer temperatures melt the glaciers and snowfields faster. When I arrived at the ridge crest, the chute down which King had contemplated sliding no longer held any snow at all. The spires and blocks of granite still piled along the upper edge of the wall, though, and I felt like an ant navigating a graveled roof, clambering over and under stones that dwarfed me in size. To my left, the cliff fell sharply off, and blocks of granite overhung the drop like stubby diving boards. For me, the melted-out chute presented the best way down. Sand and scree filled it now and I tromped through the narrow corridor losing height rapidly.

From the lower end of the chute I studied the wall down which King and Cotter climbed. There were several possibilities, any one of which could have been their route, but none looked easy and my estimation of King grew again. Psychologically, this stretch must have been hard. Each forty-foot length they gained put more of the Mount Brewer wall between them and their friends; bit by bit they cut themselves off from the only people in the world who knew where they were and what they were attempting. But forty feet was a meaningless fraction of the total distance they had yet to go to the high mountains on the horizon. Their expedition could have been scuttled in this hopeless middle territory, but King and Cotter were good for one another and spurred each other on—drawn forward, in part, by the fierce strangeness of the new country.

Though a mile broad, the amphitheatre seemed to hang above the bottom of the canyon; beyond its lower rim, the earth fell away as if into a void. King had surveyed this abrupt edge from above and thought it "utterly impassable." They trekked south through the amphitheatre, not climbing now, just hiking across frozen snowfields and talus piles, though they were tired and the slick snow and loose rocks punished them for any lapses of attention. It must have been cold, too—the afternoon was already sliding into evening and their entire side of the canyon was one unbroken shadow.

They gave up on making further progress that day and searched out a smooth stone alcove where they would have a flat place to sleep. King settled into a contented, meditative mood: "After such fatiguing exercises the mind has an almost abnormal clearness: whether this is wholly from within, or due to the intensely vitalizing mountain air, I am not sure; probably both contribute to the state of exaltation." They filled their canteen from a rapidly freezing creek and, without wood in the basin for a fire, ate a supper of cold venison and bread. King marveled at the stark scene they had come to inhabit. "Through the white snow-gate of our amphitheatre, as through a frame, we looked eastward upon the summit group; not a tree, not a vestige of vegetation in sight,—sky, snow, and granite the only elements in this wild picture." For a time the eastern wall of the canyon kept a brilliant crimson light, but this too slipped away, and in the dim gray left behind, even the rock and snow seemed to hush and retire in preparation for the coming night. The amphitheatre chilled rapidly, their creek froze, loosed stones tumbled down past their sleeping-rock, the stars glowed white and sharp overhead. The two of them huddled beneath their blankets and began a protracted, though apparently cheerful, struggle against the cold. "How I loved Cotter!" King wrote. "How I hugged him and got warm, while our backs gradually petrified, till we whirled over and thawed them out together!"

My day still had hours to spend on me, so I passed the neighborhood of King and Cotter's icy bivouac and continued to the edge of the amphitheatre. I crossed a low ridge—a precursor to the much higher divide ahead—and from its top I gained my first close view of the cliffs that we three would have to cross next. But I could hardly look at them. Further to the west, a startling new mountain lifted its jagged outline into the afternoon blue. These sudden appearances seem impossible—what can hide a mass of stone that large?—but the granite skin here is so densely convoluted that the sightlines are never simple. For the better part of a linear mile the sides of the mountain rose to the center, converging at a towering summit. All along the roofline ornate gray spires flung slender shadows down below; many tapered in at the middle and back out at the top, like stretched hourglasses, a bizarre form for perched rocks to take.

Beyond its mile-broad size, beyond the sheer weight of stone and the height of its spires, the shape of the mountain was what captivated me. In general outline it made a symmetric triangle, but closer up it blew its symmetry to pieces; all of the fine detail, its pinnacles, joints, and buttresses, was singular. The mountain framed a shapely universe but filled it with a vast population of individual creations, a local infinity of detail. Below the summit and the spires and the frost-etching and the individual handholds for the mountaineer swirled whole galaxies of minerals, flecks of black, green, and red, millions of years of rock chemistry focused on single, barely visible crystals glinting in the afternoon sun.

Looking at this peak and others, King felt sure that gothic architects had the Alps, Europe's version of the Sierra Nevada, in mind. "Whole mountains," he wrote, "shaped themselves like the ruins of cathedrals,—sharp roof-ridges, pinnacled and statued . . . innumerable jutting points with here and there a single cruciform peak, its frozen spires so strikingly Gothic I cannot doubt that the Alps furnished the models of the early cathedrals." Still, this was not King and

Cotter's mountain; it was just another Sierra peak. The big mountains hung farther off yet in the distance.

Two passes offered escape through the jagged line of summits anchored at one end by the gothic mountain. King described cliffs and a thin upper ridge, and this description better suited the eastern pass than the western one, which looked broader and icier and in their year was probably filled with steep, hard snow. So I angled eastward down talus to a creek crossing beside a massive and beautifully carved boulder which overhung its sides with smooth curves of white granite—a single rock that probably weighed upwards of five thousand tons but had tiny pink flowers, called rock fringe, sprouting from the joint between its base and a thin bank of creekside gravel.

In this part of the Sierra, everything is made of rock, from the summits to the underfooting. There is nothing soft or level here, no "ground" in the lowland sense of the word, just an endless sea of jagged blocks. When King and Cotter woke the next morning they stepped off their sleeping rock and onto another.

They began their second day with a round of frozen venison and then refashioned and shouldered their packs. What for me was unbroken talus was for them a mixture of talus and snow, and as their upward path steepened the snow covered more and more of the way until they stood upon a broad, steep snowfield. The sun had not yet appeared over the cross-ridge, and the whole surface was frozen hard. Cotter took out his bowie knife and began chopping boot-edge holds in the ice—"a slow, tedious operation," wrote King, "requiring patience of a pretty permanent kind. In this way we spent a quiet social hour or so." It's a charming image for its incongruity: the two of them perched on slippery nicks as Cotter swung his knife at the ice, slowly hacking out each new step; meanwhile they chatted amiably about the mountains or home or perhaps what their fellows were up to at the lakeside camp, so far from their world of ice and stone.

Higher up, the snow ended and the rock reemerged. Cliffs pushed out above them and above those the saddle promised passage to the high mountains beyond. And here in his writing King slipped away from reality into mountaineering clichés. His cliffs became sheer, smooth precipices, their upward course blocked by overhangs; they threw a looped end of their lasso around a spike of rock, and climbed it hand over hand while the ground dropped away below. It was a pointless lapse—the dark rocks and splintered cliffs hardly need embellishment. And the power of King's story rises from the mental courage required of him and Cotter to cast off alone into the unknown, not in the mechanics of lassos and fictional rope-climbing contests. It seems to me that King here lost sight of the essence of his own adventure. He wanted to thrill his readers, but he blunted his story's genuinely gripping moments with doubt.

In reality, the cliffs on this side of the pass are steep—but not that steep; the climbing is tricky, but not impossible, even by nineteenth-century standards. If they lassoed a spike with their rope, then ascending it would have been more like tugging on a rope to walk up the roof of an average house rather than the dangling, free-hanging affair that King described.

Still, it took me hours to reach the pass, climbing up via ledges and channels between cliffs, and though it best fit King's description, his embroidery of the details left me edgy and unsure. If my guess turned out wrong I would have no choice but to descend back down to the amphitheatre and reevaluate the clues King had left me. By then I probably would not have daylight enough to do much more than find my own sleeping rock and stare up at the cliffs.

My worries scattered the moment I sat astride the pass, a knife-edge line above two opposite cliff faces. Here, King's descriptions align beautifully with the land, with the view out over the broad Kern Valley, back to the Mount Brewer wall, and down into the deep canyon to the north (the southern fork of the Kings River—a name long predating Clarence King). The ridge divides the watersheds of the Kings and Kern rivers; the snowmelt and creeklets to the north join the Kings and head west; the waters on the other side enter the Kern and run south. On the opposite side of the Kern, the giant mountains of the crest filled the horizon—great billows of granite which seemed half rock and half cloud.

I could have relaxed into that view as into a piece of music—cellos or organs, I reckon, something deep and lonely—if I hadn't looked down the other side of the pass and discovered one last confirmation of King's account.

> Hastening to step upon the crest of the divide, which was never more than ten feet wide, frequently sharpened to a mere blade, we looked down the other side, and were astonished to find that we had ascended the gentler slope, and that the rocks fell from our feet in almost vertical precipices.

All true. Here were precipices worthy of the name. King had wasted his words on the upside of the pass. Now the cliffs had caught up to his visions.

Doubts brushed through their thoughts, but the mountain, the summit of the range, beckoned them on. If they could only get down these cliffs, the way forward across the Kern Valley looked clear all the way to the joint between valley and mountain. They couldn't resist that horizon. The power that a shapely peak exerts can hardly be countered. The mountain simply outmaneuvers the brain, reaching through the eyes and down the spine to pull directly on muscle and bone.

King and Cotter stuck their heads over the edge and studied the possibilities, pointing at features and ledges, making suggestions and rejecting them just as quickly. No solution appeared—climbing down seemed impossible—so King hatched a desperate plan. He tied a loop in one end of the rope and draped it over a projecting point of rock on their ridge. He lowered the other end of the rope down to a ledge below them and then slid down the rope himself. Cotter lowered the sacks, and then lowered himself as well. Perched on their narrow ledge together, they whipped the rope up and down until it came loose and fell into a heap of coils at their feet. Looking back up and then down again, Cotter said with his usual nonchalance, "We're in for it now, King." With that flick of the rope, they severed their route back; they could not hope to return this way. Not only were they committed to descending this cliff, they now would have to find a new, unknown path in order to reach their friends back at the lakeside camp. But they had the confidence of youth. They had the freedom of spirit to burn the morning's bridges and the evening's worries and think no further than the sunlit afternoon.

Looking down over the edge I could practically see the two of them standing shoulder to shoulder on their narrow ledge. I missed having Evan with me to say, "We're in for it now," with a cocky air and a shrug of the shoulders. There in five words is the power of a good partner, to lighten a moment with simple, eager recklessness. Alone, I found myself reaching back to King and Cotter for a share of their enthusiasm and partnership; it seemed that Cotter's voice still hung over those cliffs after all the intervening years.

I prefer my own fingers to rope-trickery; moreover, I did not trust any of the loose rocks wedged on the ridgeline to hold my rope with me on it. I left my bundle at the brink to keep it from pulling me over backward while I tested the possibilities below. By hand and eye I built a mental map of the entire cliff complex, looking for links between cracks and corners and other features offering finger- and toeholds.

A circuitous line shaped up: an awkward downward thrutch over a lip of rock, then a traverse in the wrong direction to access a corner with a finger crack between two granite planes, then another traverse back in the right direction to a set of fingerholds which led up over a small buttress, then down a rotten crack on the other side filled with loose flakes that flexed against my hands when I jammed them deep into the guts of the fissure. I descended a hundred feet by climbing twice that far, and I understood why King and Cotter chose the rope. The rock was badly shattered, a dark species of granite loosened by time and its own weak constitution. And it was still steep. Apparently gravity simply hadn't gotten around to knocking it all down yet—oversight seemed to be the only thing keeping the stones in place. I couldn't use most of the friendliest-looking holds for fear they would come loose and send me tumbling.

At the bottom of the last rotten crack I looked down over thirty feet of steep cliff to easier ledges below. This section looked loose and difficult, but better than any alternative I had found to reach the security of those broad ledges. Still, I did not want to climb it more than once, so I left that last bit untried, and returned to the ridgeline and my kit, repeating the sections of my route along the way until I had each hold memorized.

I carried my sack down the easier bits and lowered it down the steeper rock, depositing it on ledges that would not let it roll. Losing my blanket and provisions would have transformed my expedition into a bleak ordeal. But each part I had practiced unfolded smoothly for both me and my gear.

On the second viewing the final cliff looked no more appetizing than it had the first time. The rock was steep and blank except for a crust of edges—which looked more like baked-on dirt than solid rock—and a fingertip crack behind a thin scab of stone. I thought briefly of using King and Cotter's method and then arrived at a compromise. I lowered my bundle and then tied a loop in the remaining rope-end, which I draped over a rock horn. I aligned the hanging rope with the finger crack, with the idea that, if the rock should shatter, I might have time to grab the line before I fell. Facing in, I reached down and put my fingers into the top part of the crack, then scuffed my feet down along the crumbling veneer of the cliff face, while eyeing the rope dangling by my hands. I leaned out to put my weight down through my boot soles and the scab-edge flexed under my fingers, but held, and I quickly muscled myself down to the rock-strewn ledge where my bundle waited.

King and Cotter wrung their own route from the cliffs, sometimes climbing the rock, other times shimmying down their lasso. When the angle eased they leapt and bounded from boulder to boulder in the talus below, jubilant to have passed through unscathed, and when they reached a broad snowfield softened by the sun they leapt into that too, and glissaded together down several hundred feet in a single slide. King regained his feet and turned back to eye the dark wall they had descended. Its aspect surprised him, even though he had just been intimate with its fissures and shattered stones. "It seemed," he wrote, "quite impossible we could have come down there." Looking back up at the cliffs and narrow notch of the pass, I agreed with King. The stretch we had all climbed down looked chaotic and improbable, the kind of rock that seemed to demand a climbing rope and modern hardware. I wasn't sorry that we wouldn't be returning that way.

King continued his thought, and his carefree outlook: "And now it actually was beyond human power to get back again. But what cared we? . . . We were bound for that still distant, though gradually nearing summit . . . and were jolly, shouting, singing songs, and calling out the companionship of a hundred echoes." I followed in the wake of this hubbub, descending down a long talus slope, pretty tired now, toward a small bright lake that hung above a new canyon.

As I neared the lake, the walls of the talus cirque shrank, and my view of the canyon expanded. Muir wrote that there were other Yosemites in the Sierra. He could have had this view in mind. Cliffs rose sheer and strong out of the canyon bottom and thousands of feet higher tapered off into square buttresses that stuck their necks up and above the canyon rim. A whole succession of these towers lined up along the southern canyon wall, each with the kind of aesthetic lines and distinctive character that give Yosemite's cliffs their individual personalities. This canyon was smaller than Yosemite, but also narrower, and just as wildly sculpted by its own virtuoso glacier. Down on the canyon floor, a deep, narrow stream—a small river, really—curved back and forth around long bends cut through green meadows, and then dashed itself over cliffs, breaking up into white foam and spray.

The early evening sun lingered above the canyon rim. Where its slanting light struck the towers from behind, shadows pushed across the canyon, dark projections of the towers' silhouettes that seemed to have volume and substance. Where gaps allowed the orange sunbeams through, they lit hanging dust particles on fire. The canyon was filled by shadow mountains and burning air.

As a boy I read *20,000 Leagues Under the Sea* compulsively, and one part of the story always gave me shivers. Off the North African coast in the Atlantic, Captain Nemo takes Professor Aronnax, the narrator, out of the Nautilus on an underwater walk through a sunken civilization. Aronnax sees wonders that he can hardly grasp: graceful buildings of a foreign design, exquisite art of unknown origin, all the trappings of a wealthy and elegant culture. He is desperate to know where they are, but he cannot ask the question because he and Nemo are locked in their separate, airtight apparatuses. His curiosity becomes so intense that he goes half-mad and begins to pull at the helmet of his dive suit to break the barrier of silence, but Nemo stops him and uses a piece of chalky rock to scratch ATLANTIS onto a dark stone.

Walking down through this canyon, gaping at the towers that lifted their crowns so high into the sun, I felt, for the first time, the impulse that drove Aronnax to reach for his helmet. I was in an unfamiliar part of the Sierra and had intentionally ignored the map before I came. I wanted to know the names of these cliffs and towers, if they had any; I wanted to know which had been climbed, which had stories to tell of the passage of wide-eyed climbers, and which had only been visited by birds and breezes. For the first time my self-enforced blindfold chafed me and I wanted to tear it off. But, of course, I had no Nemo, and neither did Clarence King. I even felt a little ashamed by the impulse. This is one of the lost pleasures of unknown lands; traveling through a nameless place means freedom from prior translations, a chance to connect mountain and mind with no one else telling you what you should see.

The red glow of the sunlight marked a day tapering toward its end. I could not stop and stare at the towers—neither the ones made of granite nor the ones made of shadow—for as long as I might've liked. The taproot I would have grown if I paused would have been painful to sever and there was no water nearby as I was still high above the canyon floor. I was tired, and I felt awkward and uncoordinated, and regretful to be walking away. I descended on balky legs to the mouth of the canyon where the stream poured itself into a winged lake with an outline like a diving bird.

My descent carried me down below eleven thousand feet for the first time all day, though I didn't know it at the time. The lower elevation, combined with water, invited the return of greens and browns to the land. Animal tracks—deer, squirrel, rabbit, marten, and the split-toed prints of innumerable kinds of birds—crisscrossed the exposed mud around the lake rim, and birds flew back and forth through the branches of thick-trunked pines. On the eastern shore I found a flat place to camp where a pine provided a partial canopy.

My legs nearly staged a labor protest when I forced them back to the lake to get water. It had been a terrible year for the snowpack, so the lake water was warmer and cloudier than I might have liked given that I had no pump-filter or iodine tablets. But I was too tired to walk around to the outlet stream where the water might have run clearer, so I decided to trust my guts to handle anything breeding in the water. Back at my flat spot I leaned my back against a rock, let my taproot grow, and watched the high cirrus turn pink. There were many questions, and many mosquitoes. A round fold in the earth blocked my view to the east, and though I knew the mountain was close by on the other side, I did not know exactly how close or how long it would take me to reach it. I had no answers so I gave up wondering and settled into a defensive posture against the mosquitoes with my warm hat jammed low over my eyes and my blanket wrapped around my feet and ankles. As soon as twilight dimmed to dark I stretched out and slept soundly beneath my blanket despite the gentle rain of buzzing wings.

King and Cotter passed my sleeping spot with plenty of day left, and continued on across the upper part of the Kern Valley, pressing up to the highest

Foxtail pine skeleton on the upper Kern

thicket of pines below the bulk of the mountain. They walked until after dark and when they stopped they lit an entire resinous log ablaze and had their first hot meal in the illumination of the flames. They settled in for a short night, for they planncd to wake early, but they slept well in the warmth of their fire.

The next morning I woke at dawn and stuffed some raisins and peanuts in one pocket and a handful of bread in the other. I rolled my warm shirt and hat and extra socks into the blanket, along with the stove I had brought so that I could heat my food like King and Cotter but without burning any more of the thin alpine ecosystem. I wedged my bundle in the crotch of a tree and used my rope to hang the remainder of my food above the reach of a wandering bear. Put together, my load probably weighed less than King's or Cotter's—I don't think I had more than thirty pounds with me. But I figured that my eight pounds of camera gear probably equaled the weight of their level and barometer, and, short of adding chunks of venison to my roll, there was nothing more I could have brought without going beyond their impromptu equipment. My sack had worked surprisingly well. The length of the rope-ends allowed me to wrap it tightly to my back so that it moved little as I walked. I did discover that splinters of rope fiber had lodged in my fingers and palms from handling the straps. Overnight my flesh built fluid-filled capsules around the offending slivers and pushed them to the surface, and I dug them the rest of the way out with my knife.

I set off toward the mountain, food in my pocket, a brimmed hat on my head, water bottle tucked through my trouser belt, camera tackle over one shoulder, feeling light and free. I rounded the southern end of the ground-fold which had blocked the eastern horizon from my camp and received my first near view of the mountain. The land the previous day had been deeply carved and studded with spires and shattered rock, jagged expressions of the work of ice and time on bare granite. This new scape was less angular and far more surreal. Wide-open meadows pressed up into the blue sky; instead of the deep, square canyons, the broad land tilted, almost gently, into the headwaters of the Kern River. Big mountains rose up from the eastern edge of the meadows, monolithic curves of granite like ocean waves. I had reached the upper zone of the Sierra: first Evan and I had hiked through the lower, damper western forests; then I had followed King through the chaotic canyons; and now this strange, soothing upland of high meadows and cresting peaks. On the other side of the mountain, not visible yet, the desert that Brewer had looked for past his mountain spread to the east—desert that stretches, in various forms, all the way to the edge of Kansas.

The meadows between my camp and the mountain were filled with animals. Early in the morning I startled a doe and two white-spotted fawns. One of the little ones crouched and vanished—a sleight to make a magician jealous. The other, more foolish, one tried to run with its mother who bounded away on arching strides of fifteen feet. The mountain was so large and the land so open that distance proved deceptive. I walked for many hours with the mountain in plain sight before I reached its base. I found a large, leopard-spotted frog in a shallow pool of a nearly dry pond. There were few flowers, but many butterflies, delicate little windblown flutterings of color, some orange, some bright green, others pale blue. At one point I sat and rested for a few minutes, and when I stood and turned a young-looking mountain lion sprang away from fifty yards off— whether it had been stalking me or was simply surprised at my sudden change of shape, I do not know.

King and Cotter rose in the predawn, had breakfast by the light of their log, which continued to burn, and then hiked north around the base of their mountain by starlight. Dawn revealed an icy outlook. The talus below the peak was covered by a frozen layer, "an even snow-slope," King wrote, "whose surface was pierced by many knobs and granite heads, giving it the aspect of an ice-roofing fastened on with bolts of stone." Looking at the mountain in the light, they discovered that the east face "was too precipitous to think of climbing" and the northwest corner "too much broken into pinnacles and crags to offer . . .

any hope." The only chance seemed to them to be straight ahead, up the broad north face through intervening bands of ice and granite. They stared up at the peak top, which they could see now, nearly two thousand feet above them. On the summit, wrote King, "the rose of sunrise reflected gloriously, kindling a fresh enthusiasm within us."

As I reached the edge of the Kern Valley, where the land began to swell toward the mountain, the meadows gave out and rock retook the surface. Again I found no snow here in my season; where King walked on his ice-roof, I leapt and scrambled between jagged white boulders packed one against another at contrary angles and with keen, outthrust edges. I curved around the mountain's base until the north face unfolded for me, a broad sheet of granite, perhaps half a mile wide, tilted up at a uniform angle, sparkling in the late morning sun. The monolithic shape tested my eyes. I had trouble capturing something so large and unvarying. Between the northwest ridge to the right that dissuaded King with its long column of spires like the spines on a lizard's back and the sheer east face to the left, only one feature interrupted the breadth of the north face: a gentle rib running down from top to talus, an improbable-looking ripple in the otherwise smooth surface.

This rib was the feature King and Cotter chose to climb. Just as they began, the sun touched the face above them, melting out rocks which had been frozen in place but now rolled in their direction. King described their upward progress: "We climbed alternately up smooth faces of granite, clinging simply by the cracks and protruding crystals of feldspar, and then hewed steps up fearfully steep slopes of ice, zigzagging to the right and left to avoid the flying boulders."

I had no falling stones to dodge or ice to cut steps through, so the climbing was a pleasure. A different sort of granite went into the construction of this mountain. Yesterday the rock had been scabby and shattered; today's rock was crystalline and beautiful, attractive stone for both the eye and hand. The outer layer was split into plates, like a chessboard for human-sized pieces, offering cracks at the edges for fingers and crisp friction for boot soles on the squares themselves. In places, plates had come loose and were perched on top of the rib. These were best avoided—some even creaked at the touch. Beneath me the mountain tumbled down a sweeping rush of stone and sky.

Higher, King and Cotter reached a long curtain of ice hanging down from the upper edge of the mountain at too steep an angle to climb directly. They found instead a shallow gulley with a deep fissure between one cliff wall and the ice, a sort of ice moat, and they entered this body-sized crack and climbed up through it with their backs pushed against the rock and their boots pressed against the ice. "We were now in a dangerous position," wrote King. "To fall into the crevice upon one side was to be wedged to death between rock and ice; to make a slip was to be shot down five hundred feet, and then hurled over the brink of a precipice." In accordance with his disposition, King either did not allow or did not confess fearful thoughts beneath his armor of words and actions. "In the friendly seat that the wedge gave me," he continued, "I stopped to take wet and dry observations with the thermometer,—this being an absolute preventative of a scare,—and to enjoy the view."

Above this chimney-gap between ice and stone, King and Cotter arrived at one last barrier, a short, steep wall of rock, a horizontal band blocking them from the skyline above. They traversed to the left and right looking for a friendly angle or line of holds to climb, but found only smooth, unbroken stone. Only one possibility presented itself, and King turned his attention in that direction with considerable apprehension. A stalagmite-shaped icicle, broad at the base and narrow at the top, ran up from the ice on which they stood to the top of the granite wall. King worked slowly up the wide lower cone, chopping edges for his boots and hands with Cotter's knife until the icicle became too narrow and fragile to cut deeply. There King wrapped his arms and legs around the column and shimmied up "so that the climb was made as upon a tree." But this slender trunk could snap at any moment, a possibility that filled King's mind until the moment he grabbed the mountain's upper stones and heaved himself over the edge.

I would have liked to have seen their mountain dressed up in ice the way King and Cotter saw the peak. On my sunny day, climbing warm, bare rock, it was hard to imagine the icicles and frozen curtains they confronted—still, ice grips stone in strange ways, and a deep freeze can alter every inch of a mountain's personality.

The perched rocks were the only hazard I found, but I took them seriously. I learned an early respect for large, apparently rooted stones. As a teenager, climbing a mountain in Oregon, I collapsed a wall of stacked boulders on myself and was carried a ways down the mountain by rolling rocks before I swam clear of the rubble. I was lucky and walked away—my helmet saved me from anything worse than cuts and a damaged shoulder. Now I had no helmet and there would be less chance of stopping a tumble down this mountain's tilt. So I avoided detached boulders when I could, sometimes climbing steeper rock on either edge of the rib where the plates were firmly set, other times taking a direct line where interlocking stones seemed unlikely to slide en masse. The mountain steepened just below its upper edge, but edges jutted from the joints between rock layers, offering holds for hands and boots, and I quickly joined King on the summit ridge.

Lying prone on the granite with his head stuck over the edge, King watched Cotter climb the icicle. When Cotter took hold of the granite and rolled over the top they could, at last, ease their minds. "We had now an easy slope to the summit," King wrote, "and hurried up over rocks and ice, reaching the crest at exactly twelve o'clock. I rang my hammer upon the topmost rock; we grasped hands, and I reverently named the grand peak MOUNT TYNDALL."

Mount Tyndall? The name honored John Tyndall, the English geologist who wandered the Alps in the 1850s and wrote accounts of his travels that were equal parts narrative adventure and scientific theory—a model individual for King's notion of the adventurous gentleman of science. When Brewer later described King's desire to cross the Sierra in pursuit of its highest peak, he wrote that King "had read Tyndall's *Glaciers of the Alps* and thought nothing was impossible."

I like Clarence King; I enjoy his irrepressible energy and enthusiasm, his self-conscious attempts to be debonair and casual in the face of danger. But his hammer blow on the summit makes me cringe. It's an ugly gesture. Why rap the head of a beautiful mountain which has been gracious enough to allow a visitor on its summit? Maybe King didn't really do it—perhaps he just included the line for effect because it fit into the prevailing notions of man and nature. I like to think so.

I nestled into the summit rocks to stay out of the wind, enjoying the feeling of sailing along on the peak top with the air rushing over the rocks just above my head. Mount Tyndall swells up from the west, crests, and then breaks sharply over sheer cliffs to the east. From where I sat I could poke my head over the eastern edge and look straight down two thousand feet into the jumbled talus below. Mount Tyndall shares its shape with many of the other high peaks; their resemblance to waves is a product of the local geology. The western swell reflects the tilt of the entire four-hundred-mile Sierra block. The eastern cliffs mark the edge of the block that has been lifted up out of the valleys below. North and south these enormous granite rollers swept to the east, stilled on the verge of crashing down into the valleys below. Instead of a granite deluge, those valleys held only the Sierra rain shadow, a dry land of sage-green and scrub-brown.

King and Cotter took out their instruments and made observations. "To our surprise," King wrote, "upon sweeping the horizon with my level, there appeared two peaks equal in height with us, and two rising even higher." This surprise must have been feigned. These other mountains are striking sights from the Kern Valley, and from the pass King and Cotter had crossed the day before, and even from the summit of Mount Brewer. The highest mountain they named Mount Whitney for the chief of their survey, the next highest, Mount Williamson, for one of the best of California's early topographers who mapped the state and proposed a southern route for the transcontinental railroad.

Why did King and Cotter climb Mount Tyndall instead? Mount Whitney was many miles further south along the crest. Weighing that distance against the pounds of food left in their knapsacks would have hardly inspired confidence. Mount Williamson, on the other hand, situated itself immediately east of Mount Tyndall. Perhaps they had even thought to climb this higher mountain when they rounded Mount Tyndall to the north. But the west face of Mount Williamson is a jagged, foreboding chaos of granite teeth; its appearance alone could have dissuaded them. Another thirty years passed before Mount Williamson was climbed from this side, by die-hard honeymooners Bolton and Lucy Brown. Bolton was one of the first of the Sierra mountaineers to criticize King for his exaggerations, though Bolton's appraisal (he wrote that King's account "is very far from giving a true impression of the region") is probably too harsh.

Standing atop Mount Tyndall, King seems to have been overwhelmed by the stark lines of the land he had crossed and of the deserts beyond. The lighthearted tone of his narrative becomes bleaker and darker as he reels off paragraph after paragraph of description filled with funereal adjectives and the breakdown of the natural order. The colors of the sky and earth reverse so that the sky is dark and the granite earth blindingly bright. No soothing shelter for mind and body can be found. From the deserts to the mountain stones, life seems to him to have left this land. He concludes with this thought: "I have never seen Nature when she seemed so little 'Mother Nature' as in this place of rocks and snow, echoes and emptiness. It impresses me as the ruins of some bygone geological period, and no part of the present order, like a specimen of chaos which has defied the finishing hand of Time."

It is a grim aesthetic indictment of the land, despite King's assurances of the majesty of the mountains and the beauty in the sculpted granite. Perhaps this is why Bolton Brown took such offense at King's description; after all, he was a follower of Muir, who saw life in every alpine flowerbed and love in every nook fashioned by the glaciers. Despite King's attraction to the West, he still retained a New England sensibility—he wrote often of his desire for a well-kept home and garden, of the shelter offered by a room or a grove or a fertile meadow—he could never quite find comfort in this immense land built of bare materials with no apparent consideration of human needs.

King and Cotter packed their instruments and looked once more around from their summit before leaving it and the view of the cresting mountains behind. They returned to the point where they had passed the final cliff band on the north face only to find that the upper end of their icicle had broken off. Nothing remained but a gouged trail in the hard snow to show where it had tumbled down to shatter itself against the rock below. King saw no other means of access to the north face—indeed, he concluded that "nothing but the sudden gift of wings" could take them back that way. Instead they traversed in both directions along the summit ridge, and found a long, tedious, but ultimately easier route down talus and scree slopes composing an inner fold of the mountain's shape, a passage they could not have spotted from their western approach. They arrived back at their camp in the early evening and relaxed into a celebratory mood, spending the last hours of the day recounting the events of their climb. Sleep finally quieted their thicket, and King enjoyed his first restful night of deeply unconscious slumber since Brewer announced the news of the high mountains.

I, too, returned to my camp, though I had farther to go to take me back to my blanket rolled up in the crotch of the tree. It was late afternoon when I arrived, after recrossing the broad valley of the upper Kern. There I had a choice between spending the evening hiking up to a higher elevation and spending the same time sitting and swatting mosquitoes. The former seemed more soothing. After lounging against a rock for a time to eat a bite and take some notes, I reassembled my knapsack and began an hour's walk up through pine terraces separated by gray cliffs.

King and Cotter had, of course, only half succeeded. They had reached their high mountain summit; their peak would prove to be one among the handful of California's mountains that topped fourteen thousand feet. But they still had to return to their compatriots on the far side of the Brewer wall, and they would have to find a new route back as they could not reclimb the steep rock they had descended to reach the Kern Valley. That passage had been shut and locked the moment they flicked their lasso off the rock horn at the high pass the day before.

From the summit of Mount Tyndall they had examined the cross-divide and chose a wide gap between a stubby triangular peak shaped like a canine tooth and a broad mountain arrayed with dark spires. They had seen the opposite face of this pass from the Mount Brewer wall, and must have known that cliffs blocked that side. But they really had no choice; every other gap between the peaks along the ridgeline sat high atop other abrupt cliffs, each with its own unwelcoming expression.

I arrived at a string of dark, stone-bound lakes just below the toothy mountain and found a flat gravel-patch laid into a ripple in the granite for my bed. I walked up to the head of the lakes to fill my bottle with running water and startled a large rabbit, which raced off into the talus. The creek was so low that I had trouble getting water into my bottle without also catching small squads of writhing, translucent creatures. After many attempts I resigned myself to lively water. By then the sun had given up my lakes to the shadows and was busy dyeing the peaks to the east crimson. The air already wielded a chill and I could feel the cold hardening; I had gladly traded the mosquitoes for the cold, but sleeping at nearly twelve thousand feet would test my blanket and inner engine and I envied the rabbit for the warmth of her burrow.

I returned to my bed and ate the last of my dinner food. I planned to make it back to my food cache on the other side of Mount Brewer the next day. If I made it, I would get dinner; if I didn't, I wouldn't. The color on the peaks turned from crimson to russet and an irregular, musical splashing drifted up from my lake. I took my blanket to the lakeshore and sat on a rock. Dusk had stirred up the trout to their evening business of leaping for flies. I was mesmerized. Sometimes six or eight would strike all at once. The water was black and the fish silvery, and they popped into existence without warning even though their underwater world must have been a madhouse of eagerness. They were little fish, perhaps three to eight inches long, but many cleared the lake surface by three times their body length, some diving back down with the grace of miniature dolphins, others flopping and splashing belly first. The lake might have been two hundred feet across, and was nowhere more than forty feet wide, but it must have held hundreds of fish for the ripples on the surface and the cheerful sounds of splashing never died away before the next began.

A half hour later I remade my bed and watched the stars spark the clear night air one by one. The cold reached down through my blanket, clothes, and flesh and I woke often to chafe myself and push my sluggish blood out toward my fingers and toes.

◆ ◆ ◆

THOUGH MY NIGHT sky had been crisp and clear, I woke to an airborne congregation of alien starships. Elegant lenticulars and dark, puffy cauliflowers hovered just above the summits; the rising sun colored them red and inflamed their edges until they glowed—outrageous tones a landscape painter would be hooted at for using. The outlook was undeniably ominous. I decided to skip breakfast and bolt for the pass.

From their camp near the base of Mount Tyndall, King and Cotter took a diagonal route across the Kern Valley and up to the pass. Though in good condition at the beginning of the trek, Cotter's boots were now falling apart. Having followed him across so many miles of jagged talus I understood why; even my boots were wearing through at a surprising rate and delaminating at the edges. On the downside of the pass his soles came off completely, so they stopped to fashion him moccasins from strips of blanket and sections of their leather provision bags.

From the pass they descended eight hundred feet of steep rock and arrived at the edge of an overhanging eave of stone. Here, King's account tells of a near-miss: Cotter's makeshift moccasins cause him to slip and King catches him at the brink, using one hand to snatch his partner's shirt and the other to grab hold of a "pine tuft" which bears the weight of the two of them. These cliffs exist, but it's hard to know why King and Cotter would have attempted them. I found a chute in a corner, tucked against the tooth-shaped peak, that cut through the cliffs and delivered me quickly to the low-angle blocky terrain and talus slopes below. Maybe ice filled this chute in King's season. Maybe they simply missed the narrowest part of the cliff-band.

Looking back on my days shared with King, it seems as though following him was a bit like trying to climb one of the distorted shadow-mountains I had seen in the canyon the day before I climbed Mount Tyndall. I knew that the substance of his story was there all around me. Reading his descriptions, I saw the same rockscape through which I traveled; climbing up and down his cliffs taught my fingers the real dangers he and Cotter confronted; I understood just how far they had pushed themselves into the unknown, how much trust they placed in their wits to see them through. But it's as if King worried that his travels wouldn't seem adventurous enough, so he squeezed his thrilling moments for every last splash of drama, trying to give his reader the tales he thought they expected, in which men dangled over precipices clinging to bits of shrubbery and lives were saved by the lucky snatch of a shirt-sleeve. In King's version of the Sierra, it is hard to tell where the projecting shadows of story end and the real stone begins.

The three of us lurched down thigh-destroying talus, shedding altitude quickly. Mount Brewer faced us directly now, with its satellites stretching out to the left and right. Below our feet dropped the deep canyon that King had marveled at from high on the Brewer wall. We had crossed the divide further to the east this time, and now we would have to descend all the way down into the canyon before struggling back out of it on the other side. With each downward step the Brewer wall rose higher and higher above. We entered a forest, the first real forest we had seen that was not merely a thicket on this side of Mount Brewer. We slid down steep pine needle slopes and spongy layers of duff bound loosely to the underlying stones.

One more obstacle filled the future of King's tale, and I had no way of knowing whether it would be made from honest rock or embroidery. They reached the lake at the bottom of the canyon, a long, rectangular body of water that filled the canyon floor. Charged with snowmelt, the waters were high and icy; the outlet creek ripped loose from the bottom of the lake with the force of a river, carrying whole logs in its grip. King and Cotter had no chance of crossing the torrent. Their only hope was to round the lake at its head.

There was no real lakeshore; the steep talus of the canyon-side met the surface of the lake and slid below the waterline. King and Cotter traversed along these stacked boulders above the water, at times crossing snowfields and brush thickets. After three-quarters of a mile of this slow work they reached the lake head only to find their way forward blocked by a thick rib of rock which stretched down from the upper reaches of the canyon wall and plunged into the lake.

They had run up against a dangerous predicament. The granite rib fronted both the talus and the water with a sheer rock wall. Their choices were to swim the freezing lake or climb the smooth stone: hypothermia and drowning to the right, a slip and a fall straight ahead. Beyond the rib they could see an unbroken sweep of talus leading back up to Mount Brewer—a taxing, but not hazardous, course. Their safe return depended solely on finding passage around or over this last obstinate mountain toe stuck out in their way.

I was skeptical, but when I caught up with them here I found myself in a genuine fix. It is an unlikely setting: the lake channels the color of empty sky, the forests are green and soothing, flowers grow out in big bunches around boulders. And then this hard gray band of rock runs down from on high, washing its base in the water and cutting off one side of the lake from the other. Its cliffs were as steep as anything King and Cotter had yet climbed, and so fine-grained that few holds broke the clean planes of its surface. The water looked uninviting even in my comparatively benign conditions—rimmed with ice and filled with fresh snowmelt it would have been a truly grim sight.

King was a good swimmer, but he "concluded that in our exhausted state it was madness to attempt to swim it." A pyramid of ice tapered up from the lakeside and leaned against the rock. They decided to climb this to its top and then try the last section of cliff from there. From a narrow platform at the top of the ice, King climbed up a series of finger-crevices and protruding knobs for twenty feet, but there his holds ended. A few feet higher a crack split the rock, but he could not reach it from his delicate perch, no matter what he tried. Defeated by these last few inches, King climbed carefully back down, knowing that a slip would've meant crashing down onto the ice and then tumbling into the frigid water.

When King arrived back at the top of the ice, Cotter suggested that his long arms might be sufficient to reach the crucial hold. He climbed the same section of cliff that King had, and, when he reached the blank spot, coiled his body and "made a bold spring for the crack, reaching it without an inch to spare, and holding on wholly by his fingers." From there he followed the crack to the top, climbing slowly and deliberately. "It was," wrote King, "the most splendid display of slow gymnastics I ever witnessed."

When Cotter reached the top, King tied their rope around his chest, under his armpits. Cotter called down to King "in an easy, confident tone," saying, "Don't be afraid to bear your weight." The idea was that, should King fall, Cotter would grab hold of the lasso, brace his feet, and hold King in place. Emboldened by his partner's success and the firmness of his tone, King began the climb again, silently resolving to make the climb without Cotter's aid. When he reached the difficult spot, he summoned all his strength and flung himself up at the crack, catching it with his fingertips. He climbed the remaining crack with care, and pressed himself up and over the edge to join Cotter. There he had a shock. Instead of a secure stance, Cotter "was sitting upon a smooth roof-like slope, where the least pull would have dragged him over the brink. He had no brace for his feet, nor hold for his hands, but had seated himself calmly, with the rope tied round his breast." Why hadn't Cotter said anything? Cotter projected confidence purposefully, King wrote, "knowing that my only safety lay in being able to make the climb entirely unaided; certain that the least waver in his tone would have disheartened me, and perhaps made it impossible."

Safe now, and sure for the first time of their way back, King and Cotter slipped back from the edge and sat down on the granite. On King, Cotter's brave act had a profound effect, which he described with his customary flamboyance. "To coolly seat one's self in the door of death," he wrote, "and silently listen for the fatal summons, and this all for a friend,—for he might easily have cast loose the lasso and saved himself,—requires as sublime a type of courage as I know."

King's melodrama screams fraud. But looking up at their cliff, I could see its sloping top and visualize Cotter perched there. Knowing what little I do of Cotter, I could imagine him summoning an utterly selfless and foolhardy act. Studying the rock I saw only three possible routes to its roofline, and all of them looked committing and difficult. Staring at this last, impressive piece of stone, King won me over, and I resolved to stop fighting with him over the details. The simple fact that they made it this far, and managed, after days of wandering the mountains, to climb this abrupt and polished cliff (which they must have, unless they actually had been given wings), spoke more eloquently to me than the flourishes King used to tell their story. Picture Cotter up there, barefoot, or with leather flour sacks tied to his feet, making desperate moves above that shattering fall. Imagine King staring upward, willing his partner to stay attached to the stone, wondering what would become of them if he came crashing down. Their success depended on a kind of partnership and force of will worth striving for on any mountain and in any century.

Now it was my turn. Without the ice I lacked the visual references to know which exact feature they had climbed. The line closest to the water looked exceptionally difficult; the furthest uphill was a damp chimney filled with loose rock. I settled on the middle line, a deep fissure splitting an otherwise smooth face.

Broken ankles were the best I could hope for if I fell, and then I would have a slow race against starvation on my hands and knees, looking for a trail and a chance meeting with a backpacker, for no one would find me where I was. I trusted my hands, but I mistrusted the weight and bulk of my hobo sack, so I took it off and tied one end of my rope through the knotted corners of the blanket. I would climb the cliff and then pull my goods up after me. But gauging the length of my rope against the vertical distance left me unsure that I had enough yardage. So I propped my bundle up against the base of the cliff, trusting a few bushes to hold it there, and tied the other end of the rope around my ankle to add an extra body length to my tether.

The crack was wide at the surface and narrow inside, and the whole fissure angled to the right across the face. I found jams for my left hand in the back of the crack and wedged my left foot in the wider parts. The edge of the crack offered deep holds for my right hand, though I had to lean out into space to the right to make them good. I pasted my right foot against the blank face, trusting friction to hold it in place. The rock was steep and my boots were clumsy, so much of my weight hung through my arms. Each time I moved higher, new jams and holds appeared above me and the lakeshore stones dwindled below.

Halfway up, I looked down at the sack and the dangling rope tied around my ankle, and I had to laugh. Surely, something was going to happen—the branches would break and send my gear tumbling away to yank my foot from the cliff; my knots would slip and my things would spill out and roll away into the lake. I had no right to think that this would work, that forty feet of manila rope and a wool blanket would get me where I wanted to go. But it did, just as it had for King and Cotter. The rope came tight against my foot just as I topped out the cliff, and my bundle stayed together as I hauled it up.

It was only forty feet (*exactly* forty feet)—a nondescript outcrop in the larger world of climbing—but a formidable barrier when placed at the end of King and Cotter's adventure. Here was a clear line: on one side doubt, on the other the completion of the journey. Four minutes of bold climbing separated one from the other.

King and Cotter had had enough. They situated their last bivouac by a creeklet flowing down into the lake on the other side of the rock rib. But my dinner waited for me on the far side of Mount Brewer and I continued on. The upward slog through brush and boulders, then through the tree line and up more talus, endless talus, consumed hours. On a hunch which proved mistaken, I crossed the Brewer wall via a wide gap farther to the south, thinking King and Cotter had gone that way. As I reached the top of this pass it began to rain, at last, after the spectacular overture of the morning and the slow buildup during the day. The air filled with soft gray dampness, which slipped casually through my porous clothes, and I traversed back across a mile of steep, broken cliffs to correct my error.

Back on known ground, I flew down the canyon toward the familiar lake below Mount Brewer's western face. The rain let up, then began again, and continued its indecision for the rest of the evening. I cooked dinner in a narrow crawl space under a rock: mountaineer's molé, the leftover odds and ends at the bottom of the food sack, in this case a mixture of oats, lentils, powdered garbanzo beans, powdered milk, cocoa, tomato sauce flakes, and peanuts. It tasted delicious, but probably shouldn't be attempted at any other place or time.

King and Cotter slept until the sun reached the bottom of the canyon the next morning, then rose and worked slowly up and over the Brewer wall. Cotter's feet had been cut badly through his flimsy slippers, and that partly accounted for their pace, but they hardly cared about discomfort or speed now. They chatted happily and noisily, and seven hours passed by the time they reached the descent on the other side. The downhill pulled them along faster. They could feel the true end of their adventure approaching. When, at the lake, they discovered a note on a tree telling them that the camp had been moved down further for better grazing, they hardly paused, and raced through the woods, neither of them paying any mind to poor Cotter's feet. Nearing the lower valley in the last light of the afternoon, they watched the treetops for the faint ribbons of smoke that would signify the location of the camp. "We saw them," King wrote, "with a burst of strong emotion, and ran down the steep flank of the moraine at the top of our speed. Our shouts were instantly answered by the three voices of our friends, who welcomed us to their camp-fire with tremendous hugs."

The author (and hobo sack) returns from following King and Cotter to Mount Tyndall

Back up at my misty camp, a feeling of pleasant wistfulness mixed itself with my contentment. Having played their parts I found I wanted more, I wanted to go back and discover new passes and peaks for real, with my own eyes instead of King's. There is something grand and special about an era when two men—boys really—could light off into the unknown, climb mysterious mountains, and be explorers with nothing more than makeshift knapsacks and a robust belief in their own strength and cleverness. The re-creation of that experience has pleasures of its own, even beyond the thrills of the adventure; from the summit of Mount Tyndall I saw not only the sweep of the Sierra, but the unfolding tradition of California climbing. The women and men who today populate the cliffs and peaks of Yosemite and the Sierra, striving with the rock and with themselves, descend from these first ragtag explorers; they dangle at the end of long strands of accumulated knowledge, experience, and teaching. But going back, ignoring the map, and tying on the hobo sack also has its limitations. The strong emotions King and Cotter felt can be approached, but only as echoes. The feeling of the summit, of the sudden relief gained at the top of the lakeside cliff, of the first view of those faint ribbons of smoke that signaled their return—these, in their purest form, are reserved for them.

·3·

Clarence King + Mount Clark

[JULY 1866]

Mount Clark (11,522 feet), southeast ridge

THE PURSUIT OF science was an unusual choice for a young man of Clarence King's era and background. He was born in Newport, Rhode Island, in 1842, and both sides of his family had New England roots two hundred years deep. His father died when he was young and his mother set to work preparing him for a classical education at a New England institution. She polished her own knowledge of languages in order to teach him French, Greek, and Latin; she even moved their household in order to place him in the best preparatory schools. All the same, she was little more than a child herself when her son was born, and their closeness reflected both the bond between mother and son and the memories of a shared childhood. She encouraged him to follow the currents of his imagination, and this meant that after his discovery of a fossilized fern at the age of seven her house became a "veritable museum" for the rocks, plants, and other wonders of the natural world that snagged his attention.

King took to his education with eagerness and energy, but when the time came to begin his studies at Yale in 1860, he chose to join the newly formed Yale scientific school instead of the college. He valued literature, art, and history as much as any scholar, but he had his own opinion as to how these subjects should be studied. Later in life he wrote:

> There can hardly be conceived a greater calamity befalling a young man born with a talent for literature than to have him elaborately and expensively spoiled in an American classical college. Better far that he should be a cowboy, with the Bible and Shakespeare in his saddle-bags, the constellations his tent, the horse his brother, than to have life, originality, and the bounding spirit of youthful imagination stamped out of him by a competent and conscientious corps of badgering grammarians.

Yale College was at a low ebb at that time anyway. Henry Holt, the publisher, who entered Yale the year after King, had this to report: "the Yale of my time . . . was probably at its very worst, in mind, body, and estate. In mind it dated back centuries." The professors were stuck in the past and few in the college recognized the importance of the emerging sciences. Work in a laboratory was viewed by some as a degradation of the intellect, in part because the use of equipment seemed so much messier than the "purity" of reason. King had no such aversions to test tubes or mineral samples, and he threw himself wholeheartedly into the world of experimental chemistry, a subject he applied increasingly toward the study of geology.

The unknown roused King. Nothing brought out his best like a good mystery—whether the challenge was posed by an unclimbed mountain or a geologic puzzle. The problem-solving compulsions that motivate scientists and climbers are sister impulses; scientists and engineers have always been prominent among the men and women drawn to the mountains and crags. For King those must have been heady days in the Yale chemistry lab, for they were his first structured exposure to the scientific method and the rigorous process of extracting truth from nature. In his eagerness he managed to finish a three-year program in only two.

There were drawbacks, though, to his location and studies. There was no real opportunity to sally forth into his cowboy ideal of the literary vagabond immersed in the larger world. There were still woods around New Haven, pockets of land for afternoon walks and the examination of rocks, plants, and animals. But not the big unmapped, unfettered spaces that embodied Nature, capitalized, and not yet humanized.

A confluence of forces brought him to California after the completion of his degree. The Civil War must have had its effect, as it did on most everything in those years. King's family was anti-slavery, but pacifistic from religious conviction, and while King could be downright combative when it came to mountains and bears, he was far less eager to injure a fellow human being. (He wrote to a friend that killing a man would "crucify in me many of my noblest impulses.") With his student exemption from the draft at an end, a loosely regulated state two thousand miles away from the nearest battle line must have been appealing. More importantly, the Whitney survey was in full swing and King's professors followed its progress with eagerness. Brewer, of course, was a Yale man, and he sent frequent letters describing the fieldwork back to his alma mater.

On an October day in 1862, King visited one of his professors, George Brush, who happened to be reading Brewer's most recent letter. It described the ascent of Mount Shasta, and Brewer's exhilaration made the words glow. He described the strange rock forms and spires, the moonlight on the snows, the airy summit; beneath his lines ran a feeling of hardship and purpose. King was hooked. Brewer could hardly have known that he had summoned a disciple from three thousand miles away.

California had all of the ingredients for adventure King desired. Here was his horseback ride with the "constellations his tent" to an exotic location to search for Truth. By now he had read Tyndall, and Swiss-born Louis Agassiz, the father of glaciology, had become a fixture at Harvard, so the image of the adventurous man of science learning secrets on the windswept peak tops had already lodged itself in his imagination. And there were whole ranges of mountains in California still unmolested by the human boot. That was the best part. With all the far corners of the world map being filled in at a rapid rate, here was a huge blank space accessible to a New England youth. All he needed to do was cross the continent, which he did, in the summer of 1863, with his childhood friend James Gardiner, and a letter of introduction to William Brewer.

Gardiner and King were both young and poor, though not impoverished, so they took the train to Missouri and then found a wagon outfit headed west whose captain agreed to feed them in exchange for help in guarding the live-stock. They had an adventurous crossing, featuring close encounters with out-laws, vigilantes, charging bison, and other western phenomena. They parted ways with the wagons at Carson City in the Nevada Territory, as King wanted to see the Comstock Lode—the mountain of silver that had drawn so many fortune-seekers into the desert. That night a fire burned down the building in which they slept and they lost everything but the clothes they had worn to bed. They spent two more weeks there working for the funds to carry them the re-maining distance to San Francisco.

On the last day of August, four months after leaving St. Joseph, Missouri, they reached Sacramento and boarded a steamer bound for the San Francisco Bay. The ferry was packed with miners, men with sunburnt faces, threadbare flannel shirts, and casually worn revolvers. But Gardiner noticed one man in the crowd who did not quite fit. He was just as hard-looking and travel-worn as the others, but something about his eyes and the lines of his face seemed familiar, even though Gardiner was sure they had never met. Gardiner studied this indi-vidual for a while and then showed him to King, who shared a similar instinct. So, wrote Gardiner, "after dinner Clare walked up to this man, the roughest dressed person on the boat, and deliberately asked him if he was Professor Brewer." Indeed, he was! After the months and miles of travel they had chanced onto the same boat as the man they were most eager to meet. Brewer had spent the summer crisscrossing the northern Sierra, but had worn out every one of his traveling companions and was headed back to San Francisco to meet with Professor Whitney. King had never seen his picture or even heard him described, but he felt a reflexive certainty that he had found the man who wrote the Shasta letter.

Brewer was happy to see them, too. Here was a sudden wind from home, two enthusiastic college boys full of news and common memories of New England. Even better, King wanted a place on the survey and didn't mind working as a volunteer. Brewer needed an assistant, but the finances of the survey were in disarray because of political wrangling; Brewer himself hadn't been paid his salary for over a year. That night King and Gardiner stayed with Brewer at his hotel in San Francisco, and the next day he introduced them to Whitney and the other members of the survey. In a few days' time Gardiner had found a position with the Army Engineers, and Brewer laid plans with King for an investigation of the northern goldfields.

From San Francisco they took the steamship back to Sacramento, then rode into the Sierra foothills. They worked north through rough country, traveling against the grain of the land over tall ridges and down steep valleys. The towns were small and expensive for visitors. Some featured well-built houses with picturesque settings, but most consisted of miserable shanties fogged in with a desperate, avaricious atmosphere that both men disliked. Farther north, the settlements dwindled, so Brewer and King spent more nights on the ground, which they both preferred. They found each other to be lively conversational companions. What bliss, for King, to be able to argue theoretical geology with a man like Brewer over a campfire in the California wilds.

Their destination was Mount Lassen, the southernmost of the Cascade volcanoes. It was a ten-thousand-foot plug of old lava and cinders, set among remote pine forests and boiling springs. So far as anyone knew no one had yet reached its summit. They climbed the mountain twice, through snowfields and cold temperatures and up the final crumbly rock spire. The second time they ascended through the night in order to watch the sunrise from the summit.

Mount Lassen affected King more than he might have guessed. On the pre-dawn morning of September 29, from the final lava outcrop with the silvery snowfields stretched below his feet, he watched the sun call to life one peak after the next down half the length of California and up into Oregon. Lassen's blue shadow stretched a hundred miles toward the Pacific. Mount Shasta turned to gold as the red solar ellipse detached itself from the horizon. Every fold, lake, ripple, and bend of that gilded landscape reached him through cold, clean autumn air. Here was a vista for a man looking for visual poetry, looking through eyes unpolluted by color photographs, aerial views, satellite images. He had truly never seen anything like this before.

Mount Lassen was a gentle mountain—not really a climb, even then, only a hike. It offered King a brief taste of what he sensed waiting for him in the heart of the Sierra. But it was practically October and the first snows had already glazed the summits; the big mountains were settling in for their season of hibernation.

The goldfields were still undated, so, after another month in the northern pinelands, Whitney sent King back to the Sierra foothills, in the region of the outflow of the Merced River. King found the work deeply, and disturbingly, dissatisfying. Scratching and sifting through the "vulgar gold dirt," as he called it, weighed down his spirit. He far preferred to hike up to the top of a local hill called Mount Bullion, from which he had a view of the big mountains in their gleaming winter coats.

The quality of his work suffered; his lack of attention frustrated his colleagues. The survey's paleontologist, William Gabb, observed, "I believe that fellow had rather sit on a peak all day and stare at those snow-mountains than find a fossil in the metamorphic Sierra." This was precisely the kind of work that should have invigorated King. Cross-referencing a fossil from the field against the known fossil record would give them an era for the gold-bearing stone; aside from its value to pure geology, this kind of data could, in theory, enable them to predict other strata in which gold might be found. Still, he could not bring himself to care. "Can it be?" he asked himself. "Has a student of geology so far forgotten his devotion to science? Am I really fallen to the level of a mere nature lover?"

The mountains grip the mountaineer just as hard as the climber grips the stone. Many have shared King's dilemma. At some point decisions must be made. Brewer decided to leave the mountains; a year after climbing Mount Lassen, a few months after reaching the summit of Mount Brewer, he was on a boat, headed home for the first time in four years. There he found a professorship and remarried. Though he made a few excursions into the Rocky Mountains, he settled comfortably and productively into his academic calling. Evan, who traveled to Mount Brewer with me, is bending along the opposite trajectory. He has finished his chemistry PhD, but his future revolves around places like Yosemite and Moab; he plans to live out of his car and climb every day.

Back in the foothills King rededicated himself to science, at least for the moment. He broke tons of rock and several hammers churning through the slates looking for the missing key. He spent days hunting that fossil, and he found it, at last, a little cigar-shaped *cephalopoda*. And yet, even after solving the riddle, even as he imagined accolades from white-haired scientists, he could not bring himself to be excited. "There was no doubt," he wrote, "I was not so happy as I thought I should be."

King escaped the goldfields in the spring and traveled to the Yosemite Valley for the first time. The mountains were beginning to thaw and the waterfalls must have been spectacular. At the end of May, Brewer mustered the southern Sierra party and King finally reached the big mountains and met Mount Tyndall. In the fall Brewer swung by a few last western sites before returning to friends and home in the East.

King returned to Yosemite. Congress had designated it a protected park over the summer, the first of its kind, and King's new job, accompanied by Gardiner, was to survey the boundaries of the preserved area. The process was laborious, a mile-by-mile measurement with chain and transit, but King showed no discontent. The mountains were no longer far-off phantoms for him to dream about from down in the foothills. On all sides he could see nothing but peaks and cliffs, great eruptions of clean, untouched granite.

All along his circumambulation one particular mountain pulled at his attention, a surfacing fin of orange and gray rock two thousand feet high named Mount Clark, located ten miles east and a little south of the Yosemite Valley. No matter from which direction he looked at the peak a fresh set of sharp lines and angles stared back at him. Here was a mountain with no easy side, its entire bulk composed of knife-blade ridges and steep headwalls. He left Gardiner to carry on the boundary work and recruited Cotter again for an attempt at the peak. They never even touched bare rock. Their venture ended in an epic retreat through an October blizzard that buried the mountain, knocked down trees, and closed the high country for the season.

◆ ◆ ◆

WHEN SNOW MELTS off Mount Clark the waters tumble down a canyon-side and join the Merced where the river slides over a bed of polished stone. Lower, the river picks up speed, vaults two famous waterfalls, filling the air with rainbows and shreds of foam, then pauses for a time in the placid bends on the floor of the Yosemite Valley; then a new drop ends the lull and the waters rip through gaps between hundred-ton blocks of granite. Eventually, the cool blues, whites, and greens of the mountains are abandoned in favor of brown: brown dirt, tan oaks, dry grasses, dull orange rocks. The river leaves the granite country behind and digs a deep furrow through the foothills. This is the gold country. King found his *cephalopoda* fossil here, a few miles from the main trunk of the Merced.

He had names for the two ends of the river. The one he called his *zenith*, the higher state of his heart's desires. The other, his *nadir*, the lower state of work and toil in the bowels of the earth.

King had to wait two years to return to Mount Clark. By then, Cotter was working in Alaska and Brewer had returned to Connecticut. King and Gardiner were doing more work in Yosemite for Whitney and the California Survey. This time they came to the mountain in July, under an open, blue Sierra sky that made King's memories of the wind and snow of two years past seem even grimmer. Mount Clark remained unclimbed. In all likelihood no one else had seriously entertained the idea.

They brought their survey gear, and King wrote that the summit would be a station of great topographical value. But his avowal of its geologic worth is humorous, and even a little sad, stuck in among his fervent descriptions of the mountain's aesthetic qualities: the keen edge cresting the peak from north to south, the needle spike summit, the views to be gained from its height above the nearby peaks. Nervous tension underlies King's words. Those same qualities that made the peak visually striking made the prospect of the climb both frightening and thrilling.

King and Gardiner left their horses and pack mules in the woods below the mountain's southwest shoulder and hiked up above timberline bound for the rocky pass between Mount Clark and the next peak south. They hurried up the last few hundred feet of granite slabs and boulders, hoping to reach the saddle with light enough to see the stonework to the east. They arrived with the sun a half-hour above the horizon, time enough to enjoy the cliffs and ice dropping away below their feet and the miles of granite rippling on toward Mount Lyell across a basin that once birthed glaciers and now held the headwaters of the Merced River.

I joined them there, wanting the same view. And though the eastern aspect had its virtues, I could not pry my eyes from Mount Clark. Its southern ridge sliced through the sky and the sunset splashed its western half with color while the eastern side fell into darkness. Right there before me, ten million tons of stone swelled out of the ground, held upright by its own brute strength but finished with a single dainty point toward which the mountain's lines all converged. Like King and Gardiner, I settled myself in the lee of a rock that cut a chilling wind. A remnant patch of melting snow leaked a little water and I topped off my bottle knowing that the night hours would firm the snow and turn off the trickle.

I have often wondered what it would be like to live on a planet dominated by mountains, a place where continents bristle with summits from sea to sea, and rock canyons maze out for thousands of miles between the high peaks. I suppose our stories would change, religious revelations would happen in fabled grassy fields instead of atop mountains, and adventurers would bring home tales of prairies that would be only half believed. We invest foreign geographies with magic and populate them with strange creatures and feelings. No wonder, then, that among the plains and rolling hills of our flat earth, the mountains shape our thoughts in powerful ways. Staring up at Mount Clark, thinking about the build of our planet and the landscape of the mind, I admired the pattern itself, the contrast between field and summit that endows the mountains with their strange potency and enables the mind to flesh the rocky bones with wonder and awe. There is much worth imitating in the stark, quiet strength of a mountain, much to be learned about oneself from the feeling of mystery that collects around its stones.

The sun shaded down toward the horizon and the mountain flared. I did not just watch the alpenglow; I was immersed in it. The rocks around our camp on the saddle turned the same colors as those draped around the mountain's shoulders. King nourished himself on these shades; "we drank and breathed the light," he wrote. The summit triangle glowed red and sent me up like a balloon, rising and stretching through the ruddy air, as if my thoughts couldn't wait for morning and had to taste the summit right away. I assume that King felt his own version of this pleasant longing from his seat on Mount Bullion, and that Brewer knew the feeling, too, on his birthday, staring up at Mount Shasta.

On the morning of July 12, King and Gardiner woke with the dawn, had a rasher of bacon for breakfast, and walked out along the saddle to the point where the solid ridge reared up from the talus. To their left, shadows owned the forbidding southwest face; to their right the sun glinted and scattered off quartz-laden blocks of gritty stone. The knife-edged ridge joining the two cliff faces lay straight ahead. From a distance this blade had appeared smooth, but up close it revealed serrations and clefts and orange gargoyles of granite squatting squarely in the climbers' path.

Blind corners hid all along the ridge. The two men climbed up over vertical steps and balanced along narrow edges only to find the way forward blocked, forcing them to reverse the precarious moves they had made. Where gaps and gargoyles interrupted the crest of the ridge they traversed along narrow ledges above the cliff faces, empty air plucking at their heels. They never knew whether their route would continue on past the next corner. I followed along behind them, bumping up against my fair share of dead ends, even though I knew to watch for them. The sightlines were so jumbled that I gave up on thinking forward and simply followed my fingers wherever they were willing to take me. But I had the advantage. I knew the mountain had been climbed. King and Gardiner were never even sure that it would be possible.

Two hundred feet below the summit, the ridge steepened and began to merge into the southern wall supporting the summit needle. A hundred feet further the ridge died away completely, leaving King and Gardiner stuck below a blank sheet of granite that loomed above them and seemed almost to push them away into space. Pressed up against the stone, standing on a narrow ledge, their position was delicate. Two steps to the right would have sent them over the edge of the east face. To the left a chasm in the cliffside separated them from blocky ground that might lead to the summit—had it not been on the other side of that airy space splitting the granite at their feet.

But the summit was so close! King looked hungrily across the leftward gulf. He decided to leap it. "Two years we had longed to climb that peak," he wrote, "and now within a few yards of the summit no weak-heartedness could stop us . . . There was no discussion, but planting my foot on the brink, I sprang . . .

While in the air, I looked down, and a picture stamped itself on my brain never to be forgotten." He landed on a rock wedged in a crack in a corner. The stone shifted, but held, and he braced himself against the opposite walls in case his foothold should give way. Each man gripped handholds and leaned out over the drop in order to pass the instruments across; then Gardiner repeated the leap while King pressed himself deeper into the crack to give him landing space. Then they "sprang up the rocks like chamois, and stood on the top, shouting for joy."

From the time I first read King's description of their leap I had been eager to see it for myself, and when I arrived there I found a dramatic spot. The gap was hung over a thousand feet of air, the whole length of the sheer, dark southwest face. No wonder such a vivid image lodged itself in King's brain—it was a long, long, way down through that gulf in the cliff wall, and jagged, hungry-looking rocks stared back up from the talus fields below. The distance across was tantalizing, perhaps seven feet or so, not much more than a running stride though there was no room to build up speed. And the landing on the other side was entirely uncertain, the consequences of poor aim entirely grim—a few seconds of rushing air for the ears, time enough for a regret or two or maybe only panic, and then a sudden stop.

I began to toy with the leap in my mind, trying to imagine the timing I would need to catch myself on the other side. I looked around at the clean lines and square edges of the stone all around me. Then, abruptly, the idea of the jump left my thoughts, and the tension building across the gap went slack. I traversed in toward the mountain on a thin toe-ledge, and where the sides of the space converged, I leaned across to the blocks below the summit. King's leap can be skirted to the right with a bit of careful balance.

Was his flight a rank lie? I don't think so. His description is precise; besides, Gardiner narrates the jump in much the same way in his own private journal, and he was not the same kind of storyteller as King. I continued up to the summit, vexed and perplexed at this strange man. What was he doing hurdling a death-fall with a sane alternative right beside him? Maybe he didn't miss the secure route because of poor judgment. Maybe the leap was an irresistible attraction. What better way to arrive at the summit of an unclimbed mountain than through a burst of heroic action?

Sitting on the summit, my greedy eyes had their fill, north to the white towers of the Cathedral Range, west at Half Dome and the Yosemite Valley, south and east to the dark spires of the Minarets, which King named from this very spot. John Tyndall's words and insights still accompanied King in the Sierra— the Minarets closely resemble a diagram Tyndall drew in the Alps of a curiously formed upside-down icicle which he labeled "ice minaret."

I began to see King's leap as the pivot point around which his scattered desires turned. His need for the dramatic moment, for everything to hang in the balance pending the outcome of one brave act, would never be satisfied by science. The heroic moment does not fit well into the scientific method. The results of his fieldwork could stimulate the analytical part of his mind and provide their own kind of intellectual thrill. But the work itself, the methodical exploration of the *nadir* must have been crushing to his spirit after his taste of adventure among the high peaks. And yet he could not let go and surrender himself to the mountains, either as a writer or a climber. A rigorous, ambitiously intellectual part of him feared the term "mere nature lover."

King wanted to be so many things: scientist, explorer, art critic and patron, author, millionaire. And he had natural gifts that made it all seem possible: a shrewd mind, sharp memory, brilliant wit, physical strength, and the conversational charm of a born raconteur. His good friend Henry Adams wrote that "with ordinary luck he would die at eighty the richest and most many-sided genius of his day." Another close friend, Secretary of State John Hay, set down a sentiment felt by many who knew King: "It is strange that the Creator, when it would have been so easy to make more Kings, should have made only one."

But a tone of frustration runs through his mountain writing and echoes into his later years. He could never seem to find what he wanted among the peaks; he was always craving, always dissatisfied. He wanted the mountains to give him something tangible, something that would contribute to his idea of a successful man.

He drifted away from California and the mountains and started many things. His survey of the 40th parallel was a pioneering episode of American science. His theoretical work hinted at rich structures and a place in the transatlantic debate inflamed by Darwin. But King never finished those studies. He sunk his energies and technical expertise into mining corporations and consulting work, looking for the gold lode that would make him rich. He raced from prospect to prospect, full of unhesitating hopefulness. But he didn't really like being a businessman; the end-of-the-century climate of frenzied capitalism appalled him; he lacked the white-hot avarice that made the powerful men of the era. He spent too much time traveling, wandering, and thinking. He put his mining work on hold to be the first director of the United States Geological Survey, but he held the position for only two years and then returned to speculation. He often talked of writing a novel—his literary friends begged him to give flesh and blood to the stories and characters he spun so brilliantly on evenings at the high-society clubs he frequented. But when he sat himself at his desk, his characters stopped speaking to him—or the distractions of his projects and desires drove them away. Except for his early sketches of the Sierra Nevada, his literary projects remained elusive and imaginary.

Perhaps it was just bad luck, but he died at the age of fifty-nine in a tavern in Arizona, round in the middle, far from anyone he loved, coughing through lungs damaged by his mines. During the previous decade his friends had already started to protect him from himself, both economically and socially. Excesses and eccentricities had begun to obscure his talents; people were already talking about youthful promise gone unfulfilled, though many still loved him dearly and even President Roosevelt sent condolences at the news of his passing. Maybe it was not bad luck—perhaps the trouble came from his inability to reconcile the provinces of his mind. He never chased down the one pursuit that would allow him to be brave, witty, rich, and happy all at once. He could not see a future for himself in the mountains and he could not find a position for himself in regular society that equaled the wonder of flying through the air toward an unclimbed summit while looking down into the chaos of rocks far below.

· 4 ·

John Muir + Cathedral Peak

[SEPTEMBER 1869]

Cathedral Peak (10,911 feet) and Budd Lake

I N 1869, THIRTY-ONE-YEAR-OLD John Muir spent his first summer in the Sierra as a shepherd for a friend's flock. The sheep were essentially irrelevant, merely the vehicle that would take Muir into the mountains. (Later he would call the animals "hoofed locusts" for their destruction of the high alpine meadows.) The mountains were far from irrelevant and Muir spent his time roaming, studying, and climbing. In early September, in the last shreds of a short summer season, Muir spent a day climbing Cathedral Peak and became the first of many to rest upon its slender summit.

The Cathedral is a marvelous piece of Yosemite stonecraft. Sharply cut blocks of clean white granite abut the summit spire, and a long arcing ridge leads down and then back up, to the upthrust knife of its western pinnacle. Farther to the west and the east, cold blue lakes, ringed by trees and more granite, jewel the hollows formed at the feet of the other mountains in the Cathedral Range. The name is apt; the Cathedral has served as wilderness church for many generations of Yosemite pilgrims. A good friend, the man who taught my wife to climb when she was young, was married there—and we will scatter his ashes there in the summer. Jim, like Muir, returned to this part of Yosemite over and over, nearly every summer for more than thirty years, to revisit the peaks; "old friends," he called them, with a genuine warmth of affection for the stone. After climbing Cathedral Peak, Muir wrote this in his journal: "This I may say is the first time I have been at church in California, led here at last, every door graciously opened for the poor lonely worshipper."

For Muir, that sentiment was loaded. His father had quite literally beaten the Bible into him. Daniel Muir, an evangelical Presbyterian, believed in work, silence, and thrashings. Kind words might have led to pride, so no kind words were heard from the patriarch of the Muir household. Later, when John Muir wrote a letter to a friend discussing the nature of child abuse, he said that the emotional toll of endless harsh scoldings hurt more than the physical pain of the beatings. Daniel Muir's version of asceticism, rooted in the Calvinism that underlay his beliefs, crossed well over the line into brutality.

His father's zealousness acted as a goad for the voracious mind and physical stamina that Muir possessed. By the age of eleven he had three-quarters of the Old Testament and all of the New memorized "by heart and sore flesh." On their Wisconsin farm, barely into his teenage years, he took pride in working harder and more productively than the hired help. And there was no end to this work. Daniel Muir demanded as much toil from his children as they would give, and his eldest son, already possessing the willpower that would carry him through his mountaineering adventures, would not back down from any command, no matter how unreasonable.

On top of the work, there was worship: Bible lessons, Sunday school, church services, family worship (an hour every evening spent on his knees, listening to his father's fervent prayers that none of them stray into temptation). Yet somehow Muir still found the time to have an exuberant childhood. He and his brother David packed their few spare moments with play: imaginative games of derring-do enacted while exploring the woods around their home.

Even on his own, in those years Muir took his father's religion seriously. The austere aesthetic of Calvinism satisfied a desire to master his own impulses. While learning how to swim in a nearby lake, Muir grew frightened, lost control, and almost drowned. Later that night, reflecting on the incident, he concluded that "I ought to punish myself for nearly losing my life from unmanly fear." At the first opportunity, he returned to the lake with a boat and hurled himself, repeatedly, into deep water, shouting "Take that!" with every plunge. The religious message also had a firm hold on his mind. At the age of eighteen, he wrote several parabolic letters to a friend. One described a traveler freezing in a blizzard and then sheltered by a stranger. "Ah Bradley," Muir wrote, "would you ever forget that man? No Bradley . . . that man would sit in the best place in the warmest end of your heart. Where then should you put Jesus? Where *have* you put him?"

Thirteen years later, Muir seated himself atop the Cathedral. A new spirit had led him there; he had shed the dogmatic earnestness of youth and become the man proclaiming the mountaintop his church. The change was more complicated than a simple rejection of his father's beliefs. Muir still saw God in the work of every snowflake and in the construction of every mountain. "Contemplating the works of these flowers of the sky," he writes, "one may easily fancy them endowed with life: messengers sent down to work in the mountain mines on errands of divine love." Divine love is everywhere in Muir's writing, but organized religion and Jesus are notably absent.

Even as a young child in Scotland, he felt a compulsive pull toward Mystery, in the grand sense of the word. Certain mysteries, like the source of the shrill peeps coming from beneath a haycock on a walk with his grandfather, or the formative agent of the Yosemite Valley, were meant to be solved. Others—what brought the snowflakes together to make the glaciers that made the canyons, the beauty in the metallic rainbow of a wood duck's feathers—were meant for wonder, a soul-satisfying admiration for the fine workings of nature. By the time he arrived in California, Muir had already begun to rebuild his sense of the divine out of these higher mysteries. Three years earlier, he had written to his friend, Jeanne Carr, that he took "a more intense delight from reading the power and goodness of God from 'the things which are made' than from the

Bible." Now, in the Sierra, he was ready to turn his full attention to the texts written into the mountains.

Looking at Muir's early education, the God of Cathedral Peak is more closely connected with the time he spent in the woods with his brother David than with their father's injunctions and threats of hellfire. The two boys spent the same amount of time studying beetles and trees as hunting and fishing. Their curiosity extended to all of the phenomena, large and small, that surrounded their farm. And miraculous puffs of similar wonderment would occasionally escape from Daniel Muir, too. It was he who pointed out the colors in the duck's feathers, he who suggested that the boys study the frog when learning how to swim. Perhaps their father struggled mightily to maintain his sternness and piety. In the end, he withdrew deeper into his Bible, abandoning the boys to the labor of the farm so that he could remain inside and read.

After the years spent imprisoned by his father's faith, the Californian mountains must have felt like an emancipation to Muir. In his days as a wild child in the Scottish Highland, he was often threatened with hell; one particular servant girl "loved to tell its horrors" and warned him that evil boys would be cast down into it. Muir had a ready response. "I always insisted that I could climb out of it," he wrote. "I imagined it was only a sooty pit with stone walls . . . and I felt sure there must be chinks and cracks in the masonry for fingers and toes." He and David practiced by making nighttime excursions to the rooftop of their house. Now, an ocean and a continent to the west, Muir put his climbing craft to use for ascension instead of escape.

Muir was not the first to look for God on the peak tops. That search dates back much further and spans the globe, from the Andes to Sinai to the Himalayas. But much has changed in the hundred years since Muir's death. Veils have been torn off so many of the world's mysteries—too many for me to believe that God has made these peaks out of love or with some design. As pleasant as it might be to think of the mountaintop as closer to God, I can't, and neither did my friend Jim, who died of a heart attack last winter—though he was more spiritually minded than I am. Yet I return again and again to these peaks, this mountain in particular. I have climbed the Cathedral close to a dozen times, and some that I know count their visits to its summit in the hundreds.

The summit is the size and shape of a tabletop, about four feet wide by seven feet long. It has a slight southern slope, but stays flat enough for a comfortable seat. The edges are bounded only by air, the rock drops down on all sides—a thousand feet to the south, a hundred feet to the north; imagine resting on a coffee table placed atop the Chrysler Building. Nothing clutters the sightlines.

The landscape here is profoundly still. This is high alpine terrain and movement is limited to a few squawky Clark's nutcrackers and butterflies and gusts of wind. The gnarled dwarf pines that dot the meadows and find toeholds on the mountainside do not change from decade to decade. In this stasis, time ebbs and stops. All around, bare crags and stony peaks cut the air, the raw stuff of the earth frozen in place after breaching the top layer. Though I can't locate God, I do feel an absurd closeness to the stars, a sensation that comes from being pressed up against a thinning and blueing sky.

Squeezed between the mountain and the stars, it is the age of this place that calls me back. The difference in age and size between the mountain and me is very nearly infinite, a quantity that is hard to locate in cities. Here, the scale of the universe is more visual, more visceral, the human creature at its least significant. It is both invigorating and humiliating to ride on the back of something so huge, to look up into a whirlpool so deep. Muir's God lives here somewhere, in the cycles of rock and snow and woody growth that far predate man's self-consciousness and need nothing from him for their continuation.

This is a good place for ashes. There will be no quick growth here, no sudden changes to break up our memories. I will use the same handholds that Jim used and that Muir used and we can all three sit on top in the tranquility that lingers there. In terms of flesh and blood, Muir will fade away first, my images of him constructed from words, his fetishism of the peaks beautiful and strange and foreign to me. Jim will last longer, his image pressed deeper into my brain: an intense pair of brown eyes, muscle layered year by year onto his small frame, the way he leaned into a conversation as if into a headwind. The affection he felt for the mountains was more similar to my own, though Jim may have been less awestruck, more congenial. Maybe that comes with time.

I'll vanish too, of course, and give up my spot to the next generation who will try to make sense out of the summit. The constant will be the rock itself. The Cathedral, older than our temples, our gods, our graveyards, will not fade or crumble on any scale that matters to us. This mystery is about permanence, about the duration of stone and flesh and words, about the astonishing ratio between our little lives and this immense and ancient world.

·5·

John Muir + Mount Ritter

[OCTOBER 1872]

Storm clouds building over Banner Peak (12,945 feet) and Mount Ritter (13,157 feet), side by side to the right

THE SUMMER OF 1872 clung tenaciously to the High Sierra. August slipped by, September yielded to October, and still each morning dawned clear and blue, though the nights lengthened and the air grew icy teeth. Muir had been in the mountains for months, rambling and studying and climbing, just as he had every summer since 1869 when he first took his friend's sheep up into Tuolumne and climbed Cathedral Peak. But even he could not believe that summer would hold on much longer, so he headed down to the Yosemite Valley where he planned to overwinter.

He describes a mellow, pleasant kind of regret at leaving the high peaks. He looked forward to being "warmly snowbound" in his Yosemite cabin "with plenty of bread and books." But he would miss the mountains. As he descended he stopped and looked back, catching last views of the glaciers, summits, and cliffs that had been his companions and teachers. He felt a bit of sorrow, too, that he was not a better artist, and could not mirror these vistas on canvas. To anyone who has seen Muir's sketches, this wish is typical of his inability to honestly judge his creations. He had the deftness to reveal accurate and expressive details with just a few thin pencil lines, just as he could make a waterfall race with a sparkling phrase. Still, he wanted to capture colors and shades and the full glory of his mountains. One cluster of peaks in particular, the Lyell group, begged him for a portrait. "After long ages of growth in the darkness beneath the glaciers" he wrote, "it seemed now to be ready and waiting for the elected artist, like yellow wheat for the reaper."

West of the mountains he passed through Tuolumne's fairytale domelands, then continued down past Clouds' Rest and Half Dome and the big waterfalls along the Merced River, arriving, as he put it, "in Yosemite in due time—which, with me is *any* time." Waiting for him on the valley floor were two men, who had letters of introduction. They were painters. Did Muir know of an uncommonly good spot for the painting of a large canvas? It was as if his wish for an artistic hand had been enough to conjure just the men he wanted.

In a sense he truly had summoned them. This was before the foundation of the Sierra Club, before Muir's marriage and the publication of his books, before the creation of Yosemite National Park and the great environmental battles of the turn of the century. These were his years to roam the Sierra and cultivate the free growth of his thoughts on wildness. Nevertheless, his voice trickled out from the mountains; it was heard by those who came to meet him in Yosemite and by the few to whom he sent his letters, and there was a dawning realization in a few small circles that a rare mind had emerged in California. William Keith, one of the two painters, had learned of Muir in this way and had come to Muir when he wanted to find insight into the mountains of the West. It was around this time that people began to make a comparison, which Muir himself did not wholly disavow, between Muir and John the Baptist, the man behind the "voice crying out in the wilderness" who prepared the people for the first coming.

Muir told the painters to pack their things and be ready to go with no delay, as storms could thunder down at any time in October, even if the sky seemed benign. He led them back up to Tuolumne, taking two days to return to where the land pushed up toward Mount Lyell and the confluence of rock, snow, and sky made him think of ripe wheat. They arrived in the evening, turning the corner of a hill just as the alpenglow lit the peaks. Muir described the reaction of his companions: "Their enthusiasm was excited beyond bounds, and the more impulsive of the two, a young Scotchman, dashed ahead, shouting and gesticulating and tossing his arms in the air like a madman." That was Keith. He and Muir developed a lasting friendship.

Muir found a comfortable pine grove for the painters' camp. They lit a fire and discussed plans. The two men were eager to have several days, at least, to do their work, and Muir decided he would hustle south aiming for the untouched summit of Mount Ritter. He knew that his plan was audacious and that the season could turn any day. "I warned the artists," he wrote, "not to be alarmed should I fail to appear before a week or ten days, and advised them, in case a snow-storm should set in, to keep up big fires and shelter themselves as best they could, and on no account to become frightened and attempt to seek their way back to Yosemite alone among the drifts." Imagine receiving that kind of advice from a man you've just met who has led you two days out into the middle of the mountains! The next morning the artists set hungrily upon their brushes and pencils and the view, while Muir lit out for the mountain beyond the southern horizon.

I don't remember when, exactly, I first read Muir's account of his climb of Mount Ritter. But it must have been early in my teenage years, around the time I first started climbing, because the story colored my entire conception of adventure and mountaineering. Ritter was the only mountain that came near to killing Muir. His story of the climb is one of the most compelling mountain writings ever laid down on paper, a simple statement of desire, fear, and deliverance set against Mount Ritter's cold, dark cliffs. I had trouble imagining following him up there, as if the cliffs would prove insubstantial, made more of myth than rock. It was a strange, edgy feeling, not so much a fear of the climbing, but a fear of the legend itself; I wondered if I would be giving offense to some sort of cosmic hubris watchdog with my intention of re-creating this piece of history.

When I returned to his story and tried to read it over with a practical eye, I found much I had missed. I had always been swept along by the climb, but now I paid as much attention to how Muir traveled to the mountain. Twenty-five miles of rough country separate Tuolumne and Mount Ritter. Even though it was the middle of October, Muir wore light clothes, took no blanket, and carried little more than a tin cup, a notebook, and a bundle of bread. As I studied his words, the bare outline of the future took shape in my mind and it looked hard, cold, and hungry.

One of Keith's paintings from inside Lyell Canyon, where they camped, shows a river ford and a trail, so perhaps Muir walked this path for a distance in the morning. Soon, however, he left the canyon bottom and followed a boisterous creek up and over the eastern canyon-side. These alpine creeks brought him no end of pleasure. "What a fine traveling companion it proved to be," he wrote, "what songs it sang, and how passionately it told of the mountain's own joy! Gladly I climbed along its dashing border, absorbing its divine music, and bathing from time to time in waftings of irised spray." Only Muir could be so overjoyed by repeated soakings from an ill-mannered rill on a chilly morning while trying to hurry toward a distant mountain.

From the top of the canyon wall Muir descended down the eastern front of the Sierra in dazzling sunlight with a view out over the Mono desert. He had crossed over to the east in order to travel a less cumbered line toward the mountain, though forests and canyons still filled his way forward. In the distance, the black guard peaks of Ritter clawed up out of the trees, and above them jutted the sharp horn of Ritter's sibling, Banner Peak, while Ritter itself, massive and withdrawn, looked down complacently on its defenses. "Mount Ritter," Muir wrote, "is king of the mountains of the middle portion of the High Sierra . . . and it is fenced round by steeply inclined glaciers, and canyons of tremendous depth and ruggedness." The mountain, of course, had never been climbed before, though

Clarence King had tried. Difficult rock and an intensifying storm turned him away, and he called the summit "inaccessible," which was the word he used for any interesting alpine place he failed to reach.

Night-frost iced the meadows and the morning still wore gray when I walked through the lower reaches of Lyell Canyon. The river bent through long, shapely arcs, and thin streamers of vapor hung above its current. Coyote barks erupted from a grove just opposite me. Their howls were so sudden and sad that my skin shriveled and I half expected to see a mountain lion burst through the meadow with a coyote pup in its mouth or something as calamitous.

By the time the sun was bright I joined Muir atop the canyon wall. At this point I intersected a popular backpacking trail and passed two men and a woman, all heavily laden with packs that looked to weigh fifty or more pounds each. One of the hikers, an older man, huffed and glared at me. He demanded to know where I had come from, and I realized that his squinty indignation had been provoked by my unconventional kit. I must have looked a little strange. I had a tin cup, a warm hat, and three small cakes of bread (one for each day Muir spent going to and from Mount Ritter) crammed into a thin, open-topped canvas shopping bag which I had slung across one shoulder. I judged that this ration and carrier were a reasonable approximation of Muir's "little stock" of bread. Aside from my shoulder bag I had the clothes on my back and a knife and compass in my pocket. We were twelve miles from the nearest trailhead and I was headed deeper into the mountains. To the old man breathing hard under his load, I was clearly crazy or cheating or at least generally suspicious. Since I had not yet survived a night, let alone climbed my mountain, I had no particular wish to talk up my plans, so I mumbled something noncommittal and pressed on.

In all honesty, my possessions were disconcertingly light—each easy step forward reminded me that I carried nothing to defend myself against the darkness and cold. But the miles dropped by so quickly I hardly registered them passing; I seemed to float along through the woods and over the stones. As with my trek to Mount Tyndall I had no map, but that mattered less this time because I knew the general area well, as did Muir. Besides, from the moment I topped the Lyell Canyon wall, Mount Ritter was rarely out of sight. After all, it was the largest mass for miles around, though traveling toward it meant navigating canyons, ridges, cliffs, and streams. Down in a maze of creeks at the bottom of one canyon I met a glossy yearling bear with a shaggy black coat. It startled and ran before I could admire it very long. Overhead an enormous red-tailed hawk cruised by just above the treetops. On a steep valley side I passed over pink-hued granite bosses arranged one above the next like terraced mushrooms, each showing deep scratches and shiny patches of glass left by the passage of glaciers.

Muir loved this terrain; he delighted in the plants and creatures and was moved by the artistry of the last ice age. "All my first day was pure pleasure," he wrote, "simply mountaineering indulgence, crossing the dry pathways of the ancient glaciers, tracing happy streams, and learning the habits of the birds and marmots in the groves and rocks." Muir spent much of his time in those years piecing together glacial history. His discussions with the stones had convinced him that glaciers were responsible for sculpting the mountains and grinding the sediments that fertilized the garden valleys. As the creative force behind the beauty of the Sierra, the glaciers became demi-angels in Muir's mountains.

It was the scientific upshot of Muir's theories that caused Professor J. D. Whitney to call him an ignorant shepherd. Whitney had come to California seeing catastrophes in the geologic record, and no field evidence to the contrary would convince him otherwise. When he looked at the Yosemite Valley he saw earthquakes and spasmodic subsidence, cataclysmic hand-of-God events that rent the top layer and shook the earth's foundations. So when this starry-eyed naturalist with little formal scientific training had the temerity to suggest that all of that grand rockwork was the result of something as insubstantial as snow and ice long since melted, Whitney reacted with his characteristic bluster. Never mind that Muir had spent months and years sketching the geometry of the canyons, studying the weathering patterns of the granite, and crawling down among the rocks to examine places where the passing ice had rubbed up against the stone. Never mind that Muir discovered live glaciers where Whitney had said none could exist.

The shadows fattened and merged, and Muir looked for a place to pass the night though Mount Ritter was still a few miles away. He found a hollow space in a pine thicket "where the branches were pressed and crinkled overhead like a roof, and bent down around the sides." These nooks, with beds of spongy old pine needles, were some of Muir's favorite places: "snug as squirrel-nests, well ventilated, full of spicy odors, and with plenty of wind-played needles to sing one to sleep." Before retiring, Muir watched the sunset light the peaks rose and then red. "This was the alpenglow," he wrote, "to me one of the most impressive of all the terrestrial manifestations of God." No wonder Muir disliked Whitney's theories. Muir's father was the kind of man who would look at Yosemite and see a single blow of God's fist. When Muir looked he saw waterfalls, sunsets, and snowflakes. The alpenglow faded, and Muir crawled in through a "side-door" under his pine and found little birds "nestling among the tassels." Like Muir, the birds had taken refuge from the night under the protective branches of the tree.

When he wrote about the alpine creatures he wrote as a friend and compatriot, as one who shared their bowers and understood their daily needs.

I arrived in Ritter's neighborhood in the afternoon. Muir's bed under the whitebark pine sounded so snug and pleasant that I was halfway optimistic about the idea. But I looked under the hem of every whitebark for a couple of acres and found nothing at all like the chateau-Muir. Maybe I ended my day higher than Muir, where the trees were scrawnier, but I doubt it. Where I saw thin branches he probably would have complimented the star skylights, and what looked to me like minimal shelter he probably would have called a comfy home. In all Muir's writing he seems incapable of finding fault, no matter how slight, with any aspect of the Sierra. In theory I agree with him—it is the human being who inhabits the imperfect form and who should try to live up to the mountains—but in practice, on a breezy evening at eleven thousand feet with a cold night ahead, I could have used less philosophy and more insulation. I picked a narrow furrow under one scraggly pine, largely by default. The pine bodied up against a rock and between the two I thought I might have some wind shelter. The sleeping box was open on one side and loosely roofed by green branches. I threw a few extra handfuls of dry pine needles onto its floor and pushed a bundle of sticks against the open side in order to have at least the illusion of an enclosed space.

With my bed furnished, I walked over to a nearby pond and dipped some water in my cup. Fresh bear tracks wandered the mudflats all around the water. The prints were large and I would have liked to see the animal that left them, though mud has a way of magnifying paws. I sipped water and sat by the pond shore for a while on the off chance that the bear would make an evening visit, but she never did.

Back at my pine I found a rock for my back and sat with a view to the south and east. Thousand Island Lake filled the valley below me, an immense rectangular sheet of water populated by outcrops that stuck up through the surface. The lake was large enough to drown a city; the granite spires poking through suggested ancient architecture caught by a rising tide. Across the lake-head rose

Sunrise through fire haze over Thousand Island Lake

Banner Peak and behind it the summit of Mount Ritter, both of them washed in colored light from the setting sun, though I could see only slices of the alpenglow from my outlook. The mountains here are made of dark, metamorphic rock from a time long before the birth of the granite Sierra. They are holdouts against erosion; most of their generation of stone has long since been weathered away and washed down into the valleys. They *look* ancient, whether or not you know their geologic age. Their faces are cracked, shattered, and color-splotched, though the lines are still sharp and the cliffs upright, and the result is a collection of jagged old peaks that look like fossilized teeth.

I ate the butt-end of my first loaf of bread and wrapped the other two in my canvas bag to use as a pillow. I was pretty hungry, though not ravenous yet. On cold nights in the mountains I like to eat to stay warm, but that wouldn't be possible this night and I figured I would wake up pretty depleted by morning. Muir was a slight man; he called himself the "runt of the family," a condition he thought partly the result of overwork on the farm as a child stunting his growth. As a man he ate little to begin with, and when he traveled the mountains he took only enough bread to sustain himself for however long he planned to stay. Even when he carried food, he was always on the edge of fasting.

In name and temperament, Muir may resemble John the Baptist, but his actions echo Jesus more than he might have cared to admit. Muir came to the Sierra at the same age that Jesus was baptized and "led by the spirit into the wilderness." Neither of them put much stake in food. In his wilderness, Jesus fasted forty days, and then Satan came to test him. "If thou be the Son of God, command this stone that it be made bread," Satan said. Jesus replied, "Man shall not live by bread alone, but by every word of God." I can almost hear Muir's response. Yes, he seems to say, it's true that bread is the lesser need, but do you realize the stones themselves are the words of God? He had been inculcated with these stories at such an early age that it's no surprise they appeared later in his thoughts.

A few stars scattered the twilight. Reluctantly, I squirmed into my space beneath the pine, knowing that I should not let any more body heat escape into the night than I had already. I had enough room to lie flat with my boot soles against the rock and my head wedged in toward the pine trunk, and I could roll onto one side or the other to give my rump a break. I could have chosen a roomier spot, but I wanted a space that would trap my body heat. The pine needle mattress proved surprisingly comfortable.

The wind came up and blew hard. I was dimly aware of it tossing my tree back and forth, though only a few gusts penetrated my bower. I slept well enough for the first third of the night. Past that point the cold infiltrated my thin clothes and flesh, so I caught brief naps between sessions of rubbing and shaking and cursing. Many times I peered out between branches to the east, but the stars were always sharp and the sky black and the night spun on. Muir was cold, too. He built a fire outside his shelter and "had to creep out many times . . . during the night" to warm himself, "for it was biting cold." His October night was longer and colder than mine, but I had no fire, so the trade seemed fair.

The night couldn't go on forever, and it didn't; the eastern horizon turned gray and the stars lost their brilliance, and that was all the invitation I needed to shake free from my tree and struggle out into the predawn. There's not much to do in the morning when you go to bed with your boots on. By the time I was standing I was more or less ready to go.

Muir described his preparations: "I fastened a hard, durable crust to my belt by way of provision, in case I should be compelled to pass a night on the mountain-top; then securing the remainder of my little stock against wolves and wood-rats, I set forth free and hopeful." Later he added, "I had not even burdened myself with a coat." (And in the back of my mind I hear Jesus instructing the apostles to "take nothing for their journey . . . no scrip, no bread, no money in their purse: But be shod with sandals; and not put on two coats.")

I stuffed most of my second loaf of bread in a trouser pocket and, feeling obliged to fully enter the spirit of the day, I stripped off the outer of my three shirts, wrapped it around my remaining bread inside the canvas, and hung the bundle from the top of my tree. I drank off the water I had left overnight in my cup and left it below some branches with a stone inside to keep it from being blown away. Then I tottered off on my stiff legs through the murky dawn, trying to waken warmth through motion.

I felt emptied out, but not particularly hungry. I had eaten a few mouthfuls first thing, but the bread in my pocket did not badger me with temptations as I had expected. In fact I felt light and energized, as if I could race to the mountain if I could just get my legs to work properly. The first mile led me over rocky meadows sprouting short clumps of whitebark pine, like the one under which I had slept. I passed through a few denser bands of trees, but even then none were very tall. The short growing season and winter snow force the trees here into strange shapes; some grow scrawny branches on stout trunks, like old fat men with potbellies and sticklike arms, while others become spraddling creatures like crawling bushes.

I needed twenty minutes to warm up, and then my stride lengthened and loosened. The sun cleared the horizon and began splashing light and heat all around. Muir soaked up the sunrise; maybe he had learned how to ingest that instead of breakfast. "I strode on exhilarated," he wrote, "as if never more to feel fatigue, limbs moving of themselves, every sense unfolding like the thawing flowers." I felt it, too, as if the night had stripped pounds from my frame and now I could move through the mountains at ease. The trees vanished and the meadows thinned. Clear creeks poured down between rocks. Whenever I crossed water I gulped a mouthful or two—often just lying flat and sticking my face in the flow—because I knew that I would have none on the mountain.

I followed Muir up a narrow valley to the north of Banner Peak. A wall of talus closed its head; in Muir's season this had been covered in autumn-hardened snow, and he had needed several attempts to find an angle he could climb, even with his hobnailed boots. For me it held only rock and I leapt from boulder to boulder up to the crest of a small divide. At the top of the talus the mood of the land changed, the flowers and grasses refused to grow here, the atmosphere turned hushed and severe. Muir described the scene: "There, immediately in front, loomed the majestic mass of Mount Ritter, with a glacier swooping down its face nearly to my feet, then curving westward and pouring its frozen flood into a dark blue lake . . . I could see only the one sublime mountain, the one glacier, the one lake . . . rock, ice, and water close together without a single leaf or sign of life." Here at last was the mountain. It appeared to be real enough, though, admittedly, the aura of Muir's story magnified the cliffs and darkened the maze of rock and shadows.

Below me, the lake looked colder than any substance I had ever seen, like a big-bored well filled with steel-colored water that would float icebergs if its glacier took a mind to produce any. The glacier filled the crease between Ritter and Banner, stretching up from the lake to the bottom of Ritter's cliffs. Above the snow, spires stabbed out from the mountainside while avalanche grooves wound down between them. Much higher still the summit cut a simple point out of the sky, and it did look more like a geometric abstraction than honest earth.

Confronted with such a stark and foreboding scene, Muir picked his way down to the glacier feeling a hesitancy foreign to him in the mountains. "I could not distinctly hope to reach the summit from this side," he wrote, "yet I moved on across the glacier as if driven by fate." He decided not to attempt it. "The season is too far spent, I said, and even should I be successful, I might be storm-bound on the mountain; and in the cloud darkness, with the cliffs and crevasses covered in snow, how could I escape? No: I must wait till next summer." But the sky was still blue and the sun bright, with no sign whatever of a storm. While he rationalized his legs carried him on toward the peak. "I would only approach the mountain now," he continued, "and inspect it, creep about its flanks, learn what I could of its history, holding myself ready to flee on the approach of the first storm-cloud." He ascended the glacier and arrived at the base of the cliffs; and then he began to climb because he could not help himself, the fingerholds and edges worked into the gnarled stone beckoned him on toward the summit. "We little know," he wrote, "until tried how much of the uncontrollable there is in us."

He entered one of the avalanche tracks above the glacier, climbing up a narrow corridor through what he called "a wilderness of crumbling spires." In the shadows of the recess much of the rock was coated in ice, which Muir hammered off with loose stones in order to access the holds beneath. He felt terribly insecure. The mountain seemed to dangle him above gravity's clutch. Already he had passed difficult sections that he did not believe he could reverse. "I . . . began to be conscious of a vague foreboding," he wrote. "Not that I was given to fear, but rather because my instincts, usually so positive and true, seemed vitiated in some way, and were leading me astray." This must have been a sickening feeling for him. He traveled the mountains with the same kind of ready familiarity as the animals he studied. To be unsure, and conscious of fear, was an alien, unsettling emotion that made him worry not only about the physical dangers gathering on the mountain, but also about the rightness of his own thoughts and impulses.

He could not descend. Those cliffs he had already climbed were barriers arrayed behind him (and besides, the summit still tugged at him from above . . .). He climbed higher through the channel, putting more elevation and dangers between himself and the comparative safety of the glacier now far below. He arrived at the base of an imposing cliff that blocked his progress altogether. He tried to climb the channel walls to bypass it, but found them holdless. What could he do? If he sat down and gave up, no one would be along to rescue him— at least not inside the next decade. His choices had narrowed to this one square-built wall of stone.

He scanned it for holds from below, and though they seemed slight, he believed he could string them together in a sequence to the top of the cliff. He climbed up, choosing his holds with care, but his eyes and fingers failed him. "After gaining a point about half-way to the top," he wrote, "I was suddenly brought to a dead stop, with arms outspread, clinging close to the face of the rock, unable to move hand or foot either up or down." Like a spider barely holding to a slick window, he had become stuck, and paralyzed. "My doom appeared fixed. I *must* fall. There would be a moment of bewilderment, and then a lifeless rumble down the one general precipice to the glacier below."

It had been many years since Muir had felt this kind of fear, perhaps all the way back to the episode from his boyhood when he seized in the water and came near to drowning. The effect on his mind, and the outcome, echo that early test.

When this final danger flashed upon me, I became nerve-shaken for the first time since setting foot on the mountains, and my mind seemed to fill with a stifling smoke. But this terrible eclipse lasted only a moment, when life blazed forth again with preternatural clearness. I seemed suddenly to become possessed of a new sense. The other self, bygone experiences, instinct, or Guardian Angel—call it what you will—came forward and assumed control. Then my trembling muscles became firm again, every rift and flaw in the rock was seen as through a microscope, and my limbs moved with a positiveness and precision with which I seemed to have nothing at all to do. Had I been borne aloft upon wings, my deliverance could not have been more complete.

Muir did not often have need to access this unconscious level of self-preservation. But when he did his instincts reacted with a vigorous grip on life and the mountain, and his inner curtain parted to gift him clarity of mind which seemed lifted from a miracle.

Adrenaline is easy stuff to come by—a few dollars for a ticket to a roller coaster or horror movie will do. Climbing offers something far more rare and precious, which is why the tag "adrenaline sport" rings hollow to me. The mental clarity brought on by an intense instant, the moment when the world falls away and nothing exists beyond the fingertips and a few square feet of rock; this wellspring of thought and vision runs deeper than a cheap buzz. This is why climbing has been compared to meditation, though it's a state of grace built from fierce exertion instead of stillness.

Yet people would not climb mountains if there weren't risk involved, or at least they wouldn't be the same people. Risk opens the door, focuses the mind, begets a healthy distrust for the padded walls of prudence. Is it worth it? In that moment of falling would Muir have thanked the mountains for bringing him so far, or cursed his fingers for failing and his boots for taking him into the peaks to begin with? There's no answer. All of us on this side of the fall can't know. It's worth it if you live, I'm sure of that. If Muir had not been the type to gravitate toward Ritter's cliffs, to launch himself up that maze of ice and stone in defiance of his hesitant judgment, could we expect him to have had the same vision of the mountains? Could we expect him to have understood wildness so well?

I started across the glacier, and wished for Muir's hobnails because I kept sliding on the ice and falling down. Maybe I kept sliding because I couldn't stop looking up at the cliffs and thinking of Muir dangling himself from them, compelled onward by the uncontrollable within him. The last hundred feet of snow were too steep for my boots so I crossed around to a lower extension of the rock and began a delicate traverse on ice-crusted holds. Strange rock fringed the glacier. Well-developed crystals of clear quartz studded the insides of fracture planes. One cubic boulder had smooth exterior faces, but a broken corner revealed bubbly, frothy, volcanic rock on the inside. Ritter's stone began life as volcanic output, but eons of heat and pressure miles underground altered its nature and twisted its form until it became a geologic carnival of minerals and shapes. The chemical and physical torture opened many slots for fingers and boot-edges—good thing, too, because the cliffs pushed sharply out above the snow. In places the fingerholds shrank while the angle remained steep, and I dug my fingers into slight creases and pulled hard toward friendlier holds.

The avalanche tracks snaked and branched above, their true courses lost behind warped cliffs and teetering spires. I followed Muir as best I could through the maze and over cliffs cut from the channels, hanging my body on my hands and my hands on blocky edges where the mountain's mortar had worn away. The clues he left are slim and Ritter hosts a fractal bedlam of stone. I don't believe we'll ever be sure of the exact spot of his fear and escape. But I think I found it, a smooth gray cliff buttressing out from the back of its channel. The holds it offered were sparse, but tantalizing, a scattering of narrow finger slots worked in between planes of finely grained stone quite different from the rest of the mountain. I sunk my digits to the second joint and tiptoed up the bare offerings for my feet. Slot reached slot and edge brought edge and soon the air piled up below me.

I don't believe Muir climbed Ritter because of a lapse of control. I think he *wanted* to be here, upraised among the air and shadows and wild stonework. But it's uncomfortable to admit stronger imperatives than strict rationality—not just to admit them, but to embrace them. I reached the last slot and pulled myself over the cliff top, which merged into a narrow ridge winding toward Ritter's summit.

The strength breathed into Muir by his wakened inner self stayed with him. He flew up the mountain, and I followed his shadow through chutes between towers, across exposed traverses, over clutches of stacked blocks, and along the crests of sharp ridges. The mountain seemed to stretch on past the numeric limits of its elevation. And always there were holds for the hands, air under the boot soles, and vertical acres of jagged rock which even Muir called "savagely hacked and torn."

When Muir reached the summit he sat in the light of the lowering autumn sun, admired the mountains, and let the warmth thaw the fear and cold of the north face out of his muscles and nerves. Peaks filled the land, the close-by ones made of the same dark, shattered rock as Ritter, the rest built from granite that sparkled and glared. Between the mountains curved smooth basins made all of granite, some the size of a mountain's lap, a few immense enough to hold whole districts of forests and streams. Down in the basins a thousand lake-eyes looked back at Muir. "Lakes are seen gleaming in all sorts of places," he wrote, "round, or oval, or square, like very mirrors; others narrow and sinuous, drawn close around the peaks like silver zones." He called the whole scene "Nature's poems carved on tables of stone."

I found a seat below the summit and watched the wind walk across the lakes. Ripples tracked their surfaces, breaking left or right, then plunging ahead, like coyotes chasing a scent. The wind swung past the summit, too, and I stayed hunkered down among the rocks.

Muir had no intention of climbing back down what he had climbed up—one round of that sort of personal insight was enough for him for the day. He decided to descend the south face, which would take him the wrong direction but looked to be the gentlest way off the top. He shed a thousand feet down loose talus and scree, which brought him to the upper reach of Ritter's south glacier. The snow had softened all day in the sun, so Muir made "rapid progress, running and sliding, and keeping a sharp outlook for crevasses." After a half-mile, the glacier spilled itself over an icefall, breaking up into giant blocks of compressed snow-ice split by blue gaps. At first he tried to avoid this dangerous place, but cliffs fell away on all sides so he returned to the fall. He discovered that the sun had hollowed the ice enough that he could carve handholds and kick steps in its flossy outer layer, and so he excavated a set of rungs that delivered him to the lower edge of the glacier.

A circuitous route through precipices and waterfalls brought him back down to the basins east of the mountains, but his pine was still far to the north. Night caught him here. He kept the mountain to his left and the downgrade to the Mono Valley to his right and walked by starlight across bare granite canyons and boulder fields toward his bread and lake and bed. The darkness quenched the energy that had propelled him through the day; his muscles finally wearied. But nothing obstructed his return, so there was no reason to stop and he shuffled on through the sleeping land. Eventually he heard the waterfall feeding his lake, then he saw stars reflected in the water, and from there he located his nest under the tree and his small bundle of supplies.

First he stretched himself on the ground, "lying loose and lost for a while." Then, under a sky stuffed with stars, he rousted himself, made a bonfire, went down to the lake and "dashed" water on his head, dipped his tin cup, and came back to the fire to make tea and eat bread. Apparently this ritual was a necessary revivifying step before he could put himself to bed. When he did at last retire he slept long and hard, though his fire dwindled and the wind flung frigid air against his pine.

I stepped off the summit and down the loose rocks of the south face, working hard not to kick too many off, though a few rolling stones were inevitable. The glacier was a sad shadow of the vigorous ice river Muir descended. It covered perhaps a third of the area he described, and had retreated so far that the icefall no longer existed at all. It may not even be a live glacier anymore, though a few bergschrunds were cracked open across its upper fringes. The glacier's dwindling size has probably killed most of its downward motion, planting it in place, destined to become just a permanent snowfield. I stopped for a while to drink meltwater, having grown thirsty since my last drink in the valley north of Banner Peak.

Below the snow, creeks ran down to the east, gathering together to hurl themselves off tall cliffs that cut away at the lowest end of the glacier's basin. I skirted the edge of the drop to the south until the cliffs broke down enough to allow me passage along thinly grassed ledges. Down on the canyon floor Ritter's guard peaks reflected crisply in quiet, braided streams. I slogged up the opposite canyon wall, only to find another deep basin separating me from my whitebark. I began to wish Muir had chosen another way back. The miles and contours seemed stacked against us. I hiked up thousand-foot talus piles, crossed more creeks, rounded lakes, zigzagged down ledges to descend canyon walls, and Ritter and Banner looked splendid on their high thrones to my left, and all of it was gorgeous, but my legs began to lag and my bread ration was about used up. Still, when I returned to my tree the sun was just a short arc into its western descent.

I sprawled out in a meadow for a few minutes to rest my legs, sip some water, and finish the bread I had left in my pocket. But I had no particular wish to hang around doing nothing for hours until the cold came along to freeze me. So I got myself upright again and slung the sack with my cup and shirt and last loaf of bread over my shoulder, and headed back toward Tuolumne, planning to sleep wherever darkness found me. And here I entered the time warp of lightweight travel. I crossed the northern valleys, down past where I had seen the bear, up over the pink granite bosses, while Ritter receded in the distance. And still the sun floated up in the west. I took one last look at the mountain then followed gravity's pull down into the Lyell Canyon. I reached the canyon floor and followed the river. It became a war of attrition between my legs and the sun to see which would poop out first. My legs won, but not without a lot of prodding. The sky finally turned gray a ways down the canyon where the river, already fattened by a hundred creeks, swung through its long curves. I found a tree that had been recently uprooted—so recently that its branches were springy and all its needles green. I slid under it and found the densest part of its growth, where the branches pushed down on me like a heavy blanket. Darkness settled and I fell to sleep.

I woke after a time. I suppose it could have been a half-hour or three hours. The cold had begun to creep through me again. I thought, why not get up and walk out by starlight? I had traveled by starlight before, of course, and I was fairly near the end of the canyon, perhaps not more than six miles. And I was already cold. So why not walk and warm up and finish this journey in the night? Hadn't Muir returned to his camp in the dark? I wriggled out from under my tree and sorted out my sack by feel, for there was no moon and it was so black I could not even see my hands. I must have been groggy still, for this did not strike me as a problem.

I walked through the woods with my hands outstretched to feel the trees until I stumbled onto the trail that runs through the bottom of the canyon. It's a well-trod path, a smooth rut about a foot-and-a-half wide running through forest and meadow and occasionally over bare rock where its course is marked with stones. I joined it in a meadow near the bank of the river, where no trees blocked the stars, which were dense enough to make whole sections of the sky pale. And yet I could not see the trail. It floated out in front of me, a depthless stripe of not-quite-blackness amid the total dark. I stumbled along, feeling for the edge of the rut with my feet, waiting for my eyes to warm up and my night vision to improve. It never did. I thought back to the times I had traveled by starlight and I recalled snow and bare granite, reflective surfaces, not forests and meadows, these soft dark places that sucked in the faint light and gobbled it down. I had nothing to use to make light, not even matches; I had left them behind not wanting the temptation of a fire, not wanting to burn any part of the Sierra for my own foolishness.

I persisted down the trail, cold, slow-witted, and unwilling to admit that the night could stop me. The meadow ended and my trail entered forest. The vague apparition of path drowned and vanished. I tripped over roots and rocks and wandered off the track at curves. I felt ridiculous. I knew this trail, it was well made and easy to walk, but I simply could not see it, and I had no experience being blind. Short of crawling out on my hands and knees, I could not make any forward progress.

I couldn't go back either, and it was somewhere around here that I realized what I had done. I had no way to return to my fallen tree. I would never be able to find it. It hadn't been much, but at least it offered some shelter and warmth. And now it could have been on the other side of Ritter for all the good it did me.

The river was to my right, and I knew that the coldest air in the canyon would settle by the water, so I turned to the left and groped through the trees, feeling for anything approximating shelter. My fingers returned bad news, the trees were all bare, straight poles with a few sticks and twigs poking out from them. All my blind groping found nothing so much as a bush or needled tree branch to use as a blanket. I gave up, and laid myself out on the forest floor.

What followed was a frigid, windy length of blackness that felt like a week of nights. Without a watch the passage of time meant nothing to me. The trees blocked the stars so I could not even watch them wheel by. I shivered and clutched myself and tried counting games, but none of them passed any appreciable time, so I quit them. Sometimes I lapsed into a semiconscious haze, but I don't think I ever slept. My toes tingled and tossed pain up my legs, and that seemed a good sign because it meant the nerves were still alive; I kicked my feet against the ground to keep them from losing feeling.

Muir is occasionally criticized for writing purple prose. Some say he is too florid. Here is how he described the morning after his night under the tree with the birds: "How glorious a greeting the sun gives the mountain! To behold this alone is worth the pains of an excursion a thousand times over. The highest peaks burned like islands in a sea of liquid shade." Personally, I find this passage beautiful, but I did not understand it until, after my week-long-night, I saw the blueing of the eastern sky and grayness on the canyon's western wall. Muir is not just dealing in exciting visuals. He's describing a moment of transcendent gladness, the moment when night finally ends and a new day is born with light and warmth.

I spent two days following Muir to Mount Ritter and back. But Muir spent whole seasons sleeping under the pines and on the rocks. Thinking of him in this way, I began, for the first time, to see the path he walked from the church of his father to the God of the mountains. Muir had no need for the frustration of expecting Jesus to come back—why wait a lifetime for Him when the Sun offered resurrection from the darkness with every dawn? Why hunt through a book, like Muir's father, searching for God, when God burned the summits of his most beautiful creations every morning and evening? After all, which came first, the land or the book? My sunrise in Lyell Canyon would have meant nothing from under a sleeping bag inside a tent, but prostrate in the black cold, it brought such relief and happiness that I could begin to believe in this kind of salvation.

I struggled up and walked stiffly out to my truck. None of my pieces seemed well connected yet; feet, hands, legs, brain all sputtering along independently, slowly recovering the ground they'd abandoned during their nighttime retreat. I turned the heat up high and drove out of Tuolumne and down into the desert.

Muir woke the next morning and took the long way back. "I sauntered home," he wrote, "—that is, back to the Tuolumne camp." He discovered some beautiful new lakes tucked in among the tributaries of Rush Creek. It was just another day for him to explore the wonders wrought into his mountains. He spent so long poking around among the glacial carvings that it was evening before he recrossed the Lyell Canyon wall. Down in the canyon, as he approached the artists' camp, he whooped to them and they returned his call. He discovered, when he arrived at their fire, that the days had passed slowly and anxiously for them. "They seemed unreasonably glad to see me," he wrote. "I had been absent only three days; nevertheless, though the weather was fine, they had already been weighing chances as to whether I would ever return, and trying to decide whether they should wait longer or begin to seek their way back to the lowlands. Now their curious troubles were over."

Down in the Owens Valley I warmed up enough to change my clothes, and to feel appropriately humbled. I had been thoroughly routed by two-and-a-half days in the mountains with Muir. I tried to imagine what it would be like to follow him for a season, and whether I could learn enough to keep up. No wonder he had so few traveling companions. Who could have kept pace with him? Who else could have been so happy being cold and hungry and dazzled by the mountains all the time?

· 6 ·

Bolton Coit Brown + Mount Clarence King

[AUGUST 1896]

Mount Clarence King (12,905 feet), southeast face

THE SCENE IS easy enough to imagine. Dr. David Starr Jordan, president of Stanford University, sits behind his desk absorbed with one of his many projects. Jane Stanford, having outlived both her husband and her son and now devoting her full attention to the university she helped create, comes bustling in with a new edict for her president: the art professor, Bolton Brown, must be let go. The problem, as Dr. Jordan would later relate, was that Mrs. Stanford had dropped by to see a drawing class on a day when Professor Brown had procured as a model "a young lady from San Francisco, a very well developed young lady, and she didn't have any clothes on."

This was the last year of the nineteenth century and it was a tumultuous one for Bolton Coit Brown. Since 1893 he had been a professor in Stanford's Art Department—a department that he, in fact, had done much of the work to establish for the newly formed university. But now his job was slipping away. He had never dealt well with figures of authority and their commandments. Brown's father, like Muir's, used religion as a blunt instrument for control (though he employed words in favor of sticks). Unlike Muir, Brown responded with arguments and atheism rather than compliance, and would forever carry a deeply held mistrust for the moral principles espoused by the Church.

For Brown, the Victorian and Christian prudishness toward nudity not only betrayed an offensive illogic, but actually damaged the psychological health of young people badgered into a sense of shame for their physical bodies. After the episode in the president's office, the first compromise that Brown struck with Dr. Jordan and Mrs. Stanford was that he would not use nude models in "mixed" classes. He announced the new rule to his students. "I told them, in a word, that on account of outside criticisms, the boys and girls must separate to draw that woman there. And *then*—for the first time—I *did* see shame in their faces . . .

It was a horrid moment." Undoubtedly, the simple act of submission to Mrs. Stanford's orders provoked a part of Brown's discomfort, but he must have also felt that, with a single irretrievable sentence, he had burdened his students with a baggage of self-consciousness, sex, and sin.

As the political situation at Stanford grew bleaker, Brown continued to do his own drawing and painting, and during this time he created a piece that would become one of his favorites. It is a black-and-white drawing that has the look of a woodblock print. A stream flows through the center of the frame, banked by oaks and rocks. Standing knee-deep in the creek, a nude female silhouette holds out a hand to a male silhouette seated on one side, as if beckoning him to join her. The drawing carries the title *Play*.

Visions of a girl in the woods began to visit Brown's thoughts as a young man. Recalling school years spent exploring wild bits of upstate New York, he wrote that it was "lonely to be alone in such lovely places, and I felt the loneliness as well as the loveliness. The world spoke to me, but where was the companion to share my listening? A girl haunted the woods . . . I could feel her nearness in almost any sunny glade. And she would understand: she would be at home in the quiet rooms of the forest."

Brown seemed to have found his girl in 1896, at the age of thirty-one, five years before he rendered *Play*. Given his longings for a wood nymph and his partiality toward this drawing, no great leap is needed to conclude that he is the seated figure in the image and the woman beckoning is his wife, Lucy. According to Brown's sister, Ellen, "it was inevitable that Brown should fall in love with Lucy Fletcher, she being the most beautiful thing in sight." Ellen's tone suggests both a compliment to Lucy and a commentary directed at Brown for his inclination to expound on the nature of sensuous loveliness. The compliment was probably genuine; Lucy's wavy brown hair framed a willing smile and the "bluest Irish eyes." They married that June in a ceremony that seems to have brought out the worst of Brown's tendencies toward control and obstinacy. He micromanaged everything from the seating chart to the minister's words and would not let his father perform the ceremony despite Edmund's assurances that he would conduct the proceedings in any way Brown wished.

After the wedding, Bolton and Lucy set out immediately for the Sierra. Bolton had been making annual summer trips to the mountains since his arrival in California in 1893. Now for the first time the companion he had desired tramped with him and she was perfectly willing to take full part in the rough camp life that he preferred. For two months they wore yesterday's clothes from the first day to the last, had meals off an open fire, slept on the ground, and took their baths in icy creeks.

Figures in creeks—generally female, nude, and idealized as silhouettes or as medleys of plain curves—are the subjects of a large portion, though probably not the best portion, of Brown's art. These women are round, soft, sensuous creatures, but elements of sexuality are purposefully suppressed or forced to the scenic margins. In "The Crooked Tree," for example, a suggestively drawn oak trunk foregrounds a bathing party, but the women splash unselfconsciously in the water and take no notice of the onlooking tree.

The honeymoon gave Brown his first opportunity to put the ideals of his art into action—to wander the woods with a beautiful and adventurous girl without constraints imposed by institutions, ministers, and neighbors. Imagine the delight he must have taken from watching Lucy bathe. But I wonder how she felt about the women in his drawings. Were they her? Were they in competition with her? Did she measure up to his fantasies?

Of course, they did not go to the Sierra to take baths; camp life was the background, the mountains were the main subject of their travels. Here again, Lucy proved to be a hearty companion. In fact, Brown writes, Lucy "had all summer cherished a secret longing to have 'an adventure' befall us." Simply living in the mountains for two months would not satisfy her. She wanted some further test of her character. Perhaps she felt the need to prove herself. She got her chance. A month into the honeymoon, they decided to attempt a new route on Mount Williamson, the fanged mountain just beyond Mount Tyndall that had surprised Clarence King from his summit. Brown thought they might be away from their basecamp for five days, but they carried nothing more than their worn clothes and two small bundles containing food and a sheet of calfskin for emergency shoe repairs (theirs were already tattered, and Brown surely had the disintegration of Dick Cotter's boots in mind). Even the food was not plentiful, one pound each per day, what Brown called starvation rations, but it made for light packs and Brown reckoned that his weighed twelve pounds while Lucy's weighed three.

On their first night out, a major storm brought numbing temperatures and piercing rain. Without a tent, sleeping bags, or even coats, that night's fire was critical. But every sliver of wood and tinder was already saturated and the rain extinguished each spark Brown struck, so he got nothing to burn. Despite the alarming cold and desperate conditions, Lucy remained sensible and shrewd. "So Lucy," Brown described, "bending over to roof the operation with her back, took from her bosom dry matches for me to light a fire with." Perched on the edge of hypothermia, she shielded their fire with her own suffering—the grit beneath her pleasant face and gentle smile revealed in this small act. Brown must have been thrilled. Not only had he found a companion, he had found a partner.

That night they settled into each other's arms and a damp, smoky cocoon of warmth, rotating themselves at intervals toward the flames.

A Sierra coincidence: not far from the Browns' smoky fire, but more than a century later, my wife and I met a similar storm. All day we struggled to make our miles and keep our heads above the rising tide. As the light dimmed from gloom to gray, the clouds piled up in the twilit sky and the rain hammered out a violent rhythm. We could see nothing to use for shelter, just large, loose stones and scrubby trees set in a steeply pitched ravine-side. But we were tired and cold and I fixated on finding us protection from the wind and rain. I thrashed my way up and down that soggy hillside discovering nothing but dripping thickets, swamps, and jagged ground, while the daylight died and the night air sharpened its teeth. Vexed, defeated, I flung myself down under the drooping branches of a stunted white fir and declared it home despite the leaky roof and uneven floor. In my benumbed frustration I kicked over one of the sharp rocks that poked up through the ground there and exposed an angry fire ant colony. Under the circumstances, they seemed to be the perfect companions for the night.

Ashley gave me a few minutes to cool off and then offered me her hand, piercing the rain and my own fog of irritation and exhaustion. She led me out from my hole beneath the fir and up the ravine another mile to where we found a flat spot beneath the ancient arms of a grand old pine and the last coals of a glorious sunset. She had no special knowledge telling her that the pine would be there, or that the tree I had chosen was in the middle of the worst of the weather. She simply had deeper reserves of optimism and endurance on an evening when I had run out of both.

Naked exposure to the mountains teaches these lessons about ourselves and our companions—precisely the kind of education Brown went looking for. As a child, he and his friends would rush to the local lakes and creeks during storms that stirred up the waters. With thunder crashing overhead, Brown held himself to the creek bottom with his feet while storm-incited waves crested over his head. He kept his eyes open during these submersions so that he could see the shimmering sheets of water and the rippling image of the outer world from inside each wave. A later lithograph by Brown shows a young boy, perhaps two years old, being led into a creek by a girl who looks to be his sister. The sister is clothed, but the boy is bare-skinned. The piece, titled *Adventures*, seems lifted right from Brown's personal lexicon of meaningful moments, a young child's first exposure of the flesh to the power of natural forces.

For a grown-up version of these adventures, Brown went to the mountains. As a boy, he decided that the lessons of rivers and storms were learned best in bare skin, without coats or clothes to block the message. No wonder then that he carried so little when he climbed the peaks. Like Muir, he wanted his possessions to interfere as little as possible. Nowadays, the equipment that accompanies climbers—GPS units and oxygen bottles and hand drills, just to name some of our strangest dependencies—proves primarily that technology makes mountain climbing easier, while teaching us little about the mountains themselves or our own capacities.

After their stormy night, the Browns climbed the northwest face of Mount Williamson, a side of the mountain that had never before been attempted. Brown described the complicated architecture they found there as a "wilderness of flying buttresses and pinnacles" (an echo of the "wilderness of crumbling spires" Muir found on Mount Ritter). The climbing demanded gymnastic maneuvers and difficult route finding through forking slots and chimneys. When they escaped, and emerged high up the mountain on easier ground which led to the summit, Brown understood the tenuous nature of their passage. "It was as if a mouse had got upon the house roof by climbing up through the rain-water pipe," he wrote. Adventure for him required that feeling, of being a small animal clinging to the outside of a marvelous old edifice, or of being a small boy in the grip of a storm wave. And Brown's image of the climbing mice is appropriate for a man who had read Muir's early writings. Here, the people are the wild things on the outside, gaining occasional glimpses into the sophisticated inner workings of the mountain castle.

They returned to their basecamp from Mount Williamson under bright blue skies and mild conditions. Shortly thereafter they set out again, looking for unclimbed peaks. Brown particularly wanted to find a high, striking mountain that he could name for his university. In one day they climbed two new peaks, naming the first Crag Ericsson, for John Ericsson, the Swedish engineer who immigrated to New York and designed the USS *Monitor*; and the second Mount Stanford. Lucy did not accompany Brown the entire way up Mount Stanford. She was feeling tired and a little ill, perhaps from their exposed night out or from the frantic pace of their climbing spree, so she retreated before the final ridge to the summit.

Back at camp again, with the summer drawing to a close, Brown suggested to Lucy that he do one final climb, but this time alone. He had unfinished business in the area, with the peak named for Clarence King. The previous year he had attempted the mountain. Blocked within sight of the summit by an expanse of blank, vertical rock, he turned back. The mountain was still unclimbed. Brown does not say why he asked Lucy to remain in camp. Perhaps he was looking out for her health or worried that the mountain would be too difficult for her, or simply eager to travel the mountains at his own speed. Lucy has left us with no record of how she felt about this arrangement. Brown wrote that she agreed eagerly and did not wish to see anyone beat him to the summit. But it was their honeymoon, and they had spent the summer forging a particular kind of bond; I can't help thinking that she must have been disappointed to be left.

Mount Clarence King is a three-sided pyramid of white granite that presides over a lovely lake district in the central Sierra. Brewer and his team passed by the peak in the summer of 1864, after the ascents of Mount Brewer and Mount Tyndall, and after King had left the party to ride all the way around the southern tip of the Sierra in order to attempt, unsuccessfully, Mount Whitney from the east. They named the peak for King in his absence and he must have been pleased. He could not have asked for a more strikingly beautiful mountain to carry his name. During King's time in the Sierra, Dick Cotter and James Gardiner were his two primary companions; the two peaks immediately to the south of Mount King were later named for those two men.

From their camp in Paradise Valley, Brown set out for Mount King early on an August morning. He made one concession to his earlier defeat and also brought along a forty foot length of rope. He took off through the woods at a near run, having become, over the summer, fully acclimated to the altitude and the demands of mountain travel. As he put it, "When you are in perfect condition there seems to be no end to your endurance, your appetite or your enjoyment." But the way was difficult and he spent much of the morning negotiating dense brush, leaping fallen logs, and bushwhacking through manzanita thickets. He passed through the tree line at the headwaters of Gardiner Creek with relief, leaving the tangled brush behind in favor of open meadows and bare rock with broad views across lake-filled basins of the surrounding mountains.

When at last he reached Mount King, he began up its southern slope, the one side of the mountain he had not explored on his previous effort. Initially, this presented no difficulties, only steep hiking up jumbled talus. But above twelve thousand feet this side of the pyramid became narrower and steeper. To his left and right, cliffs fell away for hundreds of feet down into enormous amphitheatres, leaving him with a tapering avenue in between. He traversed back and forth to poke his head over each precipice and stared down through the empty air. The rock steps up which he climbed grew in size with each upward move until a stacked terrace of vertical cliffs, a proud guard of angular granite, stood between him and the summit.

Eventually he came to a perch beyond which he could go no higher. The mountain had stopped him again just below its summit with smooth, sheer walls that he would not hazard to climb. This time, though, he had brought the rope, and he unwound it from his shoulder and tied a noose at one end. Cowboy style, Brown threw it up and around a projecting point of rock at the top of the cliff. He pulled down on the rope to cinch the knot and prepared to go up hand over hand. Brown had read Clarence King, of course, and though he thought the man a great exaggerator, he seems to have been willing to learn from King's tactics.

Is this really climbing? I don't know what to call it. Climbers seldom use such maneuvers anymore because it seems like cheating to climb directly up a thrown rope. It's another way of avoiding the difficulties that the mountain presents instead of accepting them and finding a solution with one's own fingers. That being said, in Brown's time in the Sierra, the mountains held so many advantages over the mountaineer that his forty-foot lasso seems far less artificial than much of what we do today.

Anyway, the primary reason that climbers rarely follow Brown's method has less to do with philosophy and more to do with the dangers of trusting a rope looped around an unseen point. Brown pulled on his rope and his weight brought the lassoed rock crashing down. Balanced on his stance he had nowhere to go and could only watch the stone sail by, narrowly missing him. Determined to reach the summit, he tried again, but this time he fixed a thick knot in the end of the rope, and threw it repeatedly up and over the cliff, hoping that it would wedge in a crack. It did, at last, and he pulled himself upward and "did not dally with the job either," he wrote, "for every second I was afraid the knot would pull through the crack."

Brown had to repeat his rope toss several more times to reach an area just below the summit. Here the three sides of the massive Mount King pyramid converge into one sharp point. Perched on top of that point rests one monolithic cube of granite, the true summit. Brown called this last rock "the ugliest place of all." To stand atop the highpoint he would have to lasso one of the sloping corners of the summit cube and will his rope to stay attached long enough for him to pull his way up.

◆ ◆ ◆

THE LAKES BELOW the mountain come in all shapes and sizes, but they are uniformly attractive. Rimmed by clean, bare granite, or soft beeches made of thick grains of the same stone, the clear waters look like pockets of sky. Outside the granite perimeter, the land pitches sharply upward and deep-green firs populate the rocky soil. Little creeks, running over miniature falls, connect the larger pools. The color scheme could separate your mind from your body. Stare for too long into one of those sparkling sapphires in their settings of white stone and green wood, and you might awake in a later decade having noticed nothing of the passing time.

I stopped for lunch on a granite shore and, in Brown's honor, pitched myself in for a swim. Sprawled out naked on the rock to dry and eat, I thought about Brown's frustration with the nudity taboo. I'm hardly a body-conscious person, but I can't deny a difference between skinny-dipping alone and in company. Alone, there is complete ease, the feeling Brown tried to capture with the ladies in his drawings. Whether through temperament or force of will, Brown never relinquished his personal liberty to enjoy the outdoors unclothed. Long after leaving the Sierra behind and returning to New York, he took his daily bath in the woods without any apparent care as to who might be around to observe him. In his final years, in the 1930s, he was proud of the fact that his house was still unplumbed; he preferred the well and the creek.

The next morning I rose early, put on my hat and boots, pocketed a little food, and set off for the mountain. I left the trees behind before I reached the last lakes. Up there, the land has not been given any green cover and becomes nearly monochromatic except for the orange, green, and black minerals that dust the white granite. For a quarter of a mile, a coyote trotted ahead of me through the cliffs and jumbles of rock, but I lost her just before the highest lake. I have encountered coyotes in the unlikeliest places, far above any obvious food sources. I believe they explore for the interest of it, not simply to fill empty bellies. Humans are not the only creatures to have evolved abstract curiosity.

I scrambled up a long diagonal ledge which cut through one of the boundary cliffs of the mountain's south slope. Misjudging the solidity of a plate of rock the size of a manhole cover, I stepped on it and sent it skittering off my ledge. It struck the cliff three times before exploding on the basin floor five hundred feet below, filling the air with thunder and a smell like shot gunpowder. Thirty seconds later the basin was perfectly calm again, as if nothing had happened. The mountains are quick to retreat behind their facade of permanence.

On the south slope, the mountain's taper from its wide base to the pointed top was plain to see. From down at the base, the top looked improbably slender. That whole side of the mountain bent up toward the summit like a section of inverted rainbow. Up among the cliffs where Brown dangled from his rope, at the upper end of the inverted curve, the mountain seemed to be trying to push me over backward. I threaded my way between buttresses, finding weaknesses and passageways around the blank walls. Often these passages took the form of narrow chimneys, the joints between walls of rock, which I entered sideways and squirmed up through toward daylight with my back against one wall and my knees pressed against the other.

I followed Brown's route, but I carried no rope. The mountain holds fewer advantages over me than it would have a hundred years ago. Brown came along so early, the techniques he used he made up on the spot. My hands have the benefit of a century's worth of experimentation passed down the line by one climber to the next. The uncertainty faced by the first generation is what makes the early climbs so impressive. What would Brown find up there above the mountain's base? What would he need to do to get there? Would he be able to hold on? His head must have been filled with a hundred questions. Everything above the demarcation line between hiking and climbing was a mystery, both in terms of the architecture of the mountains and the capabilities of men.

We humans have become experts at eliminating uncertainty from our lives. (No wonder we are so often bored.) All the gadgetry and technology that we haul up mountains have essentially this purpose: to make our path, and our chances of reaching the summit, more certain. But if the only point of mountaineering is to stand at the top, we might as well save the trouble and hire helicopters. If the point is to actually climb the mountain, then the sense of adventure is just as important as the rock itself.

Mountaineering is a simple business. There is a mountain and a climber and a few odds and ends to compensate for human frailty. These odds and ends will change from mountain to mountain, but the fewer there are, the more the climber accomplishes. Why does this matter? Why bother to climb the mountains at all, if not for that feeling of personal satisfaction, the sharpening of mind and fingers against the wild places of the world, the pleasure of thinking: *I have gotten myself here.* In 1896, Brown carried nothing more than lunch and a lasso, the minimum required to climb Mount King. A hundred and ten years later, we should not need much more than that.

I could see the summit block above, but one last cliff band kept me from it. Beneath my feet, angled slabs of granite offered a roll and a tumble down over the cliffs below. Above me the mountain pushed up and out, a vertical wall of clean-cut rock where Brown used his rope. I traversed along the base of the cliff, searching for climbable stone, crystal studs in the granite slabs supporting my toes and separating me from the wants of gravity. I found a steep, flaring chimney, really nothing more than two planes of stone joined together at an acute angle, like the space behind a door propped open against a wall. On the way down, I would find a better way through a tunnel behind a boulder, but for now this would do.

I jammed my hands in the crack at the back, and pushed outward with my feet, one against each plane of rock, clumsy boots scuffing against the smooth stone, knees squashed in the middle. These are the advantages of history, knowing how to do these things, having learned them and practiced them year after year. Brown might well have looked at that crack and dismissed it as just another scale in the mountain's armor. When I looked, I saw places for hands and feet. With the passage of time, it's the eyes that change as much as the fingers. The angle between the two granite planes widened out and before long my legs were spread wide between the walls, trusting to friction and pressure to keep my boots from sliding. Then one more move, one last moment of confidence that rubber and rock would stay happily stuck together, before I reached up and grabbed the flat top of the cliff and hauled myself over to the rocks just below the summit.

What a perfect mountain! Three great ridges, three great planes of the pyramid, all converging at the mountain's apex to prop up the pointy summit block. That final rock is the size of a small cabin with four straight walls and a sloped roof that angles up to the east and ends with a single gently protruding gable. The granite is a flawless crystalline white, smooth and cool to the touch; what a wonderful piece of stone.

◆ ◆ ◆

WONDERFUL TO LOOK at, but ugly to climb, as Brown pointed out. He would need to trust that single gable emerging barely from the roofline to hold his rope and himself. With great care, he lassoed the sloping horn and formed another loop at the bottom of the rope to stand up in. That side of the summit block overhangs itself, so when Brown stood up and committed to the strand connecting him to the summit, he would have been suspended in free air, swaying at the end of the rope, wondering if each faint sway would be enough to pop his rope

Summit block (showing Bolton Brown's "gable"), Mount Clarence King

off the top. Hanging there, he pulled himself up enough to grab the top edge of the summit and then heaved himself over.

Brown's ascent of Mount King has been variously described as the most difficult climb in the nineteenth-century Sierra or, more grandly, the most difficult in all of America. Whatever title one gives it, the climb was far ahead of its time. The difficult rock, the rope tricks, the calculated risks; it feels like a day lifted from the 1930s and plopped down in the middle of the 1890s. More than anything else, it is the boldness that Brown showed on Mount King—his faith in himself to solve the challenges the mountain placed before him no matter how tenuous the solutions—that sets his climb apart.

He compared his summit favorably to the pinnacle of the Strasbourg Cathedral and called it "a true spire of rock, an up-tossed corner at the meeting of three great mountain walls." Surveying the small real estate of the cabin roof, he found it to be about fifteen feet across, though because of the slope and the smoothness of the surface, there would have been few places to comfortably stand. He looked down over each of the four sides to examine the summit block's perch and noted that "if you fall off one side, you will be killed in the vicinity; if you fall off any of the other sides, you will be pulverized in the remote nadir beneath." Eventually, he reslung the rope over the single gable, and let himself gently down to the rocks below.

◆ ◆ ◆

BROWN BELIEVED THAT his way was the only feasible one to the top of Mount King. It is not unusual for first ascensionists, particularly of Brown's era, to think this. Having worked so hard and run so many risks just to find the one route, it might well have seemed impossible that there could have been another. But there are always more ways than one to climb a mountain, and humans, like coyotes, are naturally curious. Bit by bit, in the years after Brown had moved on from making difficult ascents in the Sierra, climbers learned Mount King's secrets, including an unlikely passage up the final spire.

A massive rectangular slab of granite—weighing maybe ninety tons or so—leans casually against the southern side of Mount King's summit block. Where the two rocks touch, they leave open another narrow, flaring crack. I wriggled up through this space, cupped by those two enormous hands of stone, until I emerged in an angled trough running along the side of the summit block. Directly

155

above, far out of reach, was Brown's gable, but along this side the roofline sloped down, until, at the far end of the trough, it came just into reach.

All winter long, rain and snow polish the roof of Mount King; smooth as a cobblestone is how Brown described it. There is no sharp transition between roof and wall at this end of the summit block, nothing comforting to hang one's hand on, only clean, rounded stone. Standing on tiptoes at the far edge of the trough, I felt around among the eaves. I found two little raised crystals, no more than half a sugar cube each. Not much to hold, but better than nothing. I swung one foot up to the roof, level with my hands, and pulled, pushed, and rolled my way over onto the summit.

The same view can be seen from an airplane, and it is glorious enough. But when the view is earned, it drowns the eyes and sets the ears ringing. There is beauty up there that exists nowhere else, a splendor that the mountains share only with the tired mountaineer. The sunlight scattering diamonds over the lakes could not be more precious if the gems were real. No wonder most mountaineers are poor.

Imagine how Brown must have felt up there, straddling the crest of the summit block, drinking in all those lakes and peaks, his artist's eyes and his mountaineer's soul gorged with good things.

◆ ◆ ◆

BACK TO REALITY. Lucy Brown was down there in the woods somewhere, and the day was already dying. After lowering himself "spider-wise" off the summit block, Bolton followed his route back down through the cliffs, buttresses, and chimneys. Each move had to be undone, though he knew the way now. Past the upper stretch of the mountain's curve and safe again, he resumed his near run of the morning. He jumped over rocks and creeks and crashed through brush, while the approaching night pulled the shadows toward it like black taffy. It was fully dark by the time he reached the river by their camp and he crossed the thigh-high rush of water by feel. Then, through the riverside oaks, he "sighted the gleam of Lucy's fire, and in a moment more,—was home." What a vision of domesticity, the warrior returning to his woman who has kept the home fire burning into the night for him.

Bolton and Lucy would never recapture the intimate partnership that carried them through their storm and up Mount Williamson. In the following year, Lucy gave birth to their first child, and in 1899, when they returned to the Sierra for the summer, they brought little Eleanor with them, seating her atop a burro. Brown spent much of that expedition scouting and mapping the lakes below Mount King, while Lucy stayed with Eleanor in their camp above Bullfrog Lake. He did devote one day to his daughter's daycare so that Lucy could go herself to see what he had been exploring, but husband and wife never again rambled together above the tree line, and the little family seems to have been together rarely during their month-long stay. A year later, Brown spent the Christmas after the birth of his second daughter alone in the Sierra snow for a three-week trip with nothing for company but a sled of provisions.

Brown was politely fired from Stanford in 1902. Dr. Jordan remained unfailingly complimentary toward him as an artist and a professor, but found himself forced to act because, as he put it, Brown "didn't have any discretion." True enough, but Jordan's assessment hardly captures Brown's lack of self-preservation. At times, Brown seemed to have been fully in the grip of Poe's Imp of the Perverse, that confessionary urge to speak what is better left unsaid. After Mrs.

Stanford's first directive for Brown's removal for his use of nude models, fifteen months of arguments and compromises concluded with one final letter from Brown to Dr. Jordan. In it he explained that a colleague had become unnecessarily nervous about one of his recent drawing classes and that he wanted to set the record straight. They did have a model that day, but knowing the rules, he had her wrapped in a cloth drapery. He went on to detail the exact quantity of cloth used for this purpose (one hundred and twenty-two square feet) and wrote that it "never occurred to me that anybody could object" to the arrangement. Then, in a postscript after his usual signature, as if he could not force his hand to lay down the pen, he wrote: "The drapery is thin, but not transparent." Imagine Mrs. Stanford's reaction to that line!

The family moved back East, where Brown helped to found the Woodstock Art Colony and continued to draw and paint. The carefully groomed moustache and beard that he had sported in photographs taken at Stanford gave way to the thicker and wilder version that he had grown during the summers in the Sierra. One decade after returning to the East Coast, his marriage failed when Lucy quietly but firmly divorced him, though they would maintain close communication with each other for the rest of his life. The legal separation was carried out in secret, and in spite of the fact that Bolton and Lucy maintained separate living quarters, even their children did not know about the official divorce for several years. Perhaps Lucy became fed up with the stubbornness Brown had inherited from his father. His argumentativeness and inflexibility must have been exasperating. Brown refused to speak about their break, but he hinted at these problems to his sister-in-law, Mary, the day before he died, in 1936. "He was sorry he had nagged Lucy into marriage with him," she wrote to her husband, Brown's brother Edmund. "He knew she would have had a happier life without him."

Perhaps, too, Lucy grew tired of waiting at home for him to climb his mountains and finish his projects in the woods, tired of waiting for him to resume the partnership with her that had been hinted at by their first month and a half in the Sierra.

As an older man, Brown went balding and clean-shaven, and wore round spectacles perched on his narrow, prominent nose, giving him an owlish look. He devoted most of the last twenty years of his life to lithography, a printmaking process using stones. With a wheelbarrow, he would cart hundred-pound blocks of flat-cut limestone into the woods where he would sketch on them with grease crayons. Back home he washed the drawing surface with acid, the grease protecting the image he had sketched while the acid ate away at the blank surface. The slight difference in elevation between the grease-protected positive space and the acid-eaten negative space produced detailed prints when ink and paper were pressed against the stone's surface. Though his work rarely has been recognized outside of the art world, he became the most expert American practitioner of lithographic printmaking. It's fitting that a man who spent some of his best years and happiest moments in the midst of Sierra granite should devote the rest of his life to making art from stone. He knew what to expect from rocks; he knew how to work with stones.

At the same time he put distance between himself and his days in the Sierra. Those memories must have been bittersweet. During his later years he converted many of his earlier drawings into lithographs, including his old favorite, *Play*, the image of the creek with the two silhouettes who seem so suggestive of Lucy and him. The lithograph of the same title is very nearly an exact copy of the drawing except for one detail: he gave the seated male figure a ponytail and hips, excising himself from the scene.

Sickening with cancer and told by his doctors his illness would be fatal, he again found comfort in stone. He chose his plot and its dimensions in the Artists Cemetery in Woodstock and then began to hike through the woods near his home in New York, looking for his grave marker. Eventually he found the stone he wanted resting in a dry streambed: a tremendous old boulder that showed the work of years of water and sun on its polished surface. He hired a crew with a small crane to excavate the rock and transport it to his backyard, where he engraved it with his name and the years of his birth and death, leaving only the last number of the latter date to be carved by someone else. Even in those final weeks, Brown still clutched at the details, trying to control them just as he had for his entire life, from the day of his marriage, through the final days of his teaching career, and in each of the phases of his art. Perhaps that's why he was so attracted to rock, to that mountain stuff more solid than flesh or paper and more durable than human desire. When he engraved his images onto those blocks of limestone, he must have found the permanence of each line satisfying. His boulder is still there in Woodstock, resting in the shade between two trees.

The mountains live; they have their own pulses and personalities and moods. Most mountaineers have had lengthy conversations at one time or another with the peaks and cliffs. Given the amount of time he spent drawing the mountains and communicating with stone, Brown may have talked to them as much as anyone. But the mountains do not love us, they do not even know that we are there, and when they speak they do not speak to us; their rockfalls and storms and simple eloquence are messages to a far broader audience of wilderness listeners. When we hear them it is through our good fortune to be present and receptive at the moment of communication.

Putting my back to Mount King, I let my boots carry me downhill, down past the rock and the lakes and the trees, down through the canyons that become valleys, back down to the asphalt and the cities. Returned to a world of speed, the miles ticked by on the odometer, absurdly fast, the landscape blurring out the window of my truck. In six hours I drove around the Sierra, my sense of distance suddenly meaning nothing. Back home, I found Ashley battling her books, and winning, though the strain showed around her eyes and the corners of her mouth. She took the night off from her studies and we talked about the future, both of us looking forward to the spring when she would be free again and we would return to the mountains together.

· 7 ·

Joseph Nisbet LeConte + North Palisade

[JULY 1903]

North Palisade (14,242 feet) from the summit of Mount Agassiz

O N JULY 9, 1896, a curious encounter occurred on Mount Gardiner, the mountain rising just to the south of Mount Clarence King and named for King's friend and climbing partner James Gardiner. On the southern slopes of the peak, just below the final knife-edged ridge to the summit, Bolton Brown and Joseph Nisbet LeConte met each other, apparently by chance. Both had intended to be the first to climb the mountain (no one yet had stood upon its summit), and they had each started from different points in the Charlotte Creek drainage, taking their own paths up the long, complex talus fields on that side of the mountain. A few days earlier, and several miles downstream, they happened to have forded Bubbs Creek together, so each knew the other was in the area, and might well have suspected competing intentions to ascend one of the major unclimbed peaks in the immediate vicinity. Nevertheless, arriving just below the same summit at the same time on the same day among all the wild peaks of the Sierra must have felt a little absurd, like a moment from a wilderness opera.

Neither of the two men wrote much regarding their meeting, but we can infer a great deal about it. In 1890, LeConte named a small peak for his institution, the University of California at Berkeley, calling it simply University Peak. Meanwhile, Brown had made it a priority in the summer of 1896 to find and climb an inspiring mountain to name for Stanford University. Given Brown's personality he would have announced this plan in advance to anyone within earshot, and with the limited space to maneuver up on Mount Gardiner's final ridge, LeConte would have been a captive and ideal audience. Three days after sharing the summit of Mount Gardiner with Brown, LeConte and his friends climbed a much larger and more impressive mountain than the one to which he had originally given the "University" name. Upon reaching the top, presumably not wishing to be outdone by Brown, LeConte switched the name of University

Peak to the higher mountain and gave the smaller peak a new name, Mount Gould. Some of the earliest shots of the long and storied Stanford–Cal rivalry were fired right there in the mountains of the Sierra.

Joseph LeConte was known as "Little Joe" by his friends, partly as an affectionate joke about his height and build, and partly to distinguish him from his father whose name was also Joseph. He was six years younger than Brown, but had already spent more time in California's mountains, having been taken to the Yosemite and Tahoe regions by his father while he was still a small boy. In that optimistic year of Brown's life, as a newlywed with a seemingly secure position at Stanford, Brown might have looked at Little Joe and hoped for something similar for his own children. Brown would have known the story of the elder Joseph LeConte, and known that he had followed a similar path to California, both having moved from the East after accepting positions at newly formed colleges.

It was December 1868 when Joseph LeConte Sr. applied for and received a professorship at the University of California, which was then based in Oakland while construction of the Berkeley campus continued. Unlike Brown, LeConte Sr.'s move west marked the midpoint of a full life. He had already filled forty-five years with a surprising variety of intersections into major lines of American history. He was born on a plantation in Georgia and was an officer, though not with a combat role, in the Confederate Army during the Civil War. As a young man, he taught himself geology on an early exploration of the Great Lakes region. He studied evolution under Louis Agassiz at Harvard before the war, and spoke frequently with Henry Wadsworth Longfellow and Oliver Wendell Holmes, and occasionally with Ralph Waldo Emerson. LeConte's studies laid the groundwork for a popular book he would later write, a compromise between Darwin and the church titled *Evolution: Its Nature, Its Evidences, and Its Relation to Religious Thought*. He carried to his grave a strain of bigotry that he attempted to justify through evolutionary arguments aimed at proving the inferiority of other races.

After the war, LeConte found "the prospects for the South" to be "gloomy in the extreme"—partly because of the ravages of the fighting, but mostly because of black enfranchisement. He considered emigrating to Mexico or Brazil, but then word reached him of the new university in the West. In California, LeConte became a celebrated man. He was beloved as an instructor and admired for his contributions to the natural sciences. He has a building on the Berkeley campus and a mountain in the Sierra named for him, as well as other geographical features across the country. Three further generations of Joseph LeContes would be born in California.

In the summer after his first year of teaching at the university, LeConte traveled through the northern Sierra high country with a small group of colleagues. He had never before been beyond the Great Lakes, and his immersion in the western mountains inspired him with the Christianized nature worship he shared with many of his era. Spending a Sunday morning atop Glacier Point, he looked up at the peaks and down into the canyons and asked, "What could we do better than allow these to preach to us? Was there ever so venerable, majestic, and eloquent a minister of natural religion as the grand old Half Dome?"

During this trip, while admiring Yosemite Falls, LeConte encountered a man "in rough miller's garb," but with an "intelligent face and clear blue eye." The two conversed for a time, and LeConte learned that he was speaking with John Muir, whom he had heard of through a mutual friend. This was the year after Muir climbed Cathedral Peak; he had contrived a new job for himself—this time with lumber instead of sheep—in order to remain in the mountains. LeConte found this amazing: "a man of his intelligence tending a sawmill!" he wrote. "Not for himself, but for Mr. Hutchings. This is California!" LeConte invited Muir to travel with him up into the mountains and Muir accepted. Both had studied Agassiz's glaciology and they had much to discuss about the formation of the peaks and canyons which had so ignited LeConte's spirit from atop Glacier Point. For LeConte, and for his entire family, this first trip through the mountains began a long acquaintance with Muir and an enduring love for the Sierra.

Little Joe was born in the spring of 1870, three months before the meeting at the base of the falls between his father and Muir. He was the first of the serious climbers in the Sierra to have been a native-born Californian, and he was very much a product of the West. He liked making machines and wandering the Berkeley Hills of his teenage years with the shotgun his father had given him, terrorizing the local bird population. From his father he inherited a competitive mind and a body well suited to the mountains. The elder LeConte wrote pridefully in his autobiography of his own ability to do one-armed pull-ups, and carefully listed all the scientific papers he had published in his career (as well as the times when he had been the first to conceive of an idea which someone else had beaten him to print). Little Joe's small frame and wiry limbs made him light on his fingers and toes, and he enjoyed a keen appetite for mountain summits, particularly those upon which he would be the first to stand.

Any feelings of rivalry between Brown and LeConte that day on Mount Gardiner were not necessarily of a friendly variety. While Brown climbed alone, LeConte was followed by a party of friends, though none of them risked the final ridge to the mountaintop. Among the group was Helen Gompertz, the woman LeConte would marry five years later in 1901. In their journals and in reflections on the climb of Mount Gardiner, Brown and LeConte barely mentioned each other. But Helen, in her essay about that trip published by the Sierra Club, carefully noted that Brown "followed Mr. LeConte on to the summit."

Three years later, during the summer that Lucy and Bolton Brown returned to the mountains with their daughter, Bolton ran into Helen and Joseph again. This time the entry in the journal she shared with LeConte reveals a more complete version of their feelings toward Brown. After a long day of foot travel through the mountains they, along with a group of friends, returned to their camp and began to make preparations for a jolly Fourth of July evening. As she worked on the camp, she described the approach of a "strange figure":

> A tawny skin is thrown over one shoulder, and whilst I wonder who this modern Hercules may be, he advances, and I hear him say, "I've just come down from Bubbs Creek to get supplies." It is Brown! I immediately ask him where he has left Mrs. B. and baby B. It's none of my business, but I always like to make him confess in public to his habit of leaving his wife and baby in the wilds . . . Prof. B. came to our camp later when we were in the throes of getting up dinner. So complicated is the process that we have three fires going besides the dutch oven hole, and B. gets in everybody's way. We are awfully afraid he wants to stay . . . Finally he says, "You seem to be making great preparations." "Oh no," I reply, "We've all quarreled, and are cooking each his own dinner." He gave me a sharp look and I suppose I looked too innocent for he thereupon takes his departure. My pen cannot do justice to a description of that Fourth of July dinner, but my appetite has more than done it.

Helen's words carry the sting of truth, but I feel sorry for Brown, lurking at the firelit edges of all that camaraderie and fellowship. The LeContes tended to travel the mountains in packs of family and friends, and often they appreciated the company of visitors from other camps, welcoming them with food and drink as if they were town neighbors. Whether or not Brown realized he was being made an exception, it is sad to see him walk off into the night, though it is his loneliness more than the missed campfire session that seems lamentable to me.

These campfire socials were a new innovation in the high country. As the approaches to the Sierra and the paths among the peaks became more familiar, more and more people traveled to the mountains from the cities each summer, congregating in large crowds with mule trains to cart their possessions. Urban culture fueled by gold rush wealth had taken root in the towns of the Bay Area. LeConte described the time: "My life during the 'Gay Nineties' was one of the most delightful that can be imagined . . . We belonged to a gay social set in Berkeley and were out in society most of the time." The summer expeditions essentially transplanted this Bay Area social scene into the mountains—men and women, suit coats and petticoats, plates, knives, forks, and neckerchiefs—a strange western mix of cultivated wildness. The Sierra Club coordinated many of these trips. A group led by Muir created the organization in 1892 (both LeConte Sr. and David Starr Jordan signed the articles of incorporation; along with Helen, Little Joe was a charter member, and he held an official position in the organization for most of his life) for the twin purposes of the preservation of wild lands and the introduction of people to the wilderness. Muir's theory, which has not gone out of fashion to this day, was that people would be most likely to protect land that they loved.

Muir rarely made appearances on the larger Sierra Club trips through the mountains. He had little patience for pack animals and slow-moving groups. He did not go to the mountains to be in gay company, nor did loneliness sit ill with him as it did for Brown. If he had attended those summer gatherings he might well have been dismayed by their version of enjoying the wilderness.

Some of the stories told of the pleasure parties of this time—on both official Sierra Club outings and independent travels—turn the stomach for their excesses. LeConte liked nothing more than an evening fire, and often this meant a pile of wood stacked twenty feet high, the underbrush cleared of fuel for an acre or more. Sometimes he ignited entire standing trees just to light up the night and watch the flames. Rock rolling was another great joy. From summits and canyon rims he and two or three other men would pry off tremendous boulders to watch them smash against the cliffs and trees below. Rattlesnakes were decapitated for sport with a tally kept of the number killed; around this time the grizzly bear was hunted to extinction from the Sierra. The Sierra Club groups cheered the exclusion of the shepherds from the high mountains (the designation of Yosemite and Kings Canyon as protected areas put an end to the grazing of Muir's "hoofed locusts"). But the irony of a hundred people with as many mules lighting fires and rolling rocks and generally cutting a great swath through the wilderness while celebrating the absence of sheep seems to have been lost on them.

I have to point out that over the course of its history the Sierra Club has been an overwhelming force for good, and anyone who enjoys wilderness, or even just a breath of fresh air and a pretty view, owes the organization a great deal. During these early years the club worked hard for the preservation of the mountains, keeping the lumbermen and miners from skinning and gutting the most beautiful parts of America. The trouble was not with the organization, but with the attitudes of individuals, with the disturbing naiveté and callousness that tells a man the wilderness is so immense that a destroyed canyon-side or torched tree is of no consequence because there are a hundred more canyons and a thousand more trees.

I do not think that LeConte loved the mountains any less for what he inflicted upon them, though he may not have been the most introspective of men. He wrote about the fires and episodes of rock trundling with neither guilt nor destructive malice, but rather with simple-hearted delight in the crackling flames and open-eyed wonder at the tremendous crashing boulders. He was a Californian born at a time when the West was still vast and the conflict between man and nature was being fought with the outcome unclear. Over the course of his lifetime man essentially won that fight (the Hoover Dam dropped into the Colorado River in 1936 proved as decisive as the atom bomb hitting Hiroshima). To LeConte's credit his attitude, and the Sierra Club's in general, shifted during the first third of the twentieth century toward a new relationship with the land, a relationship which, seventy years later, we are still struggling to make functional and healthy.

But in the 1890s conservation was not a concern for Little Joe. He was interested in maps. The people who devoted years of their lives to the Sierra all sought to extract some sort of intellectual product from the mountains. Brown brought art down from the hills. The elder LeConte transformed his geologic observations into papers which he then listed in his autobiography. I am no exception, walking through the Sierra seeing one mountain of stone and another of history, looking for stories to write down in the hopes of understanding what we are doing up there. Perhaps we all need these intellectual puzzles to feed our minds while we satisfy our fingers. Perhaps we just fear being called "mere nature lovers," the term which drove Clarence King from the Sierra.

LeConte had only a passing interest in the geology of the mountains and little inclination toward literature. His copious journal entries are mostly recitations of events: mountains climbed, streams crossed, meals eaten. All is generally grand or glorious. He was a mechanical engineer; he liked measuring things and making things. So he decided to make a map—the first comprehensive map of the entire Sierra Range from Yosemite to Mount Whitney. Peak after peak he climbed with transit and aneroid barometer taking painstaking measurements of azimuth, height, distance. His notebooks are filled with the data from these observations. Year by year and summit by summit, he covered the Sierra with interlocking triangles, linking up the mountains, filling in the gaps, converting ten thousand square miles of peaks, canyons, and rivers into lines covering three yard-wide blueprint sheets. The task took sixteen years to complete.

◆◆◆

LeConte's work on the map took him to every part of the Sierra. In the middle of his crisscrossing survey lines, right near the center of the range, one mountain in particular attracted his attention through the telescope of his transit. It thrust its classic pointed summit high up into the blue, one of those spiry tops above which one might imagine the sky carefully picking up her skirt to avoid tearing the fabric. The rest of the mountain plunged down into a chaos of stone. It occupied the northern end of a jagged, eight-mile-long saw of dark granite, a ridge the original California Survey wisely named the Palisades. Depending on how one does the counting, somewhere between fourteen and twenty-five other peaks slice the air on this part of the Sierra crest. This is the wild heart of the Sierra. To the east, the largest glacier in the range buries the mountains to their knees; to the west, towering buttresses punctuate a maze of granite between the mountaineer and the summits.

The name of the mountain would once again bring LeConte into quiet conflict with Brown. In 1895, looking at the Palisades from the summit of Mount Woodworth, some ten miles to the west, Brown named the highest peak Mount Jordan, for David Starr Jordan. In his field notebook, on the day he attempted the peak in 1903, LeConte also called it Mount Jordan, but later, at home, when he typed up his notes and wrote an article for the Sierra Club about the expedition, he had a change of heart. He suggested that it would be better for such a grand and imposing mountain to have a name that "could be handed down through all time"; perhaps he also did not want his mountain to have been named by Bolton Brown for a president of Stanford. LeConte had his way (no surprise given his map and his position within the Sierra Club), and ever since, the mountain has simply been called North Palisade. In all likelihood, Brown would have been more disappointed than Dr. Jordan, who later had his name attached, permanently, to an impressive peak near Mount Stanford. In any event, the twentieth century arrived before any of the Palisades were climbed. Few had even glimpsed these peaks, other than from down in the Owens Valley, through gaps in the foothills.

For Helen and Joseph, the twentieth century began with marriage. Joseph asked her to marry him at the end of November in 1900, a proposal that even he realized was overdue given their many summers together in the Sierra, and their social evenings in Berkeley the other nine months of the year. But he had worried that she would not accept him because she was five years his senior. Both families expressed great joy. A typical response came from Joseph's sister, Emma, in a congratulatory letter to Helen: "You are so well suited," she wrote, "and both of such even sensible character that I do not see how you can fail to be happy together. You are such thoroughly good comrades, and so entirely sympathetic." Joseph, for his own part, returned home after their successful engagement in a "sort of ecstasy." Helen was equally pleased. She had an attractive, intelligent, squarely built face—her expression in those days must have been beautiful to see. In a letter to her fiancé just before New Year's, she wrote, "I'm pretty calm considering how much I expect of the 20th Century and how I must live up to my 'great expectations'." The world, and particularly California, was changing and maturing and she would step into this promising new century with Joseph to share her path.

They were married in June of 1901 and had their honeymoon in the Sierra that summer. They spent much of the time simply enjoying each other's company and "loafing," which seems to have been LeConte's second favorite activity in the Sierra, behind climbing mountains. A typical entry in Joseph's journal from their honeymoon trip might read: "July 3 The Durbrow Party turned up today. They invited us to an Italian dinner. It was a great feast. Ruddock as bartender was especially fine."

Backcountry feasts were a joy that they both shared. In his letters home, LeConte always commented on what he had eaten and reassured his mother of his health by telling her of his enormous appetite. In one such letter he wrote, "The boys declare that I have a hole in my heel where the grub runs out for otherwise they cannot see where I put it all." Between his father's metabolism and his time rambling through the mountains, LeConte could barely fill out his clothes no matter what he ate. In pictures, his trousers and shirts seem to hang on rails instead of limbs, and when he looks at the camera, a remarkable pair of intense brown eyes seems ready to leap out of his thin face. Helen enjoyed their banquets just as much. In a playful journal entry regarding a twilit decision between a hungry bivouac and a nighttime trek onward, she wrote, "I immediately began to feel horribly lonesome. I've noticed that feeling attacks me whenever there isn't much to eat in camp."

The newlyweds also had plans for serious mountaineering, and on July 8 they began a knapsack trip up Paradise Valley to climb some of the peaks on the south fork of the Kings River. They never made it to the mountains. The next evening at dusk, a friend arrived at their camp on horseback, and as he dismounted he said to LeConte, "I'm bringing you bad news. Your father is dead."

Just the previous summer, the elder LeConte had taken a horse-packing trip with his son and Helen up over Kearsarge Pass and down into Kings Canyon. A photograph shows him lying on his side in a meadow, with his head propped on one arm, wearing a black hat and coat, eating his dinner off a plate with a spoon. Even with his flowing, white, academic beard and formal attire, he looks entirely at ease resting in the grasses among the mountains he loved. But though time could not dull the pleasure of the Sierra, it finally caught up with his heart.

As the honeymooners left for Kings Canyon the next year, LeConte Sr. decided to take one last trip to the Yosemite Valley with his daughter, Sallie, arriving there on July 4. He had a day to tour the Valley, and he shared one more campfire with a reverent group of friends and old students, who gathered to enjoy his company and hear him speak about the mountains with his characteristic mix of science, wit, and poetry. He died of a heart attack on the morning of July 6. Word spread throughout the camps that "Doctor Joe" had been returned to the mountains; soon the entire valley assembled to mourn and watch the parting of the coach that bore his casket. It is no accident that these events—deaths, meetings, marriages—happened for the LeContes in the Sierra. Season after season their lives revolved around the high country.

In the summer of 1902, Helen and Joseph returned to the area they had left in haste the previous year. This time they had a more ambitious schedule and climbed many peaks. The middle of July found them working their way up Cartridge Creek, where Joseph gave Marion Lake and Peak the name his wife had lost when she changed hers from Helen Marion Gompertz to Helen Gompertz LeConte. Crossing the divide at the headwaters of Cartridge Creek, they emerged at last at the southern end of the Palisades. From there they made the first ascent of the South Palisade, though here for once LeConte agreed with Brown's name for the peak and called it Split Mountain. Split Mountain, though separated by several miles from the main Palisade crest, became the earliest major peak of the Palisades group to be climbed, and when they reached its summit, Helen became the first and only woman to have made the first ascent of one of California's select mountains with summits above fourteen thousand feet of elevation.

They returned to the Palisades the next summer with a duo of experienced Sierra climbers, their two good friends Jim Moffit and Jim Hutchinson. LeConte assembled this team specifically for an attempt on the North Palisade, as he anticipated difficult climbing. Robert and John Pike also joined the group when the two parties met along the way. Following the same route up Cartridge Creek that the LeContes had pioneered the summer before, they established a camp at Marion Lake. That afternoon, they climbed Marion Peak in order to stare at North Palisade, still some ten miles away, through LeConte's transit telescope.

The prospects looked grim. To the west, the mountain dropped down from one precipitous buttress to the next, the cliffs stacked in a haphazard and dizzying arrangement. To the south, one long knife-edged ridge swept in a thin line down to the next peak, which LeConte had named Mount Sill on an earlier expedition. They felt reasonably sure they could reach the shoulder of Mount Sill, but would they be able to traverse that endless, narrow knife-edge all the way to the summit? In places, deep clefts gashed the ridgeline and all in all it looked highly improbable. For over an hour they stared through the telescope at their intended mountain, and in the end, LeConte had to "confess at last that the odds were against us."

That night the climbing party readied their knapsacks for a three-day expedition. Helen decided not to join them. At thirty-eight, the years had accumulated around her hips and elsewhere. She took her body's gains in stride. In a letter to her husband later that year, without any noticeable embarrassment she wrote, "I wish I were with you! I'm getting fat—(fatter I should say)." And she had no reason to be embarrassed—she would spend another twenty years trekking through the Sierra—but her days of clinging to cliffs with her fingers were over. John Pike stayed with her at Lake Marion.

The next morning, the climbing party pushed north into Palisade Basin and made a camp in the austere country of stone in the western lee of the Palisades. The four men had left most everything behind in order to keep their knapsacks light for the rough cross-country travel, but the camp was hardly unpleasant. They cut their stogies in half to conserve the tobacco and ate tinned beef off granite plates heated in one of Joseph's famous fires. When the stars turned the mountains silver, each man burrowed into his own eiderdown quilt and passed the night among the rocks.

Up with the dawn they hastened through a chilly breakfast in the morning shadow of the mountains and then set out for the shoulder of Mount Sill. They found a tolerable angle and made rapid progress to the ridge crest. In certain sections, pleats in the slope protected snowfields from the sun. The summer cycle of freeze and thaw had drawn out fields of well-developed *penitentes*, spikes of snow arranged like a forest of swords. Some of these snow-blades came up to LeConte's armpits and the climbers stumbled between them while attempting to balance against their keen edges.

North Palisade came into view at last and the path to its summit looked clear. Their spirits rose with their elevation. They would reach the ridge connecting North Palisade to Mount Sill and then they would need only to balance along that final knife-edge for the thousand feet to the top point. "Boys, we shall make it," LeConte said, feeling a swell of confidence. He spoke too soon.

> A dozen steps more brought us to the top of the cross-divide, and in an instant was swept away every chance, every hope of success . . . We were on the edge of a precipice which sank for a thousand feet absolutely sheer to the head of a splendid glacier . . . The only possible route was along this edge, and this might have been feasible had it not been gashed in one place by a notch a hundred feet deep.

Mountains are tricky. They hide secrets behind overlapping wrinkles of stony hide. What had looked from below like an unbroken route to the summit concealed a place where an entire layer of mountainside had been stripped away, leaving a chasm cut through the ridge. In three directions, to the west, north, and east, volumes of free air circulated beneath their feet. If they could have walked a hundred yards of sky to bridge that gap in the mountain, the summit that had drawn LeConte's eye for a decade would have been a ten-minute scramble away.

But Joseph might as well have been staring at North Palisade through his transit telescope for all the good proximity did him.

They peered down into the gap in their ridge for an hour looking for a feasible route down into or out of it. Ultimately, they gave it up as too risky. They backtracked south along the ridge and scrambled to the top of Mount Sill, a rather easy and unsatisfying alternative even though it had never before been climbed. They gained some solace from the view, at least. Mount Sill stands off the main ridge to the northeast, providing an unencumbered view along the whole jagged sweep of the Palisades and down into the crevasses slitting the glacier below. North Palisade still looked entirely inaccessible behind its disheartening defenses.

Nowadays, climbers tend to think of cliffs and mountains in terms of route lines. Visualize a photograph of a mountain marked in pen by all the men and women who have climbed the peak by original routes. The ink tracings on the photograph represent the paths taken. Further generations of climbers have a choice: they can follow an existing line or find their own. But it's easier, of course, to follow a charted path, like learning a well-loved piece of music, particularly when the mountain has been climbed for a century and the most logical routes have all been done. For most modern climbers, this constitutes climbing: following previously established lines—playing the jazz standard or that piece of classical music. Certain routes, like certain songs, earn reputations and are trained for and written about; they are climbed because they are sensible, sometimes beautiful, ways up the mountain, but they exist because they have been written down and followed season after season.

Put a blank sheet of paper or an unmarked photograph in your hands and this is the Sierra in 1900. When LeConte arrived, North Palisade had not yet been inked; there was nothing up there to follow but the rock itself. The mountain must have looked entirely different through his eyes, a seamless product of the earth's innards, undivided by the LeConte Route and the Clyde Couloir and the Starlight Buttress. He had the pleasure of creating something new, but first he had to crack through a husk of frustrations. To be turned back just shy of the summit by an unseen gap in the mountain, budding elation killed off with a single step, is a rare experience reserved for the first to go that way.

Back down in their camp with their quilts and beef tins, the climbers discussed the possibilities. The gap in the ridge eliminated the whole southern approach to the mountain. That left the western cliffs, a possibility discussed with apprehension from atop Marion Peak and left unresolved in favor of the hope that any such hazard would be unnecessary.

When I followed LeConte, I camped right beneath the western scarp of the Palisades on a gravel bed just above one of the many stone-bound lakes of the region. I understood his unease. The cliffs and crags descended from the Palisade summits in a tumult of shadows and angles that mystified my eyes. From far back to the west or south, the mountains appear jagged but orderly enough. From up close the maze of rock is so overwhelming that the summits themselves are often hidden or disguised by tricks of perspective.

LeConte was hardly hopeful about their prospects. "It appeared a useless venture as well as a dangerous one," he wrote. "But finally it was decided to give one more day to the work—to at least creep around the foot of the giant." They had another full day's worth of food; there was no good reason to give up without another attempt.

Lying on my back in the gravel, next to a creek trickling happily toward the lake through a little alpine garden of its own making, I stared up at the mountains. On the approach trek, I had tried to flush the lines from my mind, but they were still there, superimposed in front of the peaks. I have spent half my life studying routes and route descriptions and I will not be able to unlearn that habit in a season or a year. But I have begun to see the limitations imposed by the lines we draw. When exploring a foreign city with a guide map, one tends to walk through a track on the map rather than through the city; one sees what the map author has suggested one should see. The danger with a climbing guidebook is the same: that one will end up climbing the line instead of the rock while staring at the paper mountain instead of the one made of stone. There's nothing necessarily wrong with this, but it does make climbers more passive and reduces the climbing itself to a physical exercise by eliminating the need for creativity.

The climbers arose before dawn the next morning. Pike had already satisfied his desires for adventure, so he remained enveloped in duck down while LeConte, Moffit, and Hutchinson departed for the mountain. They had a rudimentary plan. The day before, when they had stared down into the notch that separated them from North Palisade's summit, they saw that the gash in the ridge formed a chute which "cleft the western precipice from crest to base." So today they located the lower end of this channel and scrambled up the loose scree and talus piled on its angled floor, bypassing the steep cliffs to the left and right. They could see all the way up to the notch that had stopped them the day before, but they knew what waited for them there. There was no point in climbing back to the notch; they would have to escape from the chute before the cliffs above hemmed them in.

Halfway up, the angle steepened and they climbed bare slabs of granite, polished smooth by springtime runoff, when melting snow and loosened boulders send avalanches thundering down the gulley. Here they began to search for an exit to the north, looking for a hidden passage leading to one of the other deep chimneys splitting the western cliffs. Even if they found a way out of the channel, they would have no idea where it led. All they knew for certain was that the higher they climbed the cleft toward the notch, the less likely their chances of finding an exit.

Hutchinson discovered a fissure in the left wall, an up-slanting crack that seemed climbable. He and Moffit tried repeatedly to work out a sequence that would deliver them from inside the cleft, but nothing they invented seemed proof against a nasty fall onto the rocks below. LeConte scanned the lower reaches of the chute. He discovered "a ledge along the wall which had been invisible from below." Just as the mountain had disguised the immense notch above, it hid this small shelf, camouflaging it among the speckled granite until LeConte looked at just the right angle to catch its outline. He called the others down to him and set out along his ledge.

It began as wide as a narrow sidewalk, but damp and sloped outward. LeConte crawled along and with each move forward the ground dropped farther and farther away below. The ledge tapered until it was barely more than a foot broad, but now at least it had leveled. At the end of the shelf Joseph turned a corner to find blocky ground leading up to another deep chimney. What an exhilarating moment that must have been! The careful search for a way out of the cleft solved by a truly hidden passage, the blind moments on LeConte's catwalk yielding at last a way to the upper mountain.

But they were not safe or near the summit yet. They entered the dark and narrow chimney above them. It gripped them tightly, allowing one man at a time to squirm his way up, pressing with elbows and knees against parallel walls of

View from inside the ice chimney, LeConte route, North Palisade

stone. Thick icicles hung down from boulders wedged in the chimney, forcing the climbers out onto finger- and toeholds etched into the chimney walls. Move by move their view of the lakes and peaks to the west expanded, always framed by the sheer dark walls of their narrow groove.

They did not want to believe too much in success, but when the narrow chimney ended and they had the day's first unobstructed view of the summit, they could hold their hopes back no longer. Excitement hurried them along. "One who has not been in a similar position," LeConte wrote, "can never realize our feelings as foot by foot the upward path was won, and nearer and nearer came the tiny rounded cap above." They entered a large amphitheatre beneath the peak top. Steep rock led directly to the summit, but a more practicable angle took them to the right and up to the ridge crest. There the "stupendous panorama of precipice, glacier, and desert" burst upon them. From the knife-edge they had at last put beneath their boots, they could look down into the sagebrush scrub of the Owens Valley ten thousand feet below, then back up to the summits of the White Mountains, and beyond into the deserts of Nevada.

They could have hit North Palisade's summit with a thrown stone from their spot on the ridge, but huge rectangular blocks of granite stacked above them still separated them from the top. They latched their fingers over the upper edge of each block and hoisted themselves up, step by step. To the east, the mountain dropped one or two thousand feet down to the glacier, and to the west a hundred feet to the amphitheatre, and they rode the narrow divide in between. For ten years LeConte had studied North Palisade from afar; for two seasons he had explored on foot the Palisade region; the approach to the mountain had taken a week; the final two days of route finding and rock climbing had brought him at last to the steep point of North Palisade's summit with the roughest part of the Sierra unwinding in all directions beneath his feet. With a heave over one final stone edge they were delivered to an angled slab leading directly to the peaked summit, where they "crawled out upon the crown, victorious at last."

◆ ◆ ◆

MOUNTAINEERS TOSS THE word "victory" around pretty freely. But what have we won? And whom have we defeated? Is that what mountaineering is all about—defeating and subduing the world's last wild places? I hope not. But our vocabulary (and our modern tendency to unholster a drill at the least provocation) sometimes makes me wonder. It would be easy to conclude that we climbers are at war with the very places we love the most. I think we are at war with ourselves. When we reach the summits we have not overcome the mountains, only our own fears and physical limitations.

Lying on my back, staring up at the mountains and the gathering storm clouds, my thoughts were interrupted by a marmot wandering through the edge of my vision. Marmots are contented creatures who inhabit the alpine meadows and talus fields and hibernate under rocks in colonies for the winter. A cross between a guinea pig and a bear could yield a marmot's shape; in terms of size they are about as long as a squirrel but twice as wide. They are placid. A full afternoon might consist of a sunning session perched atop a warm rock followed by an amble across a meadow to investigate the napping options on the other side: fat, serene, little orange Sierra Buddhas. When I think of Brown and LeConte and myself rushing around to make our maps and books and paintings, and I see the marmots seated on their sunny rocks, heads up, absorbing the changing light reflected off the peaks, I suspect they know something about appreciating the mountains that we forget.

The only problem with marmots is their tendency to chew the vital items of a mountaineer's kit. After watching my visitor nose around the rocks for a while, I considered moving to a different post for the night. I had no desire to have my sleeping bag shredded and deposited underground as a marmot's winter insulation. But I figured I would be just as likely to find another marmot (or three) at the next spot so it seemed pointless to relocate. Using a kind of caveman logic, I thought I might keep the marmots away by marking my territory, so I emptied my bladder in an arc around my little camp. As it turns out, human urine acts as some sort of marmot salt lick. An entire congregation of marmots appeared and spent the afternoon capering around and digging in the damp spots I had left behind and generally undermining my elevation of their dignified character. Precisely at three o'clock, they all vanished, leaving me alone to enjoy the afternoon thundershower that arrived fifteen minutes later. Sensible creatures, those marmots.

The rain stopped before dark, but the clouds choked off the stars for most of the night and I woke the next morning to a meager dawn with clouds on the southern and western horizons. It would rain again. The dawn sky was unequivocal about that. The only question was what time the storms would start. I leapt out of my sleeping bag and off my gravel bed and ate a hurried breakfast on the way to the mountain.

The cleft began amid a splendid bedlam of granite. On all sides towers and cliffs appeared to lean at odd angles and I could not tell whether my eye, or the mountain itself, was actually off-kilter. Mazes, whether drawn on paper or made of hedgerows, always fascinated me as a child, but this seemed to be the best labyrinth of all, built huge from Mother Earth's own stone, with something precious stashed at its end. With a boy's pleasure in a good mystery, I began my search for LeConte's ledge.

I found it immediately, not because it was obvious, or because I knew what to look for, or because my eyes were any better than his, but because someone had built an enormous rock pile to mark it. This first cairn was not alone. Above, at twenty-foot intervals, on ledges and flat boulders, marched a single-file army of its relatives all the way to the base of the upper chimney. There were big cairns and micro-cairns and cute cairns with rocks balanced in funny ways. I climbed past an old length of rope hung down through the chimney, tied at the top to a boulder. Above the chimney, the marching cairns began again, winding their way up the amphitheatre to the summit. Just below the peak top, someone had wrapped two boulders in yard after yard of bright red webbing to make a rappel anchor in order to avoid climbing down from the summit blocks. It looked as if someone had tp'd the mountain with Day-Glo tissue.

It was ugly and discouraging, like finding garbage in a meadow. Uncomfortable, too—climbers had done this; I couldn't even blame it on tourists who don't know any better. The cairns here had just one purpose, to save a mountaineer from the heavy burden of thinking. Now instead of studying the mountain and evaluating the rock and solving the puzzle built into the peak by the work of a million years, one connects the dots, pulls on the rope, rappels off the top, following a track of trash and stones, the line lifted off the guidebook page and laid down on the mountain. I knocked all the cairns down and scattered their pieces. I cut the rope out of the chimney and the webbing off the top. The mountain purred.

I couldn't stay mad on top. The summit was too beautiful, the mountains in all directions too wild. To the south, the Palisade crest ripped along in defiance of all things horizontal; to the north, hulking Mount Humphreys, all alone in its immense basin of stone; to the west, the Sierra lakes, deep pools of blue; to the east, and far, far down, the desert, filling the Sierra rain shadow. The summit itself was made of the best Sierra granite: compact, smooth, hard stuff that had the feel of age under my fingers, like touching the bones of the earth.

What I find astonishing is that Muir already understood so much about the future of wilderness in the 1870s, when most of the West had not even been

Summit shadow, North Palisade

granted statehood. He wrote his famous line, "I never left my name on any mountain, rock, or tree," at a time when his Sierra Club followers could not have known what he meant by that, or why it should even matter. Somehow he already knew that it was time to walk the woods quietly, without leaving traces of his passage. Many generations later, we are still trying to catch up with him.

◆ ◆ ◆

LECONTE AND HIS friends returned to camp in high spirits. They woke Pike from an afternoon nap and the four of them descended to a warmer elevation for the night. They celebrated with a fire, an enormous meal, and whole, uncut stogies. I descended North Palisade under thickening clouds which enveloped one mountain after the next. By midday, raindrops that seemed as big as marbles were splashing off the ground. Flights of thunder swept by, crackling off the tops of unseen peaks in the damp, smoke-colored sky. The storm lasted thirty-six hours, an unusual length for the summer Sierra. By the time it was over, mountain, forest, and man had all received a penetrating soak.

After North Palisade, the LeConte family continued on its march through the mountains and the years. Helen and Joseph had two children, a girl and a boy to whom they gave their own names. They took the children into the Sierra just as Joseph had been taken by his father. The eldest Joseph LeConte took him up Mount Tallac, near Lake Tahoe, when Little Joe was only four years old. For most of the way, his father carried him in his arms, one of Joseph's earliest memories. For his children's first mountain, Joseph selected Mount Dana, a high hiking peak on the eastern edge of Yosemite with views down to Mono Lake and across to Mount Lyell.

Occasionally, Helen and Joseph spent time apart. During these absences they sent sweet, love-struck letters to each other. In one, Helen wrote, "I look at the moon every night and feel that I am quite with you then, for I know you too are looking at it and thinking of me, perhaps?"

LeConte inherited his father's tendency to play supporting roles in famous historical moments. These intersections with history happened every few years with remarkable regularity. When Wilhelm Röntgen discovered X-rays in 1895 and published his findings, LeConte quickly built the necessary cathode ray generator. He grasped the medical potential for the device immediately; when a local boy was shot in the arm by a friend he had the boy brought to his laboratory and used his X-ray machine to show the surgeon the location of the bullet. Though his methodology can't be recommended (the poor etherized lad was given an X-ray exposure of "an hour and a quarter"), the procedure marked one of the earliest medical uses of X-rays in America. In 1903, when President Theodore Roosevelt paid his famous visit to Yosemite and went camping with John Muir, LeConte traveled with the president's party. And when the great 1906 earthquake struck San Francisco, Helen and Joseph LeConte were in Berkeley, having left the city a few hours before after a night at the opera. Joseph helped with San Francisco's reconstruction, perhaps most importantly through his work testing the massive pumps for the city's new firefighting system.

Joseph covered the events matter-of-factly in his journals; Helen was the one who recorded the family mood. For many years, they had dreamed of touring Europe and at last they cleared a summer of other duties and packed their bags in May 1914. In the San Marco Square in Venice they heard of Archduke Ferdinand's assassination; in Chamonix they saw headlines proclaiming war between Serbia and Austria; onboard a train to Munich the shout went up that war had been declared against Russia. As an American stranded in Germany at the beginning of the First World War, Joseph wrote about difficulties with paperwork and currency and the crowded boat ride home. Meanwhile, Helen had this to say about their eventual exodus from Germany on a train chartered by the American ambassador for U.S. citizens caught by the war:

One thing more reminds me of the tragedy lurking under this smiling cover. All the people who met us and smiled at us and pelted us with flowers were women, children or old men! Only the guards at the bridges were strong able men! I cannot think this thought through to its end—without a shudder. Are all the nations of Europe to become peoples made up of women, children and old men? . . . Alas! The little children of to-day will shoulder a burden such that no one has ever dreamed of before. And the women! Their burden is beyond all dreams. I cannot think it. It hurts too much.

LeConte family on the Vernal Falls bridge, left to right: "Little Joe," Helen Gompertz, Joseph LeConte Sr., Caroline LeConte, Anita Gompertz (Photo courtesy of Bancroft Library)

As the world spun faster, LeConte held his own life steady. Following the example of his father, he became a beloved and admired member of the faculty at the University of California at Berkeley. He continued to spend summers in the Sierra—forty-four trips in all, a staggering number of expeditions to the high peaks. Like his father, he also continued going to the mountains until his heart forbade it. But it was no longer 1901; improved hospitals and medical care allowed LeConte to fight a lingering battle against heart disease and diabetes. He proceeded gamely and optimistically, just as he always had. When hardened arteries forced the amputation of his left leg, he adjusted his expectations accordingly. In his last journal entry, which described a lunch with his friends, he wrote, "I think I did pretty well with my 'wooden leg,' and two canes. Went up and down a lot of steps and never fell once."

The physical changes he lived through are hard to fathom. The world he entered as a child was immense. In his early memories, prairie stretched from the Bay to the forested Berkeley Hills with the interruption of just a few farmhouses. For his first trip to Yosemite, he left Berkeley on horseback. By the time he was confined to an oxygen tent in the hospital, the automobile had been invented and consecrated, America was paved, two world wars were fought, two atomic bombs were dropped, and America and Russia had begun their grim race for power over a much smaller and more jaded world.

On February 1, 1950, Jim Hutchinson came and visited him in the hospital. Helen had died twenty-five years earlier; in 1929 Joseph married a close friend of theirs, the woman who had cared for Helen in the last weeks of her life and now cared for him at the end of his. Adelaide pulled back the plastic curtain of the oxygen tent and said to Jim, "Talk to him about the mountains. He loves that." So Jim took Joseph's hand and asked, "Joe, remember our climb of the North

Palisade with Jim Moffit?" Joseph tried hard to speak, but he could not, so he listened instead. Jim wrote, "All this time he was looking intently at me, smiling, his bright eyes full of intelligence and delight. It was a great joy to him to hear about his beloved mountains."

Jim returned home that afternoon and received a phone call from Adelaide. Joseph was dead; he had slipped away with his friend's stories of the mountains still echoing in his ears.

· 8 ·

James Hutchinson + Mount Humphreys

[JULY 1904]

Mount Humphreys (13,986 feet) from the Humphreys Basin

BEYOND THE PALISADES, the Sierra crest swings to the northwest and slices a diagonal line through an area of peaks named for the early evolutionists: Mount Darwin, Mount Mendel, Mount Haeckel, Mount Huxley. Farther north, past Mount Lamarck, the mountains abruptly dwindle in stature, like the spines on a submerging sea monster's back. An immense granite basin filled with lakes and marmots and very little else opens up here. Billows of smooth stone roll to the east and west. The horizon looks unstable without mountains to anchor it, as if the granite will just dribble away down into the Owens and San Joaquin valleys. Massive Mount Humphreys presides over this strange land, alone at the highest end of the basin, thrust up like the head of the resurfacing dragon.

Joseph LeConte made an early try for Mount Humphreys' summit. The year was 1898, a time when he must have been very much in love with Helen, but still too unsure or shy to make his feelings known to her. Four hundred feet below the mountaintop, blocked at that tantalizing distance by yet another vertical cliff face, with a storm moving fast toward him, he wrote Helen a hasty note on a postcard.

Nearest point attainable to the summit of Mt. Humphreys
July 7, 1898

Dear Helen,

For the last week we have been struggling with Mt. Humphreys, and we are still 400 feet below the summit, but we are satisfied we have done all that could be done. For 4 days we tried to get our animals up this basin of the stream that drains it, but had to abandon it. So we took the bull by the horns, left our packs 15 miles away in Lost Valley, and took our knapsacks on our backs yesterday. All day yesterday we worked our way up the rugged cañon, reaching a point 4 miles from the mountain in the P.M. Long before we started up the mountain we gave up all hope of getting to the top. The eastern and western faces are absolutely perpendicular for 2000 feet. First we tried the southern edge but could not get higher than 13200. Then we tackled the northern edge and are here 13550 feet. Summit about 14000 feet. Weather cold and cloudy. We'll probably get wet.

Good Bye,
Joe

It's a strange letter, given the location. The data it contains, the mileages and elevations and difficulties moving mules, are exactly the sorts of things he noted in his journals—but he could just as easily have done that back at camp instead of high on the mountain with a storm brewing. Perhaps he was lonely for Helen, and wanted to share a moment with her through the only means available to him. Perhaps, also, he was frightened of Mount Humphreys and the terrain he would have to descend, and should the mountain shrug him off he wanted to be found with a letter to Helen in his pocket, no matter how mundane the contents. That final "Good Bye" was not his usual written farewell to Helen, and it makes me wonder at the feelings hidden beneath the words.

Mount Humphreys guards itself well and LeConte's description only hints at the features of the mountain. Long gashes score its sides for hundreds of feet and conceal hidden buttresses and ice runnels; once past the lower barriers, the topmost spire is still walled round with high, vertical cliffs. LeConte may even have taken a perverse kind of satisfaction back to camp with him. Sometimes, it is good to meet a mountain that sends you away frustrated, a reminder that the peak tops aren't made for our pleasure. Mountaineering would become a tedious exercise without the possibility of failure; birds surely find no thrill on high summits—that treat is reserved for creatures who struggle to get there.

The summit was still untouched five years later when LeConte climbed North Palisade with James Moffit and James Hutchinson, two men with whom he maintained lifelong friendships. He was particularly close to Hutchinson, who was called Jim, or Jimmie, by his friends. In later years, the LeConte and Hutchinson families frequently vacationed together in the Yosemite high country, and the two men would spend days puttering about camp together, cleaning and oiling their cars, or fussing over the tents. Later still, Hutchinson would write obituaries in the *Sierra Club Bulletin* for both Helen and Joseph.

But the younger years were for climbing mountains, and when Hutchinson stood atop North Palisade with his friends and looked to the northwest and "saw looming in the distance, entirely isolated, the rugged, spiry, and unscaled summit of Mount Humphreys, its eastern and western sides falling in precipices and . . . its whole aspect one of defiance," he felt an immediate attraction to the mountain. It was not just the geometry of the peak itself, but the whole desolate area of lake and stone that the peak inhabited. He recalled the words of Theodore Solomons, who had explored several high routes through the mountains and had called the region between the Palisades and Mount Humphreys the "scenic culmination" and "final triumph" of the Sierra. So, Hutchinson reasoned, "If this region was the heart of the High Sierra, then, in truth, the very center of this heart was Mount Humphreys." Within minutes of reaching the summit of North Palisade, he had already begun to imagine an expedition into the Humphreys Basin.

In those years, Hutchinson and LeConte often traveled the mountains together. Between LeConte's mapmaking and geologic studies and appetite for unclimbed peaks, he was usually the de facto leader of those parties. Looking back on this arrangement without a trace of resentment, Hutchinson wrote, "I have often felt as though I was his man Friday; I was always learning so much from him and doing the best I could to help him." In truth, Hutchinson let his modesty get the better of him, for he was a strong and knowledgeable mountaineer himself. He was another charter member of the Sierra Club, and he held official and honorary positions within the club on and off throughout his life. He had a long, lean body, well suited to vertical climbing. In photographs taken in the mountains, he often wears a circular hat with a shirt or some other bundle of cloth wrapped around its upper brim, making it look a bit like a mushroom cap with his long, thin, sun-lined face standing in as the stalk below. In one of those pictures, black, knee-high riding boots and a vest over a collared shirt round out the image of a man who, intentionally or not, had the airs of a madcap mountaineer and looked out at the world through warm, bemused eyes.

The summer after the North Palisade expedition, LeConte was occupied showing geologist Grove Karl Gilbert around the Sierra. Hutchinson returned with his brother, Edward, and two other men, Charles Noble and Albert Whitney. From San Francisco, they traveled to Fresno and on to Shaver Lake, then up the Red Mountain Trail, and along the upper reaches of the South Fork of the San Joaquin River. The excursion had a single objective—Mount Humphreys—so upon reaching the upper creeks of the San Joaquin they immediately began to search for a passage for their donkeys into the Humphreys Basin. As LeConte had discovered in 1898, the cliffs and ridges bounding the basin were rocky and steep and difficult enough for foot travel, let alone pack animals. First they explored the Piute Branch of the San Joaquin, then Evolution Creek, but eventually came to the same conclusion as LeConte: the animals would have to stay picketed in a meadow, while the men crossed the divide to the mountain on foot.

From atop this divide, Hutchinson had his first clear look at Mount Humphreys since standing on the summit of North Palisade. The intervening year of preparation had done nothing to diminish the mountain's size or wildness. "There, alone in solitary grandeur, rose Mount Humphreys, the king of all the peaks," he wrote. "Such a fascinating scene of desolation I never expect to see again." He was closer to the peak than he ever had been before, and could make out more of the foreground detail. Low cliffs and domes populated the basin floor, and lakes of all sizes, hundreds of them, nestled into the spaces between. Creeks drained the lakes and glazed the basin white where they spilled their waters over bare stone. Erratics, huge stones carried on the backs of glaciers and dropped to the ground at the end of the ice age, were scattered liberally about, many left in startling locations on dome crests and cliff edges. Here and there, a light fuzz of alpine grasses and shrubbery clutched at pockets of thin soil.

The four men threaded a careful descent into the basin through a narrow corridor between a wall of rock on one side and a tongue of hard-frozen snow on the other. From there they walked a crooked course through the granite bosses and lake hollows toward Mount Humphreys. They wanted to end the day with a full view of the mountain, so they left behind warmer, more protected spots in favor of a high outpost where they made camp against the walls of a small gulley with a level floor. They spent the afternoon staring at the mountain and cooking a dinner of tapioca soup, fried ham, hardtack, and tea.

LeConte's tales of precipices and chancy climbing on Mount Humphreys had only increased what Hutchinson called "the fascination" of the peak. But now, staring up at the mountain, they had to confront the discomforting reality that Little Joe, who had mentored Hutchinson and spent so many years climbing these Sierra Mountains, had failed on this peak. As the declining sun sharpened the features of the mountain, they handed around their single pair of binoculars, taking turns studying the convoluted face, trying to tease out its secrets from their alcove on the basin floor.

When I traveled to Mount Humphreys, I found a similar spot for myself. I had their same criteria in mind: a full view of the mountain with whatever little shelter I could afford, and I ended up at a chilly elevation hunkered down in a depression with a gravel floor and an eye-filling view. Flat-bottomed ravines are ten-a-mile in the Humphreys Basin and there's no telling which they actually chose for themselves. Still, there was a pleasant feeling of camaraderie in the idea that the wall I put my back against to watch the mountain could have been the same piece of stone they used to steady their binoculars.

I had read LeConte's and Hutchinson's accounts, and I knew essentially what I would find up there on the mountain. Even so, I caught myself straining to read the details and uncover the hidden features of the route. The mountain looked so perplexing and difficult that it was hard to trust the hidden channel they climbed in their stories, a channel that is nothing more than a shadow behind a long cliff wall from a seat in the Humphreys Basin.

LeConte made his first attempt from this direction, the southwest side of the mountain; his second attempt was from the north and he wrote his letter to Helen from the highpoint of that second effort. Whatever he told Hutchinson about that northern line removed it from consideration; the Hutchinson party concentrated all its collective scrutiny on the mountain's broad southwestern face. Here the tremendous slashes cut through the outer surface of the mountain, leaving broad diagonal troughs with unseen bottoms. Their examination of the peak relied on guesswork and inference, judgments made by perspective and shadow. LeConte had picked the most likely cut and worked his way up it as high as it would take him; eventually a layer of ice plastered to its insides stopped him.

Scanning the entire face, Hutchinson and his companions eliminated one potential route after the next until a single pick remained—the very same line that LeConte had chosen for himself. Hutchinson hardly seemed surprised at this verdict; LeConte would have chosen the best-looking path. He probably wanted to have a go at LeConte's route anyway, for a chance to see what kind of obstacle a mountain could erect that would stop his friend. That was part of the fascination of this peak. Hutchinson would simply have to hope to be more innovative, or at least luckier, than LeConte had been six years before.

Blame the mountain's curious geology for the trouble needed to ferret out a manageable climbing line. Hutchinson described Mount Humphreys as having two bands, the lower fifteen hundred feet colored like chocolate, the upper cap of a thousand feet like terra-cotta. The chocolate layer is old stone, an ancient bed of metamorphic rock laid down long before the granite Sierra poked its head up through the earth. Not much of that old layer is left in California's high country, though in places whole mountain chains, like the Minarets and Kaweahs, are made of it. The early mountaineers mostly avoided those dark peaks (Muir's climb of Mount Ritter is one exception), with their rotten rock and jagged, foreboding spires, leaving them for a different kind of climber who would emerge in the first decades of the twentieth century with a hunger to be tested by the last unclimbed peaks in the range. Mount Humphreys is not quite of that category— pure, hard granite makes up the mountain's insides. Hutchinson's terra-cotta layer is that rose-colored heart showing through; with this mountain, the new granite wears a vintage robe of the last era's fashion.

Heirlooms left out in the rain and snow for a hundred million years tend to show their age, and Mount Humphreys' brown mantle has the worn threads to prove it. Loose stones ranging in size from sand grain to boulder have piled so deeply below the mountain that the first five hundred feet of the peak are buried in a steep cone of debris. The falling rocks funnel through the jagged channels that cut the mountain, scouring their depths. Time has sharpened Humphreys' features and it bristles with sharp edges and deep shadows.

With the sun now very low and the decision for the next day made, the four climbers settled down into their feather sleeping quilts and lit their pipes. Cheerful conversation and a small fire chased the gloom from the twilight. They recounted the day's doings. A particular episode probably supplied a great deal of fireside merriment: one of their packs had burst open as they slid it down the snow-tongue during their descent into the Humphreys Basin, and Hutchinson had been forced into a difficult bit of snow climbing and step-cutting just to retrieve their supplies. A single climber, or a well-matched pair, makes for fast, light, nimble mountaineering. But a group of four has laughter on its side and the right number of voices to ease the tension that gathers below formidable peaks.

Theirs was an oddly composed group, not necessarily suited to hazardous mountaineering, but brought together by Jim Hutchinson's enthusiasm for the mountains in general, and for this mountain in particular. He was the young-est of six children born to pioneer parents. The second-youngest son, Lincoln, was far more outdoorsy than their older brother Edward; Lincoln made several excursions into the mountains and, with Jim, created the Sierra Ski Club. But Lincoln was unavailable for this trip so Jim recruited Edward instead. The two brothers were both bachelors, though Edward was far more confirmed in his bachelorhood, being forty-two years old at the time of the Humphreys expedition and still living out of his parents' home while working as a miner. Jim was five years younger, but had studied at Berkeley, Harvard, and the newly formed Hastings School of Law in San Francisco. Three of the six siblings pursued law; perhaps they were inspired by their father who was a bank cashier and would have been privy to that walk of life. Leaving Hastings a member of the bar, James set up a thriving private practice in San Francisco.

Charles Noble and Albert Whitney, by contrast, were family men. Noble taught at Berkeley, and joined both Hutchinson and LeConte for other trips into the high country, but not for the same reasons. Neither he nor Whitney felt the same kind of gravitation toward the summits as Hutchinson or LeConte. Muir may have nicely, though perhaps ungenerously, summed up their motivation when he wrote that "thousands of tired, nerve-shaken, over-civilized people are beginning to find out that going to the mountains is going home; that wildness is necessity." Hutchinson, on the other hand, was not simply looking for a balm for the wounds of civilized living. He was looking for a test, a moment to try his muscles and nerves in a way that could not be found in the courtroom or any other location in San Francisco. To be fair, his companions had at least enough of this adventurous streak to follow his lead.

I sat through my afternoon, waiting for the next morning and my own chance to visit the mountain, shamelessly eavesdropping on their hundred-year-old conversations. They worked well together, despite their varied backgrounds. Albert found their camp and built their fire. Charles and Edward constructed a low wall to keep out the wind. Jim prepared their lunches for the day on the mountain. Each pitched in with industry so that they could relax into the day's end with their pipes and quilts.

I had little to do but make dinner and watch the mountain. With the sun still golden and not yet pink, an ultralight glider cruised up over the mountain's west shoulder, a startling sight in the stillness. The mountain and the plane seemed detached from one another, as if the two were from separate but overlaid reels of film and not actually in the same scene. The glider spiraled through an updraft until it was a mile above Mount Humphreys' summit, then pointed itself east and slid down off the Sierra crest into the Owens Valley. Expecting an "energetic" day, the Hutchinson party turned in early, and so did I.

◆ ◆ ◆

UP AT DAWN the next morning, they quickly fried a bacon breakfast and set out toward the mountain. First light recalled a line from Tennyson's *Princess* to Hutchinson's mind: "morn in the white wake of the morning star came furrowing all the orient with gold." It's a becoming image for the Sierra, where sunrise does seem to fill each ripple in the granite with a golden pool.

They hiked through the last of the rolling granite bosses separating them from Mount Humphreys and then skirted a broad lake at the mountain's foot. Each wore hobnailed boots for traction on ice and polished granite alike, and Hutchinson carried an ice axe, as LeConte had recommended, and a fifty-foot rope. Above the lake, each step up the scree fields covering the lower mountain filled their boots with gravel and yielded little net gain after the inevitable downward slide, but eventually they slogged up to the beginning of the difficult climbing. Here Hutchinson found it hard to tell which slash was the one they had chosen from camp, even though they had carefully studied the mountain's features. Up close the larger trends of the mountain's shape and weaknesses were lost behind a multitude of individual cliffs and stones rushing forward, crowding his eyes.

Hutchinson picked a chimney to the right and the others took a parallel chimney to the left. Working back toward the middle, the four climbers converged on the channel they had scoped from below, entering it at about the same elevation on opposite sides. Above them vertical walls of rock hemmed in the steep chute, which had been polished by the yearly passage of meltwater and avalanches of snow and rock. The surface was so smooth that Hutchinson worried that it might well "baffle" them, but at regular intervals open joints between layers in the stone cut horizontally across, leaving chinks for fingers and toes, and so they pulled and balanced their way past bands of glassy rock.

A bank of hard snow marked a split in their upward passage. The main channel continued up and slightly to the right, running a straight line toward Humphreys' southeast ridge. To the left, a narrow, V-shaped opening cut a diagonal line of a thousand feet to a notch just below the summit. LeConte had pursued this latter course; his ice wall hid itself somewhere along that path. Hoping for an alternate passage, Whitney climbed straight up the wider channel, but when he reached the southeast ridge he found it sheer on both sides and blocked along the ridgeline by towers and pinnacles. Descending back to the snow bank, he rejoined the others and they entered the confined leftward alleyway.

They had just crossed from the chocolate layer to the terra-cotta, from the old metamorphic rock to the new granite, when the icy rampart that had turned LeConte around blocked their own passage. The underlying rock was smooth and "steep as a cathedral roof" with a quarter-inch layer of ice frozen to it. Their axe was useless, the ice being too thin to hold chopped steps. It was plenty slick, though, and sent Hutchinson sliding and tumbling down to the ramp below the ice wall when he attempted to climb the cliff directly.

Hutchinson inspected the sidewalls, searching for a solution. On the right side, a small chute gained him fifteen feet, and above this he found a thin, offset fissure running diagonally up and over the ice wall. Digging the nails of his shoes into the offset, he curled his fingers into the crack and leaned back against his hands. The opposition of forces between his feet pushing against the rock and his hands pulling away from it held his body in check and he shuffled his boots up one at a time while sliding his hands up the crack. Modern climbers have a term for this technique—liebacking—and time is spent teaching and practicing it, but Hutchinson discovered it for himself on the spot in order to solve the riddle Mount Humphreys had posed him.

Imitating him, the other three leaned and pressed and climbed the crack, joining him above the ice wall. They had reached unfamiliar ground; they would no longer be following LeConte's shadow or his advice. The right-hand wall of their channel swept up a thousand feet above their heads to form the great wall of Mount Humphreys' southwest face. To the left, a knife-edge ridge detached from the main wall blocked their view out toward the Humphreys Basin. Their passage lay down in the vertex between the two cliffs and ran up toward the summit parallel to the Humphreys wall. From their camp in the basin they had not been able to see this section of their route—they could see only the shadows cast by the ridge, hinting at the gap behind it. Now for the first time, their course to the summit was laid before them.

Immense blocks of granite ejected from the cliff above had fallen down into the channel and become lodged in the angle between the two sides. Each year's runoff rounded these rocks, giving them the feel of monstrous river cobbles.

Some were practically welded to the mountainside; others appeared to be so lightly perched that the climbers dared not touch them. Each had to be circumvented, either by delicate use of holds weather-etched into either cliffside or by worming and wriggling up through the awkward clefts left between the wedged stones and the outer walls. Under one of these boulders they "found suspended many long icicles the size of broomsticks or larger." They rested there for a moment, breaking off icicle tips to placate their dry throats.

Above each boulder they found another, but each solution they devised brought the top closer, and before long the channel widened out into a broad, rocky bowl headed by the notch below the summit. Hutchinson pressed up toward this notch, reaching it before his companions. "Suddenly," he wrote, "and almost unawares, I came upon the knife-edge of the Sierra crest and looked over into a yawning abyss, down two-thousand feet, to a wide spreading snow-field held in a granite-walled amphitheatre." A chute to mirror the one he had climbed ran up the north side of the mountain, and now he was perched on the thin divide between the two with thousands of feet of free air circulating on both sides. Though a cliff blocked the summit from view, Hutchinson knew that the highpoint was just a few hundred feet above. This cliff would be the last barrier, but there was no way to bypass it—it had to be climbed head-on, and it was the steepest place they had yet encountered. His blood must have been up, for he did not pause even long enough for his companions to catch him, but yelled down, "I think we can make it," and cast off toward the summit.

◆ ◆ ◆

FOLLOWING LECONTE'S ADVICE and Hutchinson's lead, I too brought an ice axe and found it just as useless against the ice wall. The layer frozen to the rock was such a thin skin that it offered nothing for the axe to bite into, while still robbing the stone of any usable friction. But my year was a dry one and the breadth of the ice narrower, so I had less trouble finding bare rock to the side for my escape.

The sky was clear but the Humphreys Basin had not yet emerged from the morning shadow of the mountain. The lake under Mount Humphreys' western toe hid itself beneath the color of dull metal, waiting for sunlight to bring it back to life and make it sparkle. The whole basin still seemed unconscious, drowsing through the gray predawn while the sun finished its work in the east. I turned away from it and entered the hanging alley.

Just as the Hutchinson party had discovered, each boulder wedged in the bottom of this passage required its own peculiar gymnastics, particularly the unstable ones. Several of these were large and I had to climb directly through their fall-lines and up and over their protruding curves without touching them. Halfway up the passage I came in sight of a massive rock capping a recessed area filled with black shadows and glittering ice. Closer, the shadows separated and the ice hung down in long strands, some stretching six feet in length, as if the upper jaw of the leviathan had been wedged below the boulder. Here the members of the Hutchinson party sat for a moment, crunching on icicle tips and marveling at the thin joint between mountain and boulder where the ice sprouted directly from the stone. Given the heat of my summer and the lack of snow and the passage of time, I had not expected to find Hutchinson's icicle cave so distinctly unchanged.

The Hutchinson party paid their visit to Mount Humphreys just six months after the Wright brothers made their first flights at Kitty Hawk. That summer,

209

the territory above the mountaintops was still empty and unattainable despite the exciting news. They could hardly have conceived that jetliners would soon crisscross these mountains on regular runs to San Francisco and San Jose, that military planes would rumble along the Sierra crest on practice flights from the Edwards Air Force Base, that a pilot in a glider would go up for an afternoon spin around the summit of Mount Humphreys. As recently as 1894, the elder Joseph LeConte had written an article for the *Popular Science Monthly* on the impossibility of a flying machine.

In the hundred years that have passed since the Hutchinson climb, we have filled our skies with airplanes and our clear nights with mechanical satellites, which are now more conspicuous over the Sierra than falling stars; in just one century we have altered the heavens themselves. And yet here on Mount Humphreys, in wet years and dry, the same icicles sprout beneath the same boulder summer after summer. It's as if these mountains are held apart from the yearly upheavals that we have come to expect as a regular feature of the present. With the exception of a few stray rockfalls, if Hutchinson returned to his mountain today, he would find things pretty much as he left them in 1904.

The night before their climb had been cold, and Hutchinson woke often to warm himself. Once, he rose to stir the fire as the setting moon cast a "ghostly light over the snow-fields, which appeared like great white sheets laid over the bones of the mountains. The lakes were a mass of molten silver and the glacial polish was burnished brass." Hutchinson was a religious man in a functional sort of way. God is present as a background fixture to his impressions of the Sierra. Later, contemplating his mental image of that nighttime view, he turned to the Psalms to express his wonder. "As I looked over this weird scene," he wrote, "from the setting moon to the million brilliant stars, and then across the glaciated basin to the snowy peaks, and finally to the great black wall of Humphreys, I felt as never before the force of the words, 'The heavens declare the glory of God and the firmament showeth his handiwork.'"

Up among the peaks is a land that has changed less over the last century than the night sky itself. No wonder so many find God on the heights. If you are moved to believe in the hand of a maker, the mountains are one of the last places on earth where you can go to see his work as if he had only just now finished, his designs unaltered. In this case the secular experience is not so different from the religious. Whether you feel, as Muir did, that God planned these mountains stone by stone as an act of cosmic poetry, or whether you believe simply in the strong fingers of unconscious nature, equal comfort can be taken from being near to something so ancient, solid, and magnificent in the midst of our leaps toward an ephemeral future.

A quarter of an hour and five hundred more feet of pleasant rock-work carried me from the icicle cave to the notch below the summit. There I found pole-monium, also known as sky pilot, a flower rarely seen much below thirteen thousand feet. Out of a bed of thick, short-leafed stems, polemonium lifts up a merry pompom of tiny purple florets. There's no soil at this altitude; the plants seem to grow straight out of cracks in the stone or in little deposits of alpine gravel, cheerfully greeting wind and lightning and light-footed mountaineers alike. Polemonium has been a favorite of climbers since Muir's time, the companion to the high summits, infusing the dry upper airs with its thick, spicy scent.

As summer ripens, the florets turn pale and begin to come off their stems in tatters, a mournful-looking surrender to the end of the season. The window is short—when I arrived at the notch, the local polemonium had already dropped half their blossoms. Here, too, the mountain performs its magic. Winter subjects the summit of Mount Humphreys to snow and cold and months of darkness. The snows withdraw to reveal stark outlines and bare rock. And then—*poof*—these delicate flowers appear, with a tight grip on their small clefts and ledges, happily soaking in those few precious weeks of the height of summer. Every year: the summit, the snows, the rock, the icicles, the polemonium.

◆ ◆ ◆

ABOVE ME, AND above the flowers, Hutchinson found trouble. The final cliff between him and the summit would not let him pass easily. Steep enough to feel vertical, it shot up from the knife-edge separating the mountain's eastern and western sides, becoming a smooth wall of clean, compact granite. Hutchinson gained thirty feet by following a line of narrow hand and foot edges sculpted into the stone. But even these holds petered out, leaving him pressed against the rock with nothing above but the unbroken upward sweep of the mountain. He searched the wall to the left and right in the hopes of finding a traverse around the impasse. Then, in "an unguarded moment" he looked down, to see if he could retrace his steps.

From his elevated vantage, that glance down revealed not a line of retreat, but instead the entire reach of the precipitous drop on both sides of the mountain. All of that empty air piled up against the divide filled his eyes. The view seized him. "A cold chill crept down my back," he wrote. "My knees began to shake." A moment of doubt and the view below woke a part of his brain which had been, until then, tranquilized by his confident progress.

Hutchinson owned a strong will and was not one to allow his emotions free rein; nevertheless his response to the sudden quailing of his courage is awfully stoic. "The alarm was momentary," he wrote. "I saw the uselessness of fear." If only it were that easy! I don't believe it was, but his time in the mountains, and in the courtroom, may have taught him how to cool his nerves and shut away clamorous instincts. Instead of trying to fight the jangling in his head, he simply worked to box it up. He turned away from the gulf below and put his "face to the wall, determined not again to look downward."

Revived from his moment of panic, he reexamined the stone with a new power of clarity. The same thing happened to Muir on Mount Ritter and to many climbers since who have suddenly found themselves staring at the rock through eyes like magnifying glasses after a bout of the terrors. Hutchinson looked to his left and discovered an edge that would support one side of his boot. He leaned over and stood up on the edge, and suddenly his hands were in range of a new set of fingerholds, which led to a crack set behind a detached pinnacle, and then a series of grooves which he climbed by pressing and bracing between the parallel walls, with occasional fissures for his fingers between hard scales of rock, and then at last the summit ridge and his first near view of Mount Humphreys' highpoint. There are holds everywhere in the mountains—few pieces of stone are truly blank. Climbing is largely a matter of perception and faith that fingers and feet will keep one from being dragged off by gravity. Climbers are limited far more by their ability to see solutions inscribed in the stone than by the gross statistics of their muscles and the lengths of their bones.

By the time Hutchison arrived at the summit ridge the others had gathered in the notch and were waiting for word from above. He climbed back down the easier upper section and stopped at a stance above the difficult part. One of the three tossed Hutchinson the rope, which he looped around a projecting point of rock near his stance. His brother came up first, pulling against both the rock and the rope as he "hauled" himself up. When he reached his brother's stance, they lowered the rope back down again, but Noble and Whitney had had enough. First the tenuous ice crawl, then the difficult moves around overhanging boulders, and now this vertical wall of rock where Hutchinson had struggled while they looked on—the mountain was asking more from them than they were prepared to give.

Married Men's Point casts its shadow (and the author's) on the final steep cliff leading to Mount Humphreys' summit ridge

They christened a minor pinnacle adjacent to the notch "married men's point" and, with great good humor, declared themselves "moral heroes" for refusing the temptation of climbing higher.

When I parted from the polemonium the sun had intensified, but still sat low in the east. It lit the rose-colored stone with slanted, early morning light, and swirls of clear mica embedded in the rock glittered like gold dust. The whole sheet of rock might as well have been fashioned from steel; no fracture lines or loose scabs marred its surface; the holds were shaped directly into the flowing granite. Those holds, at least at the beginning, were as welcoming as ladder rungs, each one an invitation to climb higher and disregard the angle and the drop. They shrank only incrementally, losing a few tenths of an inch with each upward move, hardly noticeable in sequence, but as I neared the spot where Hutchinson had been temporarily thrown from his stride, I became aware of being perched far less securely than I had been at the start. The granite had receded out from under my hands and boots. But the stone still held its beauty and was warmed and burnished by the sun, and though I had less of it to touch, it felt so good and solid under my fingers that I hardly even paused at the blank section, crossing over it with a long reach. Some days the air seems full of oxygen and invincibility and the rock itself practically boosts you up. Other days feel cold and squint-eyed and the rock bristles against the touch. Both feelings are illusory. The rock is the same on Monday and Sunday and every day in between, and gravity pulls equally on the lighthearted and dour. The difference is only internal, but I have never been sure which set of emotions actually puts a climber in more danger of parting ways with the mountain.

The holds remained crisp and friendly—some hardly wanted to let my fingers go—all the way to the summit ridge. From there I followed Jim and Edward along easy ground across the roofline of Mount Humphreys. To the left and right the rock dropped steeply away and then disappeared from sight beyond overhangs shaped like eaves, while a course straight ahead required little more than walking across a narrow island in the sky. The true summit, a few hundred feet distant, was a last remnant plug of metamorphic rock, looking odd and clumsy amid all the granite of the upper part of the mountain. In fact, Jim worried that "the whole top should break off and fall into the great abyss to the eastward," but nevertheless the brothers hoisted themselves up onto this final mass of dark blocks and "no longer looked on things above, but rather on things beneath."

They sat on top for an hour or so, and I shared their seat for half that time. Jim studied the mountains on the northern and southern horizons, and the lakes and plateaus closer by. His descriptions show more than a casual knowledge of the Sierra's geologic history. He also describes the Owens Valley: the square farms laid out "like a checkerboard" and "miles and miles" of green alfalfa fields. He did not know it at the time, but he was looking beyond the protective sphere of the mountain's timelessness. Not much remains of those farms but sagebrush desert and a few herds of cows. Less than a decade after the Hutchinson brothers stood atop Mount Humphreys, the county of Los Angeles began to siphon away the water in the Owens Valley through a series of pipes and crooked deals.

They found no evidence that anyone had preceded them to the summit. "Probably," Hutchinson wrote, "no one had ever stood where we then were, unless perhaps during the early Jurassic period, before the mountain was fully sculptured. Then the mariners of that age (if there were any) might have sailed upon the waters of the Pacific close to the base of the mountain, and, there landing, have climbed up its gently sloping sides." In fact, his Jurassic mariners would have been able to sail right over the top of what would one day be Mount Humphreys. The Sierra is only timeless when measured against the history of human civilization.

At the end of their hour, the brothers began a cautious reversal of their route up. They met Whitney and Noble at the notch, and the four of them together worked back down the alley to the ice wall. Disaster nearly found them here, when, despite their vigilance, Jim and Edward knocked loose an avalanche of debris. Noble and Whitney were several hundred feet below and directly in the fall-line with little room to maneuver. What began as a few rocks rolling down beneath the brothers' feet quickly spread and filled the whole passage with tumbling stones. The brothers yelled warnings while the crashing rocks pushed echoes down the alley; Noble and Whitney barely had time to dash into a small niche set in the cliffside before the "torrent" went "shooting by them." From then on the party stayed closer together so that any dislodged rocks would build less speed before rolling by. When at last they reached the Humphreys Basin, the four climbers emerged with a strong collective sense of relief.

Though they were all tired, none wished to spend another night at their exposed camp. That pre-climb desire to be pressed up close to the mountain had evaporated into the rarified air about the summit. So they quickly packed their sacks and descended to a secluded spot in the densest grove of trees they could find. They spent a cheerful, celebratory afternoon hurling themselves into a lively creek and narrating the events of the day while lounging among the pines. A plunge into the water "had the magical effect of making us whole again," Hutchinson wrote. "How comfortable and cozy seemed our combined kitchen, social hall, and bedroom!"

The next morning they recrossed the divide between the Humphreys Basin and Evolution Creek via the same narrow slot between the walls of rock and snow. Despite worrisome bear tracks encountered along the way, they found their donkeys unharmed where they had been left to spend three quiet days eating grass. One day later they caught back up with Little Joe, who was delighted to see them and hear the news of their climb. LeConte surely would have loved to stand atop the summit with Hutchinson, but he felt no rivalry toward his friend. "Here we found the Hutchinson Party camped near us," he wrote in his journal. "How glad I was to see them. Jim Hutchinson and his brother Ed had succeeded in climbing to the summit of Mount Humphreys. All honor to the first climbers of the most difficult peak in the High Sierra." LeConte's assessment was right enough. Mount Humphreys joined the Grand Teton and Mount Clarence King as the most difficult mountains yet climbed in America.

Back on the summit, with the land spread out beneath me, I could see all of these places and more: my camp, likely locations for the Hutchinson camps, the Snow-Tongue Pass, Desolation Lake, Mount Goddard. If I squinted I could see four pale figures striding across the granite to and from the mountain. Emerson wrote that "the health of the eye seems to demand a horizon. We are never tired, so long as we can see far enough." There is no finer place to know the truth of his sentiment than the summit of Mount Humphreys, where one can see a hundred unencumbered miles in any direction, and even further into the past. Here, adventures from another age are still plainly visible on the stone.

◆ ◆ ◆

EMERSON HIMSELF HAD a close brush with Mount Humphreys. He toured the west in 1871, at a time when his creative work was finished and Muir's was just beginning. The two men met at the sawmill below Yosemite Falls—this was the year after the elder Joseph LeConte happened upon Muir at the same location. Though Muir had not yet published any of his books, Emerson knew of him, and was eager for a meeting. Emerson returned to the sawmill every day of his time in the Valley to talk with Muir, and later they traveled together to the Mariposa Grove of giant sequoias. Two years later, while studying the headwaters of the San Joaquin River, Muir named a "grand, *wide-winged* mountain" after Emerson. "Its head is high above its fellows and wings are white with ice and snow," he wrote. This was, in fact, Mount Humphreys, and Muir found out only later that the Whitney Survey had beaten him to it. The mountain retained the name of Andrew Humphreys, a soldier and engineer who distinguished himself during the Civil War, while Emerson's name was moved to a smaller mountain immediately to the south.

·9·

Ernest Clayton Andrews + Mount Darwin

[AUGUST 1908]

Mount Darwin (13,831 feet), north face

THE DEPREDATIONS AT the mines in the western foothills of the Sierra esca-
lated even after William Brewer left the state in 1864. Hydraulic mining
had taken hold. Men fired water cannons at hill slopes to transform them to
mud to be channeled through their flumes and sluice boxes. Enormous fires were
built so that the work could go on day and night. Entire hills melted away from
the force of the water, all for a yield of a few ounces of gold. The debris had to
go somewhere, and it did—into the rivers and down the valleys. Clear waters
turned brown were the least of the worries. The mines flushed down so much
sediment that river levels rose and entire towns and farms were flooded with
mud and gravel.

The downstream farmers fought back. They sued, and they won, after years
of agitation and litigation. In 1884 a judge in San Francisco placed a permanent
injunction against hydraulic mining. But the gold fever in the foothills didn't
pass, it only went dormant. Twenty years later, the miners and their stakehold-
ers were ready to try again. Gold had increased in value and wheat had fallen.
Sensing favorable timing, a consortium of mining interests asked for a review
of the evidence against hydraulic mining by the U.S. Geological Survey. The
survey assigned one of its most distinguished scientists to the problem, Grove
Karl Gilbert.

He went to work surveying mining sites, measuring stream flows and sediment loads. He calculated that over a billion and a quarter cubic yards of rock
and dirt had been washed out of the Sierra foothills—nearly eight times the
amount removed for the entire Panama Canal. He described a "debris wave"
running down the Sacramento River system toward the San Francisco Bay, and
estimated that it would take eighty years for the wave crest to run its course.
If the miners had hoped to find an ally in G. K. Gilbert they must have been

disappointed, just as they had been with Whitney and Brewer before him. But Gilbert went further. He pointed out that soil erosion from heavy agriculture had a comparable effect downstream of the farm belt in California's Central Valley. Moreover, the conversion of riverside wetlands into arable fields by farmers had eliminated a natural sink for flood debris, passing mud and floods on down the Sacramento. The end result? Gilbert predicted that the tidal bar outside the Golden Gate would grow and move inland, bottling up access to the Bay. Ship captains knew the truth of this; dredges were already working shallows that, a few decades earlier, had been deep enough for passage.

Modern environmental scientists would appreciate Gilbert's *Hydraulic-Mining in the Sierra Nevada*. He understood that the foothill streams, trunk rivers, delta, and bay were all interconnected pieces of a complex system. Put pressure on one part (say, by dumping in a billion yards of extra dirt), and other parts of the system would necessarily react to the disequilibrium. Gilbert had an environmental conscience, but he was not primarily an ecologist. His work on hydraulic mining gave him the chance to study the geological problems that fascinated him. He searched for principles that behaved like laws of physics but which governed subjects like stream flow, erosion patterns, sediment deposition, and bank and gravel bed formation. One colleague compared him to Darwin and Lyell for his ability to "see the main principle emerging from the merge of details."

In the summers Gilbert took time away from his official duties to travel the High Sierra. Though he had never been to San Francisco or Berkeley before 1899, and though he did not see Yosemite until 1903, he quickly fell in with members of the Sierra Club and the University of California at Berkeley. The reason that Joseph LeConte was unavailable for Jim Hutchinson's climb of Mount

Humphreys in 1904 was that he was occupied touring Gilbert around the Sierra that season. Gilbert was then sixty-one, but still physically powerful, his trail muscles hardened by years as an expeditionary geologist. He was just over six-feet-one-inches tall, so he and Little Joe must have made quite a pair walking the Sierra together.

These summer excursions into the mountains were pleasure trips, though for Gilbert pleasure was to be found where interesting earth puzzles could be tried and solved. As he put it, he "studied a great deal when not working," a habit he applied equally to books and mountains. He had a reputation as a recluse, but he delighted in the company of likeminded thinkers and observers. For his 1907 summer Sierra trek he wrote a summons to a group of close friends: "You are cordially invited to join my house party in August; my cellar is the Yosemite Valley, my drawing room the Tuolumne meadows, my attic Mono Pass, and my stairway the Tioga road." By then his red-brown hair and beard had trended silver; during the trip his companions took to calling him Charlemagne.

Gilbert was choosey about his scientific companions, but ready to welcome newcomers if they possessed the right spirit. Around the time of his first intro-duction to Yosemite, he came across a paper describing the glacial fiords carved into the south island of New Zealand written by a young Australian geologist, E. C. (Ernest Clayton) Andrews. The paper contained worthy insights into gla-cial corrasion, and Andrews had succeeded in using photographs as eye-catching scientific tools—something Gilbert had attempted with less luck on a recent trip to Alaska. But what really caught Gilbert's attention was a side trip Andrews took into the psychology of science. In the paper Andrews noted that he had trained his eyes and geologic imagination in the valleys of New South Wales— valleys that had not been touched by glaciers. So he credited his ability to see the inscription of glaciers in New Zealand to contrast. He had never seen anything like the shapes of those fiords, so they stood out to his eye. This struck Gilbert as an instructive moment in the practice of science. Their work was based on observation and perception, their primary tools were their eyes and thoughts, and so an understanding of one's own mental landscape was just as important as knowledge of the mountains themselves. "I think it quite possible," he wrote to Andrews, "that geologists that frame such curious arguments against the actuality of ice sculpture have never seen anything else, and are therefore not sensitive to the contrasts between the two types of sculpture."

Gilbert was fond of an anecdote from his early life as a geologist. He was in Utah, on a high plateau, riding through a narrow band of prairie bound by forests of pine and fir. He had two companions, an army topographer and an assistant, and the trio were exploring and mapping unknown country. Quite suddenly, the prairie floor ended, a long cliff fell away at their feet, and below them stretched an expanse of sandstone desert filled with "cañons, buttes, and cliffs, all so bare that the brilliant colors of their rocks shone forth,—orange, red, chocolate, blue, and white." Gilbert and the topographer were spellbound by the view, struck wordless by the shapes, colors, and desolation. The other man looked around for a moment, then harrumphed and said, "Well, we're nicely caught!" All he could make out was an obstacle to their forward progress. Gilbert told this story as a parable of the limits of perception. "We saw what we had eyes to see," he wrote. "Our point of view was the measure of our perception and appreciation."

Gilbert sent Andrews a copy of his own work on Alaskan glacial fiords. The men struck up a trans-Pacific correspondence, and when Gilbert learned that Andrews planned to travel to England via America, he suggested that the

Australian join him for a few months of geologizing in the Sierra. Andrews later wrote that he considered Gilbert the finest American geologist, so the invitation must have pleased him. As if he needed further convincing, Gilbert hinted that the expedition could include the ascent of one of the High Sierra's unclimbed giants.

Appropriately, Gilbert chose the Evolution Group between the Palisades and Mount Humphreys as their destination. Mounts Mendel, Huxley, Spencer, and Wallace kept the geologists company as they investigated cirques and hanging valleys or tracked ancient glaciers. Theodore Solomons had distributed these names in 1895 when he first explored the region, memorializing the original evolutionists with Sierra granite. One mountain in the center lifted its head above its neighbors, and Solomons reserved Charles Darwin's name for it. Mount Darwin, tall and broad shouldered, decorated with spires and grizzled with ice and snow, played mountain king to Gilbert's Charlemagne. This was the mountain Gilbert had in mind when he offered Andrews an adventurous climb and a lonesome summit.

They made a lively party, joined by another Gilbert protégé, Willard Johnson. Gilbert's mind never rested. From the graceful curves and peculiar joint planes of the granite domes to the paraboloid web of a particular spider living in a sequoia grove, there were always causes to search for and architecture to understand. He taught Andrews the names of the alpine flora, and took the Australian creeping through the shrubbery to see the water ouzel, cougar, and woodpecker. When a disturbance in the mule train caused a halt he demanded logic puzzles from the others to pass the time. Andrews wrote that his own "stock of questions on maxima and minima, on astronomy, on motion round curves, on inertia, on flywheels, on nodes of curves, on physics, were soon used up, as Gilbert could see through a problem very quickly." When the mules were in motion, Gilbert would reel off lines of poetry and stop mid-phrase, expecting his companions to spontaneously compose completing verses. At night he told stories of Clarence King and John Muir, and when the dinner fire was extinguished and the men stretched out in their sleeping bags he named the stars and constellations.

◆ ◆ ◆

I STEPPED DOWN off the Lamarck Col over talus. Mount Mendel's sharp ridges arced above me; behind and above them the square head of Mount Darwin pushed up out of its northern glacier. Below me a string of slender lakes filled the bottom of a crease between Mount Mendel and Mount Lamarck. Each lake occupied a long step in the canyon floor, with a waterfall or tumbling creeklet spilling its waters onto the next step down.

These terraces of lake and stone are exquisite enough to make an artist hang up his tools in despair. Muir could have pointed to them as a prime example of a place where God pushed a glacier into motion with the desire to give beauty to his beloved creatures. But the new geologists were looking for mechanical principles, not aesthetic ones. In a paper he delivered two years after his visit to the Sierra, Andrews wrote a detailed work order for the construction of this species of "step" and "tread" canyon; he described lines of force and pressure, reassembled ancient glaciers through vector diagrams, and sent them into motion with formulas of mass, gravity, and friction. As a young man on the farm, Muir designed and built functioning clocks made entirely of wood—he had insight aplenty when it came to mechanical systems. In all likelihood Muir and Andrews would not have disagreed over much with each other. Each might only have felt that his counterpart had missed the primary point while dwelling on details of less consequence.

I found a boulder set into the southern canyon wall with a hollow space beneath it that I could use for nighttime shelter. I left my pack there and walked back to the nearest lake, watching the wind scoop its thousand hands through the water. Muir liked to call a Sierra lake an eye, and there is more symmetry than fantasy to this image. Most lakes here have bare, sandy bottoms and elevated rims of densely piled stones; the result is a bony, hemispherical socket filled by a clear blue iris. These eyes you *can* dive into—but after taking the plunge and hauling yourself back out onto the rim to dry off in the sun, you might begin to think: *what a strangely perfect shape for a lake to take.*

This, at least, was Gilbert's thought. The entire Sierra Nevada is covered with loose stones—and this makes sense, because when the glaciers melted at the end of the ice age, they scattered the rocks they had been carrying on their backs evenly around the mountains. So why, Gilbert wondered, should the bottoms of lakes be free of stones, while the rims of lakes are so tightly packed with them that they seem to form carefully stacked walls?

He laid out the answer in an article titled "Lake Ramparts." All of the lakes in the Sierra freeze to a depth of several feet in the winter. Water expands as it becomes ice, but ice, like other solids, shrinks when it becomes colder. So, if a lake surface is frozen, and the temperature drops, the ice contracts and cracks. (Here, Gilbert pointed out that as a boy growing up in the Northeast, he and his friends used to thrill themselves by leaping lake-cracks on their ice skates.) Water from below fills these cracks and, coming into contact with the frigid surface air, freezes, turning into what Gilbert called "wedges" of ice. When the temperature rises again, the ice expands, but with the new wedges in place it cannot return to its original dimensions. Instead, the outer margins of the ice sheet are pushed out against the lakeshore. Normal fluctuations in temperature continue the cycle, so the ice sheet continually expands, shoving outward toward its rim.

When the ice reaches deep enough it grabs hold of any loose rocks below. As the ice expands, it drags the stones along with it. Year by year the ice hauls the rocks to the edges of the lake, industriously stacking them there at the margins, until the lake is cleared, the ramparts are made, Muir's lake-eyes look out from their orbits with sparkling radiance, and lake-lovers dive into clear, deep water without worrying about opening their noggins on unfriendly stones.

Gilbert pointed out the marvel of this kind of science. "To pursue such a line of study," he wrote, "no preliminary training is necessary—nothing but attention." The principles involved—lake surfaces freezing, the expansion and contraction of ice—are understood by boys on skates. Beyond those basic facts, one needs only a questioning outlook and imagination.

Of course, even though geology was then a young discipline, a great deal of study was necessary in order to accomplish anything original. Along with the natural sciences, the professional geologist used physics, calculus, and chemistry to help him interpret the anatomy of the Earth. "For him," Gilbert wrote, "attention is not the only requisite; he must have systematic methods of work, and he must acquaint himself with the work of others in his chosen field." Even so, the practice of the groundbreaking geology of the era was not strikingly different from the work Gilbert used for his short study of lake ramparts. Gilbert spent his years in the field staring at the land and thinking about the invisible forces that shaped it. The instruments he used most frequently were the same simple topographic tools carried by Brewer and King, along with a pendulum to take gravity measurements. He had one of his most important epiphanies on fault structure while looking out the window of a transcontinental train.

The recognition of the Wasatch Fault from behind his railcar window indicates the power of Gilbert's insight into the dynamic forces muscling against the land. Though it took him weeks of fieldwork to prove his argument, he knew what he was looking at the moment he saw it: one block of the Earth's crust thrust up above another by tremendous pressures from below. Gilbert downplayed his own discoveries, feeling that they were right there "for the seeing." But when he brought other scientists to the Wasatch they did not recognize the process taking place before them—even when Gilbert explained it to them—and years passed before his description had general acceptance among his colleagues.

Which brings us back to Gilbert's most basic insight: we see what we have eyes to see. He meant, in part, that some see more than others, but also that we each wear a personal filter between our eyes and the land. Gilbert, Andrews, and Johnson rambled around the Evolution Group, seeing invisible forces pushing ice, carving rock, cleaving mountains; meanwhile Gilbert showed his companions tiny alpine flora, Muir's tracks, and the bathhouse of the water ouzel. I looked at the same peaks and Mount Mendel's narrow ridges swung up into the sky and filled my mind with images of granite tightropes; the mountain played me like a marionette, tugging at the strings that run through my eyes down to my fingers.

After Gilbert's death in 1918, four years after Muir, Andrews tried comparing the men. He wrote that Muir's "reflective faculty was not so evident as in the case of Gilbert" and that Muir's "imagination was more poetical, less disciplined," though he conceded that "each found truth in his own way." Gilbert himself would have been disinclined to make any such comparisons in the first place (though he did once complain about Muir as a houseguest because Muir was needy and refused to learn the street system). I think that Gilbert might have realized that, though he and Muir studied the same phenomena and searched the same mountains, they were looking for two different kinds of answers.

The sky dimmed and I settled into my alcove beneath the boulder. A picture of the three geologists stretched out in their sleeping bags came easily to me. I could imagine the way they would talk about the mountains, how they would conjure up the stones in the dark and turn them over with their words; I've spent plenty of nights in the Sierra doing the same. Geology and climbing seem born of the same basic impulse. We see puzzles built into mountains and we're compelled to get our hands on the rock and solve them. But I doubt that the problem-solving motive touches the ground floor of our desires. Probably it's the other way around: the attraction to the mountains the root impulse, the climbing and geologizing the conscious justification.

Night took hold and turned the mountains to cutouts against the stars, but not for long. The full moon rose over the Sierra crest and poured itself across the pale granite, rekindling the peaks and flooding the canyon with white light, like a second day, as if the Earth belonged to two suns.

◆ ◆ ◆

THE THREE COMPANIONS circumnavigated Mount Darwin, reading the histories scrawled across its stones by the passage of the ice—and searching for a climbing route. Three sides of the mountain looked unmanageable. The fourth, rising up above Evolution Lake, offered a broad face full of wrinkles, chutes, and gullies, but at least it tilted at an angle that didn't make them fear for their lives.

Gilbert left the climbing to the younger men. He would root for them from camp and look forward to hearing about their adventures when they returned.

Johnson and Andrews rose early on a chill morning. Frost covered the entire lake basin. They crunched through frozen meadows, the individual flowers cased in sparkling glass from bloom to stalk. These crystal fields captivated Andrews. He called the flowers "living glories" and imagined them as wicks for candles made of ice.

Ice on the mountain treated Andrews less kindly. Johnson led them up a chute to a narrow chimney hung with so many icicles that they "coated the sides of the cleft." Andrews attempted it, but slipped back each time he tried to press his way up between the glazed walls. While he struggled among the icicles,

Mounts Darwin and Mendel in the distance across lake-ice below Muriel Peak

Johnson traversed to the left and found another chimney with less ice in its belly. They climbed up through its insides until it widened out into a broad gulley bound by ridges like granite jawbones stuffed with jagged, snaggled teeth.

The bottom of the gulley gave them free passage until it dead-ended into steep cliffs. They traversed into another channel and scrambled up to the slender ridge forming the fine-boned left shoulder of the mountain. Johnson continued in the lead, climbing just below the ridge crest, traversing along ledges and dodging back and forth around monstrous boulders. Above them, Andrews wrote, teetered "huge blocks, thousands of tons in weight," which appeared "to lie loosely against each other almost without support."

Up ahead Andrews noticed that Johnson had dropped thirty or forty feet farther down below the ridge before continuing their traverse. As Andrews reached the edge of a large block, Johnson shouted back to him, "Window." Andrews was puzzled by this. "I had no knowledge of the word 'window' in climbing," he wrote. But Johnson had already carried on, so Andrews "sprang" after him. "To my astonishment," Andrews continued, "I nearly fell through a great aperture leading to the other side of the sharp arête. Johnson had given the warning, but I had not understood, and I was almost precipitated down the fearful face of the Darwin Glacier."

He recovered and followed Johnson's line below the loophole in the mountainside, and they pressed on to where the ridge merged into the broad summit plateau atop Mount Darwin. For hours they had clambered through a narrow world of clefts, gullies, and ridges, and now at the top of the mountain, surrounded by sky, they stood in the middle of a flat granite plain. It was level enough to play football on if it hadn't been covered with an even layer of irregular boulders pushing jagged edges in all directions.

Johnson prepared to take observations from the highest edge of the summit field, but Andrews was not yet satisfied. He noticed a skinny pillar, detached from the edge of the plateau, which lifted its top above them. That was the true summit, but a deep gap separated them from it. The spire hung out over the dizzying east face, an improbable granite column planted right on the edge. Johnson had no interest. He had not climbed three thousand feet of stone to risk his life for three more yards. "He explained to me," wrote Andrews, "that we could consider we had ascended the mountain, the last six or eight feet being unscalable." But that idea did not sit well with Andrews. The top of the mountain was there—and he clearly was not on it—and the highest stone called to him with its finality, demanding his attention.

Andrews was not normally a daredevil, but on this morning in the summer of 1908, he was fully gripped by the spirit and could not resist the mountain. He begged Johnson to allow him to attempt the final spire. Johnson forbade it. "But," Andrews wrote, "I was full of disobedience that day, and having seen him pass away to the other side of the plateau to make observations and secure possible photographs, I dropped down the crevasse." Reaching the spire would not be easy. He climbed down off the plateau into the gap between the body of the mountain and the summit. To his right and left, steep defiles fell away. He traversed out a narrow ledge above the leftward drop. Sheer, blank stone cut by jagged cracks made Andrews shy away from the side of the summit spire facing in toward the mountain. He traversed all the way around to its far side, using a fat icicle as a handhold at a blank spot, hoping for better holds and a less vertical cant. The long drop gnawed on his imagination and boot soles as he edged out onto the eastern front of the mountain.

On the outside of the spire the mountain poured away down into empty air. Andrews had pinned himself to massive exposure, holding the final spar of the peak like a spider clutching the prow of an ocean liner. But at least the rock now gave him something to hold. Horizontal cracks split the granite into blocks and shelves and Andrews fit his hands and boots into the spaces between. He climbed the ladder of cracks until nothing but sky capped him and the final rock, and he flopped his arms over the summit, hugging it to him.

Standing on the square top of the tower, without room to take more than one step in any direction, his summit fever cooled fast, and he found himself scared. "It dawned on me," he wrote, "that the descent was more perilous than the ascent, especially as I had the terrible abyss below in full view the whole time." Looking down between his legs for his footholds, he could not help but stare down the entire length of Mount Darwin's eastern face. "My knees shook," he admitted, "and I cowered, for some minutes, on a remarkably narrow ledge, a few feet from the edge."

Johnson returned from the other side of the plateau. He could not see Andrews, who was stuck on the outside of the summit spire struggling with his sudden terror. Johnson called out to him, fearing that he had fallen off the edge of the mountain. He continued to call, and Andrews found that his partner's concern cut through his own panic, at least enough to put him in motion again. He climbed down off the tower, feeling sure that he could not handle the exposure of the summit a second time, and undid his traverse to the plateau where he "received," he wrote, "a severe scolding from Johnson."

◆ ◆ ◆

Summit tower, Mount Darwin

JOHN WESLEY POWELL, the famous one-armed major who took a wooden rowboat down the Colorado River and through the Grand Canyon in 1869—when the river was almost entirely unexplored—and who replaced Clarence King as director of the U.S. Geological Survey in 1881, was a close friend and colleague of Gilbert's. They had a tight scientific partnership, particularly during Powell's years as director, and a brotherly affection for each other.

Powell wanted his colleagues to understand that "a mountain was more than a mountain, it was a fragment of earth's history." He saw lineages stretching back from every pinnacle and cliff. "A mountain has structure," he continued. "Every hill has an appointed place and every river runs in a channel foreordained by earth's evolution." Though Powell did not take his mythology as far, the hand of Muir's God is visible in the background of Powell's thought, pushing glaciers into motion, uncovering canyons, revealing mountains.

When Gilbert looked at a mountain he did not see a fossil or a crumbling archaeological relic. He saw a pinch of earth held between an equilibrium of pressures. While Powell looked back over the chain of geologic history, Gilbert saw a vast present, in which competing forces pressed against one another and plucked mountains out of the earth, holding them upright through their opposition. Uplift versus erosion. Deposition versus transport. Ice versus stone. Any landscape could be understood by the ratios embedded within it.

I like Gilbert's vision. It suits the Sierra, where the highest mountains look so much like cresting waves held between the swell and crash. A faint scent of death drifts from Powell's view: the mustiness of crumbling castles, the dust of old bones. Watching the cliffs of Mount Darwin glowing in the sunrise, the mountain looks too pink and healthy for that, its profile quivering between strong hands, not winding down into ashes. Gilbert's mountains are the rocky flesh of living forces, and time, for him, merely puts numeric boundaries on the eras of equilibrium.

Climbing through Mount Darwin's clefts and channels—down among the complex lines of consensus among ice, water, and rock—it is easy to imagine the tension underlying the stone. Without moving a centimeter, the mountain seems to be teething, jagged spires pushing up through its jawbone ridges, rocky gums peeled back year by year. Looking out at Mount Darwin's neighbors, they seem caught in the act of leaping from the earth. It would be hard to look at the east faces of these mountains, where the cliffs split straight up from the rocks below, without sensing the enormous power of something pushing from deep under the surface.

As I climbed up Darwin's broad chimneys, I tried to visualize the mountain the way Gilbert or Andrews would have seen it, trying to open my eyes to frost thrust and glacial corrasion and crest-line asymmetries. The geology of their time appeals to me for the same reasons I am drawn to their era's climbing. Few implements stood between the men and the peaks. Their tools were their own raw and imperfect senses, which they sharpened and polished against the stone and the ideas of their fellows. They opened their lids wide and tried to shove entire mountains straight through into their minds.

This kind of study—and this kind of climbing—leads to an intimacy with the mountains and with one's own hands and eyes that can't be had amid a clutter of instruments and gadgets. High up on Mount Darwin's ridge, I wandered over the rocks, pleased by their square corners and by the cracks at their backs where winter ice shoved them a hair's breadth closer to the edge each year. I thought of the positivists in the 1930s, tenaciously clinging to their notions that real science could only be done directly by the hands and eyes, even as they were buried by an avalanche of machines in a new age of science and technology. They might have found some solace in the mountains. I stuck my fingers in one of the frost-wedged cracks and leaned out over the edge to look down the drop to the north.

Tied to a rope, I could have let go and it would not have mattered; I'd drop a few feet and bounce around at the end of the line with no worldly consequences. But the feel of the hold in the rock would have been different—the connection between fingers and granite looser, my security farmed out to a device instead of dependent on muscle and trust. I know my hands, I know they won't let go, so I can lean out over the edge to look around. This, in his own way, is how I imagine Gilbert must have felt around a mountain, trusting his insight and his eyes and his history with the stone.

I crossed the plateau, leaping between the jagged blocks jumbled across Mount Darwin's flat roof. Lazy clouds puffed up to the south, but they were clean cotton and nonthreatening. Some of the blocks had lit on fulcrums, and when I landed on their upper edges, they rocked, like ten-ton seesaws.

I arrived at the edge of the plateau, across from the summit tower. I could practically see Andrews there, staring at the true summit, his summit fever smoking out the objections of his conscience. There's no telling what kind of a person will be susceptible to a summit's witchery. Here was a fellow from across the Pacific, who grew up in the swampy outpost of West Botany killing snakes with his barefoot school chums—but in the Sierra, in a landscape unlike anything he recognized from home, he saw the summit and knew exactly why it was important and what had to be done.

I dropped down off the summit plateau. The rock changed, as if I had struck a rotten cavity in the mountain's top enamel; loose stones stuck together with granite sand seemed to wait for nothing more than a firm breeze to tumble off the mountain. A crooked line took me back toward the summit spire following a crumbling ledge between the gap above and the drop below. Good, square-cut, crystalline granite made the spire itself, but it overtopped the gap with its steepest, gruffest profile. It's just as well that Andrews knew so little. A dozen years' worth of more experienced climbers walked Mount Darwin's roof after Andrews and every one of them declined to attempt his spire. As late as 1921 it still had not seen a second ascent.

I remember reading John Tyndall's study of the Alps (Tyndall had a prominent place in Gilbert's pantheon of geologist heroes) and being pleased to no end by his methods. He cast his mental net far and wide. When he decided to investigate slatey cleavage he spent time in the slate quarries, but he also studied iron fibers, ceramic tiles, cheese, and had "several practical lessons in the manufacture of puff-paste and other laminated confectionary." I can't help a grin every time I think of Professor Tyndall having lessons in the bakeshop with his mind in the mountains, turning rock into dough, kneading it, pressing it, watching the layers and cleavage planes forming right before his eyes.

No one taught Tyndall the right way to study slate, and no one taught Andrews the proper techniques and protocols for climbing alpine spires. Had someone existed to do either, Tyndall might not have understood so much, and Andrews almost certainly would not have attempted Mount Darwin's final summit. As Gilbert pointed out, ingenuity thrives in unfamiliar soil.

I sank my hands into the crisp rails on the outside face of the summit tower, pulling up toward its top edge, my boot toes slotting into the holds my hands had just vacated. I hope Andrews had enough time to enjoy his summit before the exposure dizzied him and chased him away. A climber could not ask for a grander mountain pedestal, a flat square to stand on propped right at the brink. I looked back over the plateau and its plunging cliffs, at the unreal junctions of its horizontal and vertical lines, at the dark mountains to the south and the bright lakes at their feet. Then I hung my legs over the eastern edge, staring down into the deep well of air below my boots and over the desert peaks and valleys beyond.

· 10 ·

James Hutchinson + Black Kaweah

[AUGUST 1920]

Black Kaweah (13,765 feet) from the west ridge

THE MILES DROPPED away faster than expected; the three of us reached Precipice Lake at four in the afternoon. Evan had joined me again, and another good friend, Bryan. We were chasing Jim Hutchinson into the Kaweah Range, a remote part of the southern Sierra filled by tall peaks that look so crumbly a hard wind could knock them all down.

I always carry a book in the mountains, in case of storm days or empty afternoons, but my friends had not planned for any downtime. I stretched out on the rocks by the lake and propped my head on my pack and *Beowulf* on my chest. Bryan and Evan fiddled with their things and sent jealous looks my way. Our spot nestled itself into the head of an immense cirque called Valhalla. On all sides granite peaks and pillars propped up the sky roof, and it was easy to imagine massive phantom Vikings pounding backs and spilling ale. I had not consciously chosen Beowulf for the setting. I pulled it off the shelf because my copy weighed two ounces.

Bryan solves restlessness with speech: "Dan," he said. "What's the first line of that book?"

Lo! We have heard the glory of the kings of the Spear-Danes in days gone by, how the chieftains wrought mighty deeds. Often Scyld-Scefing wrested the mead-benches from troops of foes, from many tribes; he made fear fall upon the earls.

"Hey, that's pretty good," he said. "Why don't we pass it around?"

This was an intriguing idea. Bryan, like Evan, is technically inclined; he designs circuitry for satellites and imagines efficient solutions for energy policy. I had not figured either to be the type to get excited about musty literature. I read the first chapter out loud and tossed the book to Evan.

Then Beowulf of the Scyldings, beloved king of the people, was famed among warriors long time in the strongholds . . .

The effect was amazing. Beowulf should be read aloud and in a place like Valhalla. The repetitions and tangential tales make sense when they're spoken; the canyon walls compass enough space to hold the sprawling story. Listening to Evan and then Bryan, I stared at the crags and watched the ancients fight monsters and enemies and each other against the stone backdrop. We were hooked from the moment the ship's captain "unlocked his word hoard."

Angel Wings, Valhalla

The Los Padres forest was burning and westerlies pushed the smoke up into the Sierra. Fire haze filled Valhalla that night, and when the sun set, each particle of smoke glowed pink, the whole mass of air coloring from side to side. Down-canyon, the light bounced off the Angel Wings' half-mile height of ethereal white granite, and it looked as though the rock was live flesh with a pulse. We read on, and the blood dripped from swords, and the sky behind Hamilton Dome turned orange and purple as if a volcano were erupting in place of the sun.

Eventually, the volcano died, but the story kept us up and the stars came out. With numb fingers we finished by flashlight lying side by side in our sleeping bags, watching shooting stars arc the canyon.

◆

IT WASN'T UNTIL after we returned, and I reread Hutchinson's account of his climb, that I consciously noticed a passage I had slid right past before: "there are good friends gathered in the camp-fire's genial warmth, listening as Mrs. McDuffie reads thrilling tales of James Capen Adams, mountaineer and grizzly-bear hunter, Clarence King, and other wild tales of adventure." The mountains have a way of propagating human echoes. King reads a Sunday sermon to Brewer and Gardiner and Cotter, and Hutchinson listens to stories of King, and we read other old adventures while following Hutchinson; the threads of experience creep through the years and across the mountains to link us whether we notice it happening at first or not. Footnotes and offhand comments plant themselves among the peaks—where no sudden changes will uproot them—to wait for the next mountaineer to follow the pattern and add another branch of story.

Hutchinson enjoyed the presence of kindred souls—the more the better—when he traveled the mountains. On this expedition he had the company of a dozen other people. They built a mule trail from the Roaring River, over the Great Western Divide, and down into Kern Canyon. They explored passes, climbed peaks, swapped yarns, prepared campfire feasts. All of these things made him happy. "What is more glorious than these evenings in camp?" he wrote. Fellowship; clean, hard work; and easeful nights were what he was after. "The fire dies to glowing coals," he continued, "and as the moon rises over the great wall of the Western Divide, flooding the basin with soft, mellow light, each one seeks his tamarack bedchamber for a peaceful sleep, to dream of untrodden trails, unpassed passes, and unknown Kern-Kaweahs beyond."

But he also had a destination and a plan. Each day brought them closer to the Black Kaweah, a jagged hulk of fractured rock with its summit perched high above and behind a tangle of winding ridges. From early on Hutchinson had learned to covet first ascents of big mountains. Now, twenty years later, he still felt that urge to be first and claim new territory, even though he had reached the age of fifty-three.

Sleeping bags of one sort or another were now commonplace in the Sierra, flashlights accompanied trekkers, new trails connected valleys and canyons, but not much else had changed, except one thing. Major, unclimbed peaks had grown scarce. Only a few prizes remained—and that was how they were thought of, with a spirit of friendly but earnest competition. The peaks that had not yet been climbed generally had been passed over for a reason: too hard, too dangerous, too remote. Black Kaweah fit all three of those specifications. Time and the leverage of ice had shattered its rock beyond the limits of structural integrity; nothing on the peak looked solidly attached, from individual handholds to entire ridge spans, as if the whole thing might collapse into a cloud of dust on any given afternoon. Yet the mountain still held itself proudly vertical, with steep cliffs, narrow ridges, and a high summit tower. Visions of stacked-up buttresses of loose rock held in place by rickety chance alone had kept climbers away for decades.

If Hutchinson felt nervous about the mountain, he didn't let on about it in his writing, though few of his era admitted any tremulousness before a climb. He dropped hints, though, that he anticipated serious business. After a lengthy examination with binoculars, and consultation with other men who had studied the peak, he chose the mountain's west ridge for the attempt. "It looked pretty fair," he wrote, "but I must confess there were some deep ugly gashes in it, which did not appeal to me greatly." Whole sections of the ridge had fallen completely away as if the mountain had lost a few molars; glassing its profile, Hutchinson could see all the way through these gaps in the jawbone ridge. "The sight of the Black Kaweah," he wrote, "had thrilled us again and again as we circled the peak."

◆ ◆ ◆

DAWN SAW US up and moving toward the highest end of Valhalla. When we reached the Kaweah Gap we gained our first unimpeded view of the mountain. The west ridge strikes the eye hard—long, jagged, and not the least bit inviting. And yet it's the only continuous feature headed toward the summit, so its selection makes a certain sense; all the other potential routes on the mountain seem to lose themselves in a confusion of dead ends and dark cliffs. At least on the ridge one could hope to be above falling stones.

Evan had decided earlier not to tangle with the bad rock we expected to meet, so he peeled off from us here to climb two other local peaks made of welcoming granite. Bryan and I descended into Nine Lake Basin. Bryan is built like a horse; he's six-foot-four, with legs that would be more natural on someone two or three inches taller. When we travel together I have to take three steps for every two of his, and we always go fast. We crossed the Big Arroyo by leaping across stones, then hiked up through meadows and scattered trees toward the lowest end of the ridge.

Two other members of the 1920 expedition joined Hutchinson for his attempt on Black Kaweah, two men with delightful names: Duncan McDuffie and Onis Imus Brown. Each in his own way did much for California's wilderness seekers. Brown worked as a mule packer hired on to expeditions to manage the animals. He did not often occupy himself with climbing mountains. But, Hutchinson wrote, he "was always in for trying anything once—the more difficult the better."

McDuffie was a real-estate broker in the Bay Area, and a conservationist. Over the years he held a variety of Sierra Club offices, including president. He led the effort to establish state parks in California through his work with the Save the Redwoods League. Those who enjoy the preserved areas up and down the length of California's coast and foothills have McDuffie to thank for them. When he wrote about redwoods his words took on a hushed, reverent quality. He had a strong, handsome face that was broad across the cheekbones, and a long frame well suited for striding through the Sierra.

His friendship with Hutchinson went far back. Along with LeConte they had explored the entire length of the Sierra during the summer of 1908, completing Theodore Solomons' original idea for a trail along the Sierra spine, a trail that eventually came to be called the John Muir Trail. In a picture of him taken at the end of that trip he has a tin cup hooked to his belt and enjoys an amused smile under an enormous conoidal hat, like a bishop's, which peaks a foot above his head. The man had a sense of humor.

Hutchinson, McDuffie, and Brown left camp early in the morning, walked up along the Big Arroyo for a mile, then scrambled up over talus to the true start of the ridge. "The view of the peak from this point," Hutchinson wrote, "was absolutely appalling—the knife-edge running up to the peak, and the peak itself seamed, cracked, scarred and broken by weathering as on no other mountain we had ever climbed." They searched out alternatives, but found none. The crest of the knife-edge still looked like the only route forward. "The whole ridge seemed to be disintegrating rapidly," he continued. "McDuffie jestingly said we had better hurry over before it should fall to pieces."

After slogging up the lower thousand feet of talus, Bryan and I joined Hutchinson below the ridge. Gravity and the hundred intervening years might have removed most of the individual stones Hutchinson saw, but the overall effect was largely the same—an ugly, serrated edge of rock so clearly corrupted that it might as well have been draped with a DON'T TOUCH! banner. The summit jutted up in the distance. We had expected it to tower above us, which it did, as the Black Kaweah is close to fourteen thousand feet high. But we had not anticipated just how far removed it would be, and how much of this blasted, contorted ridge we would ride before we got there. It ran along for more than a mile—twisting, turning, breaking up and down—before colliding with the summit pillar off on the horizon.

Hutchinson and his compatriots cast off into a confusion of decaying stone. The way was never simple. They teetered along the crest, climbing over shattered blocks which seemed no more than temporarily perched; sometimes they dropped below the ridgeline, clutching scrappy plaques scabbed onto cliffs, or tunneling under fallen cockscombs of stone. Hutchinson described their course: "We went up and down, around, across, over, and under boulders and broken slabs of granite." They could never relax, for there was almost always air below them and a broken hold or rolling stone could send one of them over the edge. The rock was not actually granite, but instead another archaic metamorphic layer, like Mount Ritter, only more timeworn and unfriendly.

Bryan and I followed along. I couldn't have chosen a better partner for this kind of rockscape. We know the same tricks: when to knock on holds to test their strength through sound, how to pull down through creaky flakes instead of levering them out and off, where to distribute bodyweight across two or three fragile features rather than commit to a single dubious hold. I trust him not to go pitching off the mountain, and not to knock stones down on me—at least not too often. When hard-pressed we both will admit to a guilty pleasure in climbing repulsive rock.

We carried on, not paying too much attention to the still-distant summit, focused only on the rock right in front of us. The sightlines were rarely clear and we crept along by feel. I'd lead for a time, until I rounded a corner and hit a traverse too dangerous to cross, and then Bryan would branch off while I backtracked. Eventually he would hit his own dead end—a difficult cliff or sudden gap—and it would be my turn again to find the thread toward the summit. Talking about the rock and Hutchinson and the old days when the mountains were brand new, we handed the lead back and forth like this, knowing the other would make the right decisions when they mattered.

Climbing with a good partner eases the mood of a mountain. On my own, the forking paths nag at me. *Should I backtrack? No, hate to lose the time.*

Might not be any better anyway. Forge ahead? Might get ugly up there. Wish I knew what was on the other side. With a good partner it's as simple as asking a question—"Bryan, what do you see around the left of that pillar?"—as if one has two sets of eyes and hands. The experience is different and so are the rewards. Alone I find the mountain bigger, the summit higher, the sense of satisfaction a ballooning rush of self-centered pleasure. A close partnership multiplies the individual effort, pushes back the barriers of the impossible, and offers a synergistic gladness that comes from two minds intent on one task.

Hutchinson, McDuffie, and Brown arrived at a deep notch in the ridge, the largest of the gaps Hutchinson had studied with his binoculars. Up close it justified his fears. Both sides were sheer. After a long, slow effort, they connected enough flakes and cracks on the near wall to descend into the notch. But the far wall was even worse and offered nothing for their fingers to hold with any certainty. "The whole situation looked hopeless and desperate," Hutchinson wrote. They could not go forward along the ridge, and the north side of the notch spilled out over empty air. "It was practically vertical for a thousand feet down onto an extensive snow-field," he wrote, "and we turned away for all time from any hopes on that side."

That left the southern face of the ridge, and though it fell away too steeply for comfort, it was not as steep and sheer as the north face. They picked their way down a series of shelves separated by bands of disintegrating rock, shedding the altitude they had worked so hard to gain. When these shelves extended eastward the climbers traversed deeper in toward the peak, turning lateral ridges and shuffling across narrow ledges above long drops. They did not want to give up, and climbing back through what they had already navigated was not a compelling alternative anyway. Eventually they reached the crease where the western ridge merged into the bulk of the mountain. The rock here had been smoothed by tumbling ice and stones, the perennial avalanches that scour the mountainside. Despite the work of the falling debris, piles of loose rocks still toyed with gravity, like kids dipping their toes in a lake, waiting only for the impulse to tumble in.

The crease curved up toward the summit like the beginning of an enormous spiral stairway. The men climbed up through the irregular steps, difficulties provided by short, steep cliffs that required ticklish finger and toe work. Brown had climbed out a hundred feet above Hutchinson when he knocked a stone loose, despite all of their collective care. "I heard a warning shout, 'Look out!'" Hutchinson wrote, "and knew that something was coming. I ducked my head behind a boulder just in time to prevent its being hit by a rock the size of a football, which came tearing down. The rock struck my knapsack a glancing blow and bounded off." As usual, he gave just the facts, with neither King's bluff humor nor Muir's psychological self-study. But he knew, of course, that it could have been a sad end to the climb and to a twenty-five-year association with the mountains, and I wish I knew his thoughts in the minutes after the rock bounced by.

I wonder how close these falling stones really come to us. Inches, I know, but I'm not sure I know what that means. The degree of alignment chance requires to point nature's blind gun directly at one of us is a fuzzy value in my mind. One day a few years back my wife and I were climbing unroped up an obscure route in Yosemite. I was thirty feet above her and I stepped on a foothold that was actually the upper edge of a disguised loose block. My weight levered it off instantly; I caught myself and bellowed at her and looked down to see the rock, the shape and mass of a fireplug, clip the outside of her backpack and tumble off into the trees below. She had had the time and space to take one step forward. Now, if I believe that nine inches of air were the only difference between the rock tapping her pack and crushing her skull, should I give the mountains up? And wouldn't we have to give up driving on the freeway and all the other things we do with margins measured in inches and seconds? And what's the alternative—to believe that close calls require such absurd collections of variables that the chance of one actually connecting becomes vanishingly small? I don't know. I don't know whether Hutchinson was lucky to be alive or unlucky that the rock came so close in the first place.

The spiral staircase steepened as it curved up toward the summit, forcing the climbers to traverse back out onto the western ridge. They were now high above the gap that had forced them to abandon the ridge earlier. Here the crest was more uniform and less tormented, a steep stripe of stacked-up blocks with tremendous exposure on all sides. And then they ran out of ridge to climb, and stood on the summit, and "spontaneously set up a mighty shout of joy."

At least for the day, Bryan and I had no appointments with flying rocks. Friction and chemistry—or marmot spit and eagle turds, whatever actually keeps Black Kaweah together—held the stones in place and we were given another reprieve from thinking about fate and luck. We followed Hutchinson along the narrow catwalk of the west ridge, stopping once to lie on our stomachs and poke our heads out over the sheer drop to the north. From the summit the other Kaweahs spread to the east: Red Kaweah, Mount Kaweah, Kaweah Queen; the name comes from a Yokuts tribe called Kawai, and was first applied to the river that spills west from the peaks. (My favorite interpretation of the name is "crow water.") To the north the peaks of the Great Western Divide marched up toward Mount Brewer and curved east toward Mount Tyndall. Due east of us, across Kern Canyon, the gray flat-topped head of Mount Whitney bulged up from among other high mountains on the Sierra crest.

The Hutchinson party left a note and took an eagle feather with them from the summit. They retraced their steps down the ridge and then down the inside curve of the stairway. When they reached the cutoff back up to the western ridge they decided to take their chances with the untried stretch of mountain below them. The day was already dwindling and the prospect of climbing all the way back to the ridge crest and then along its entire length again pleased none of them. So they continued down the spiral stairs, finding difficult climbing but nothing worse than what they had already done. In comparison to the dense troubles of the ridge, their descent unfolded rapidly and they were quickly off the mountain and into the talus below. Not many people climb Black Kaweah, but those who do have mostly adopted this as the standard route, leaving the western ridge alone to disintegrate in peace and on its own schedule. The three men reached their camp and the larger group of friends at dark after fourteen hours on the move.

Bryan and I sprawled out among the summit rocks, eating lunch and naming peaks up half the length of the Sierra. When the time was right, and our eyes sated, we let gravity pull us back down the ridge and through the southwestern crease, and down into the jumbled talus fields where the mountain's cliffs died away. Meadows and shrubs began to retake the mountainside. Bryan found thickets of ripe gooseberries and we waded deep into the thorns in pursuit of them. Bellies full, we plunged down through forests, recrossed the Big Arroyo, and hiked back up to the Kaweah Gap. We found Evan at upper Precipice Lake where he was trying to replicate Ansel Adams' famous picture of streaked granite rising out of cold water. We returned to our packs at the lower lake and it wasn't long before we sank into our sleeping bags and burrowed deeply against a fierce wind that tore through Valhalla all night long with a sound like a spring river.

◆ ◆ ◆

THE NEXT TIME I saw Bryan was at his wedding ten months later. His hair was shorter and his face smooth, but he was the same Bryan, his laugh and stride calibrated for the mountains and too big for indoor spaces. Many of his friends I knew well; others I knew only from Bryan's stories. A few of the familiar faces looked strange, and I realized I wasn't sure whether I had actually met them or not, an odd feeling of hunting through memories of uncertain origin. One squarely built guy and I spent twenty-five minutes running through a catalog of every time we had been to Yosemite in the past five years trying to figure out whether we had actually intersected there or whether it just felt that way from swapping tales with Bryan.

Some of my favorite climbing partners I see only once or twice a year, or once every other year. Jobs and relationships and private quests have scattered us across the western states. When we do get together—either for a climb or a stopover while passing through on a road trip—it's as if the conversation hasn't missed a beat. Living through a beautiful or scary morning together, sharing a summit or a storm-bowed tent—a day in the mountains can bring two people closer than a year spent occupying the same neighborhood or office. The barriers of tepid politeness just don't survive when you find yourself squatting trousers-down against your harness, filling a paper bag, while your partner sits three feet away in the portaledge making his supper. You either develop an earthy, resilient friendship or end up hating each other.

A few years after the Black Kaweah trip, Hutchinson and his brother Lincoln formed the Sierra Ski Club. It was Lincoln's brainchild, and the group met on his property at Norden near Donner Pass north of Lake Tahoe. They built a lodge there, and in summer and winter they met for weeks at a time to hike, ski, or snowshoe. LeConte was a member, and so were Charles Noble and James Moffit, as well as famous Sierra Clubbers like William Colby and Walter Starr. McDuffie managed to spend time at the lodge nearly every year. He also hosted an annual dinner in Berkeley for the club, and would call out each member individually with a friendly witticism he had typed in advance on a stack of index cards. Over the course of the evening stories were told and letters from truant members read amid good food and drink, self-effacing jokes, and general merriment spread around an enormous rectangular table.

Most of the Sierra Ski Club members lived in California, but a few lived elsewhere. They still kept in touch and passed time at the Norden lodge when they could. After a particularly fine summer session in 1936, McDuffie received a letter from one out-of-stater who had returned to his professorship in Madison. "What a wonderful gang it really is!" he wrote. "You fellows to whom it is just part of your daily environment can't possibly appreciate it as poignantly as I do, I think. A group of twenty or thirty men, who just frankly love each other, and who try desperately to conceal it, of course, and whose friendships date back to the beginning of things!"

Our stories bind us together. That's why I thought I knew some of Bryan's friends I'd never met; that's why LeConte wanted Jim Hutchinson to talk to him about the mountains through the walls of his oxygen tent on the day he died. I think I could knock on the door of the Norden lodge—if I could just reach back that far—and slip right into the noisy doings on the other side without feeling out of place. I would know these people, even though I'd never met them, and they might recognize me too. I could probably even give Jim a hard time for leaving his white handkerchief fluttering from the top of Black Kaweah to signal its surrender, and he could poke fun at me for being so concerned for the feelings of a lump of rock. And then we could get down to the business of scheming up the next expedition and the next climb and the next chance to have a good tale to tell, because Jim was always looking ahead at future adventures and so am I.

· 11 ·

Francis Farquhar + Middle Palisade

[AUGUST 1921]

Middle Palisade (14,012 feet) from Disappointment Peak

O N VALENTINE'S DAY, 1958, Ansel Hall dropped by the house of his old friend Francis Farquhar. Neither of them was a young man anymore; Farquhar had just turned seventy and Hall was in his early sixties. They were both still spry, though, in mind and body. The two men went down to the basement library, Farquhar taking the stairs with the light step of a man twenty years younger, both of them speaking with lively voices. The room was large, originally used for billiards by the previous owner of the house. Now, books lined shelves from floor to ceiling and wall to wall. Their contents were eclectic; Farquhar had a collector's eye for fine printing and a capacious memory that allowed him to read widely across an incongruous run of interests: from bookmaking to archaeology to tax reform, to name just a few. Of course, certain subjects took up more wall space than others. The history of mountaineering, the history of exploration, and most particularly, the history of California and Californian climbing filled shelf after shelf and shouldered the other parts of his collection aside.

At one end of the room, by a window, Farquhar had his desk, a wide surface stacked neatly with papers (he had recently taken on the editorship of the *American Alpine Journal*, and he had manuscripts to read). File cabinets stood close by, filled with notes, clippings, and correspondence. There were also many comfortable, overstuffed chairs. The Farquhars thrived as hosts, and this room in particular had become a famous meeting place for climbers from all over the world. One friend wrote, "Probably more expeditions, first ascents, and other escapades were hatched in the Farquhar library than in any other incubator of American mountaineering. When two climbers met in some remote mountain area of the world, the password often was, 'Remember me? I met you at the Farquhars.'"

The history of climbing was in the process of cracking wide open again, the second time Farquhar had seen it happen in his lifetime. The previous summer, 1957, Royal Robbins, Jerry Gallwas, and Mike Sherrick had climbed the north-west face of Half Dome—the sheer face that stares down at Yosemite and had filled Josiah Whitney's mind with images of the earth being split by the hand of God. The climbers spent five days and four nights living on the wall, the biggest and boldest thus far of the next generation of roped climbs. They hauled their food and water up in a single "torpedo sack" and slept on narrow ledges or in claustrophobic alcoves on the face. Not to be outdone, Warren Harding was now in the middle of his yearlong siege of El Capitan. The biggest cliffs in the world were being climbed, and Californians swung their hammers at the rock and the word "impossible," developing new tools and techniques, and most importantly, a new mindset. Robbins, who understood the spirit of Yosemite in the 1960s as well as anyone, wrote of that time, "The terror barriers are down."

Farquhar paid careful attention to these ascents and to the evolution of mountaineering at home and around the world. He kept a thick file folder of newspaper articles on the Harding climb of El Cap and he read the reports (and occasional ravings) of the new generation in the *American Alpine Journal*. He had given up on dangling from his own fingers but he still visited steep places in his mind and in the pages of his library. And yet, despite all the excitement bubbling up out of Yosemite, Farquhar still favored the past, as he always had, and that's where he and Hall planned to go the day of Hall's visit. With the help of a historian at the University of California at Berkeley, Farquhar was in the process of recording his oral history, and when he learned of Hall's visit, it became the perfect opportunity to add a piece of his friend's story to his own. So they sat down in the comfortable chairs of Farquhar's library and turned on the tape recorder. Farquhar assumed the role of interviewer, though the transcript of their conversation reads more like two old friends chatting about youth.

Hall had first come to Yosemite as a boy, and the mountains had gotten into his blood. "I was inoculated with the Sierra Nevada fever," he said, "and from that time on an outdoor career was inevitable." As a summer job in high school, he worked for Camp Curry in the Yosemite Valley. Then he took a forestry degree at U.C. Berkeley, graduating just after Congress created the National Park Service. In 1917 Hall began work as one of the first two rangers in Sequoia—which meant, as he put it, that he was "turned loose" in the southern half of the park with a horse, a mule, a rifle, and some tools. He felt romantic and dashing. There he was, twenty-one years old, living alone in the middle of the mountains, tracking cougars and fighting wildfires. The attentions paid him by the Maxon daughters, who lived with their father on a homestead just across the park boundary, completed the ballad. He called that first summer as a ranger "one of the most glamorous in my life."

◆ ◆ ◆

TWO STORIES COME up over and over. In one, a boy is taken to Yosemite or the northern Sierra around Lake Tahoe by one or both of his parents in the summers, and the granite, lakes, and pines become the bedrock of his mind; he never truly leaves the mountains, even when he's not there. That is Joseph LeConte Jr.'s story, and Ansel Hall's as well. In the other, a young man travels from elsewhere and, discovering California's mountains, the trumpet-wielding angels descend and play waterfall thunder through their horns while tearing back the curtains hung before his eyes. That is John Muir's story, but not his alone.

When Farquhar received his bachelor's from Harvard in 1909, he had never heard of Yosemite or the Sierra Nevada. His family, firmly planted in New England, ran a slate-roof business in Massachusetts. They were expert craftsmen, with an impressive list of clients and connections up and down the eastern seaboard. Farquhar remembered as a boy having a tour of the Department of the Navy, and at the White House an introduction to President William McKinley by his father, the two men being old friends.

For Farquhar, the notion of a stable place in the world ended when his father died just before his high school graduation. Soon after, his mother and younger brother moved to Chicago, and he found himself abruptly rootless. He threw himself into the college experience, and though he worked hard and developed his mind and character during his years at Harvard, he finished his degree with little idea of what he would do with himself. Six months later he received, through a friend, a job offer at a publishing house in San Francisco. Farquhar had spent three years writing for the Harvard *Crimson*, and had vague notions about a career in journalism or printing. More importantly, he felt restless. With no reason to stay in the East, he took the position and resolved to find out what the West had to offer.

He traveled by train from Boston to Los Angeles and then north to Oakland. He took the ferry across the bay and had his first look at San Francisco from across the water. "I felt a thrill at that time," he said, years later, "and knew at once that I was going to like this part of the world."

He spent a year designing advertisements for Bancroft-Whitney, a publisher of law books. He learned methods of fine printing, and enough about the publishing business to conclude that he hadn't yet found his profession. He also met several members of the Sierra Club and began to hear stories about California's mountains.

Growing up, Farquhar had spent his summers in the woods in Maine and New Hampshire canoeing and hiking. His older brother had traveled in Europe and done some climbing in the Alps; Robert brought home with him a rudimentary idea of the spirit and practice of mountaineering, and the two brothers applied those notions to peaks in Maine and later in the White Mountains of New Hampshire. Of course, those were East Coast mountains, with about the same elevation as the Sierra Nevada's outermost foothills. Farquhar had still never seen anything like the Sierra.

On a spring day in 1911, Farquhar visited a friend in St. Helena, a picturesque spot north of the Bay Area now known for its vineyards and hiking trails. His friend had been on several Sierra Club trips and the two men talked about the mountains and the club. "By the end of the day," Farquhar recalled, "I had decided that I would resign my job and go on the Sierra Club trip that summer if possible." He remembered that another friend of his had mentioned a relative that had a connection to the Sierra Club. He called her to ask about an introduction. As it turned out, her brother-in-law was William Colby, a disciple of Muir and a legendary figure in his own right in the Sierra—and, at the time, the director of the club. Farquhar had dinner with them the next night and Colby brought maps and pictures of the mountains, the beginning of a long friendship between the two. "I remember," Farquhar said, "that I never had a more exciting evening in my life. I could hardly wait to get into the High Sierra."

◆ ◆ ◆

I TOOK THE long way to the mountain. It was early August of a dry year, and my trail held inch-deep drifts of loose dust that lapped over my shoes. Nervous crickets colored gray and black hung out on the trail margins, looking just like chips of granite until they flinched and leapt away. Thunderheads rolled over the summits and spread out across the eastern canyons. Before too long the rain began, an outburst of heavy drops that seemed to have more than gravity behind the percussive sounds they made against my hat. They cratered the dust and drenched me, but the land still seemed unsatisfied, never giving up its parched expression despite the downpour.

The east side of the Sierra is a border place, where a long day's walk can lead from the snout of a glacier to a sagebrush desert. Water teases the land. Storms drop most of their load on the west side of the mountains; by the time they've floated up over the crest they have little rain left for the east. Just like the ground, the air seems to stay dry even in the rain.

All afternoon, individual storm cells, each about a mile broad, broke over the crest and quickly dumped out the rain they'd hauled up with them. Then the clouds would drift out over the valley and the sun would blaze down again, drying the trees and the ground and my clothes in about the same amount of time the rain had taken to soak us all in the first place. At my elevation, below the tree line, the air remained thick enough to hold the sun's heat, so the downpours were cheerful, like summer and a garden hose. When the thunderstorms finally finished their business with the mountains, the clouds wilted back until they vanished, delivering a mesmerizing run of clear blues and starry blacks.

◆ ◆ ◆

FARQUHAR NEEDED ONLY one trip to the Sierra to know that he would make his home in California. "From the moment I entered Yosemite I knew that I was in the place where I wanted to be and have close at hand all my life," he said, looking back on his first summer with the Sierra Club in 1911. The officers of the club, including Colby, knew that they, too, had found a kindred spirit, a man well tuned to the joys of the mountains who also had the practical ability to guide others among the peaks and teach them to experience those joys for themselves. By the end of the summer, even though it was still only his first season in the Sierra, Farquhar found himself in charge of small parties on mountain-climbing forays.

Summer became fall, the Sierra Clubbers returned to the Bay Area, and Farquhar needed a new job. He went to work as a bookkeeper for the Federal Telegraph Company. Farquhar had an orderly mind and liked detail work; he enjoyed gathering data, sorting it, verifying it, using it to produce precise conclusions. It was an interesting time for the work. The excesses of the end of the nineteenth century, the financial chicanery and wild speculation and purposefully loose record keeping that had all contributed to Clarence King's miseries during much of his last decade, had finally resulted in a backlash and a move toward transparency and order.

So Farquhar began his curious double-life: suit-and-tie accountant spring, winter, and fall; mountain climber and explorer upon the arrival of each summer. He was not alone in this division of vocation and avocation (though Farquhar genuinely enjoyed his career, so perhaps he simply had two avocations). The Sierra Club of his era was filled with lawyers, professors, bankers, and businessmen. The sounds of relief, of neckties loosened and city clothes flung in closets and office doors shut and locked, must have echoed across both sides of the San Francisco Bay in the late spring when snowmelt filled Yosemite's waterfalls to the bursting point.

◆ ◆ ◆

I LEFT THE trail dust behind and broke off cross-country through forested moraines. I had far to go. I needed to cross to the opposite side of the Palisade chain and that meant grinding up over two passes, one above eleven thousand feet, the other above thirteen thousand, with miles of jagged talus between.

Francis Farquhar climbing on Mount Haeckel (Photo courtesy of Bancroft Library)

I crossed the first pass and slid down loose scree on the other side. I descended to the upper fringe of the tree line, where junipers sent their roots straight down between planes of granite and crooked their branches out like the limbs of old men. I scrambled through a short maze of stubby cliffs, and dropped down into a hanging valley filled by a small blue lake that glinted in the sun. Granite slabs surrounded the water; the sun had spent the morning warming them. Above the lake, talus piled up so high it nearly blocked out the mountains. Creeks poured over the boulders, splashing waterfalls and foam over the down-steps. Below the lake, cliffs cut away and the outlet creek disappeared over the edge. I found a body-shaped curve in the granite above the water and stretched myself out against the warm stone.

Ten minutes passed and it was time to get up and start walking. Nothing happened. The sunlight itself seemed to press me down into the rock. I noticed monkey flowers in a thick carpet on the far lakeshore that I hadn't seen before. They sprouted up from between blocks of granite and dangled inch-long golden trumpets over the water. More minutes passed; I'm not really sure how many. Nothing in that pocket seemed mobile: the lake, the stone, myself, the clear, warm air—there was nothing to hang a passing minute on.

Little blue-eyed Marys, like painted four-leaf clovers puckered into lips, bobbed up and down in the spray pushed out by the cascade feeding the lake. Single stalks of tubular purple penstemons grew out of soil pockets in the rock just beside me. An obstinate corner of my brain tried to guilt me upright with words like "lazy" and "soft." But the effort fell far short—the rest of my brain simply ignored the harangue without even bothering to reply. I was utterly becalmed. I couldn't move. Swallows wheeled around the lake, rolling and diving to snatch fat bugs hovering above the water.

I can't tell you where exactly my mind went during those hours I spent by the lake. I'm not sure myself. Back, I suppose, into the cellar of the brain, to some distant part we share with lizards and other creatures that bask motionless on warm rocks.

◆ ◆ ◆

FARQUHAR SPENT THE summer of 1920 on the Sierra Club outing up the Middle Fork of the Kings River. Middle Palisade tugged at his thoughts; the peak stood within view all along their route and from the summits of the other mountains they climbed. "There were many inquisitive glances cast at its fluted sides in search of a possible way up," he wrote, "for it was reputed to be still unclimbed." If that proved to be the case, then Middle Palisade would be one of the tallest unclimbed peaks left in the Sierra, and with its plunging cliffs and narrow summit blade, one of the most intimidating.

The opportunity for an attempt never presented itself—perhaps Farquhar lacked a partner, or was too busy with his leadership duties to the club—so he left the Sierra at the end of the summer feeling disappointed and unsure as to whether he would have another opportunity at the mountain.

Next spring he took a different approach to his summer plans. Rather than tie himself to a large group for the entire season, he planned to spend at least several weeks knapsacking in the mountains with Hall. With no mules to tend or novice mountaineers to guide, they would have complete freedom.

The two friends met for the first time in the summer of 1919. Hall had returned from a year spent deforesting France with the Army Corps of Engineers in order to supply lumber to the Allies, and Farquhar had reestablished himself in the Bay Area after his wartime post of cost accountant for the Navy. They met in Yosemite, introduced to each other by a mutual friend, Stephen Mather, the first director of the National Park Service.

Hall was then in the process of transitioning from park ranger to park naturalist. It would be a new turn both for him and the fledgling Park Service. Rangers had been conceived of to protect their wilderness and their visitors; now they would also study the land and teach natural science and history, just as Muir and Colby had done for years on Sierra Club outings. Hall purposefully followed Muir as he devised his idea of the role of a wilderness guide. In an essay explaining the new role of rangers as scenic interpreters, he began with an homage: "The friends of John Muir delight to tell of his eternal willingness to halt by the trailside to name a tiny flower or to point out with reverence the ice-carvings of the Master Sculptor on great granite walls. Nothing in nature was too small to claim his attention nor too great to be included in his apprehension." Soon, Hall would throw himself into the assembly and management of the Yosemite Museum, the first of its kind, a shoestring operation at first that would grow and become the model for other national parks.

Hall and Farquhar must have hit it off immediately, for they had the same interest in studying the history, both human and natural, of the mountains. Soon they were reading each other's draft manuscripts and competing with each other to see who could acquire the most complete collection of obscure mountain literature. "Look out, old scout, I'm catching up to you!" Hall wrote in one letter to Farquhar late in the spring of 1921. "I've now a full set of the Sequoia annual reports and a full set of the Mt. Whitney Club Journal."

◆ ◆ ◆

GETTING BECALMED WILL slow one down. By the time I left the lake the sun had already stepped down off its highpoint above the mountains. When evening arrived I was still east of the crest. I slept in a deep bed of pine needles under a foxtail and awoke at first light the next morning. The mountains—the whole Palisade chain of jagged summits tied by sharp ridges—slipped from red to orange to gold while the sun rose and I repacked my sleeping bag. Staring up at the parti-colored summits, I felt their familiar tug. I started walking as the last trace of gold faded and the granite resumed its hard daylight colors—stark brights and glittering darks that burned spots into my vision as I trudged over the high pass.

Despite its enormous size, Middle Palisade shies away from prying eyes. I had looked at it from the summits of North Palisade and Mount Sill, and had passed it long ago on the John Muir Trail, and what did I know? A shape like the dorsal fin of a continent, a narrow summit ridge that seemed to hang in the sky, a tangle of glaciers and canyons at its base. Nothing useful for the ascent. From a distance I'd had no sense of where the mountain might let a climber pass and at its base, I felt no wiser. The mountain filled the eastern sky, a wall of rock stretching left and right for what looked like miles. Grooves ran down the face of the wall at regular intervals, but they all looked disturbingly steep and cluttered with dead ends. It's just perspective, I told myself. You'll see when you get closer. It can't really be that steep.

◆ ◆ ◆

AS THE SUMMER of 1921 approached, Farquhar sent Hall a series of letters, each with a rising tone of mountain fever. In one, written June 20, Farquhar wrote, "I am getting my affairs into shape as rapidly as possible so that I can leave for the Sierra in July with a clean slate. You bet I shall be glad to strike Yosemite. I shall arrive with the supermob about the fourth I suppose, but bet I can beat anyone to it for the last available camping spot above highwater mark." The waterline he jibed about was the nightly flood of the Merced caused by the downstream arrival of the afternoon's snowmelt. On a past occasion he had installed himself in an apparently ideal spot, only to have the river become "intimate" with his toes around midnight. Another letter, ten days later, written to "Dear Anselmo," exclaimed, "The binding ropes are loosening and another struggle and I will be free . . . Then off for Yo-semite!" In this note he seemed to have given up on his hope of beating the holiday crowds to a campsite. "I am bringing my sleeping bag," he wrote, "and intend to park under the shrubbery somewhere."

For two weeks Hall and Farquhar rambled through the mountains. They crossed the Sierra crest twice, their path a broad loop with Middle Palisade in the center. With their circuit three-quarters closed, they hooked in toward the mountain. "A magnet seemed to draw me in that direction," Farquhar wrote, "and I confess that I willingly submitted to its influence."

They trekked south, crossing boulder fields and ridges, passing North Palisade and Mount Sill. Middle Palisade's narrow, elongated shape finally ballooned up before them, and inch by inch its massive western wall rolled into view. They made camp in a nest of whitebark pines by a creek below the mountain. Then they spent the rest of the day studying the peak, trying to make some sense of its strange design. Their foreshortened perspective caused all sorts of optical tricks. The summit crest ducked in and out of view behind cliffs and buttresses; at first it was not even clear which part of the ridge stood highest.

The true summit appeared to be a spire on the right-hand side of the crest. A deep groove cut through Middle Palisade up to the ridgeline just north of that spire and they chose it for their route. They could see little of its insides, but it still looked more promising than the blank rock and vertical cliffs on the flat face of the mountain. They returned to their beds in the pines, planning to start early the next morning.

Dawn on the west front of the Palisades meant only that the night turned gray. Farquhar and Hall walked up over bare granite and through the shadows hiding from the sun on their side of the mountain to the talus cone spilling out from the chimney. A short, difficult stretch over a smooth cliff gave them access to the guts of the cleft. From there they made rapid progress, though they had to be careful not to knock rocks down on each other, for the chimney was filled with loose rubble.

They climbed higher and higher. There were challenges, but nothing more serious than a tricky move or two, usually with a ledge below and a good chance that a fall would be less than catastrophic. Their excitement grew. No major obstacles checked their upward progress, and nothing above looked any more difficult than what they had already climbed. They picked up speed, moving fast up ledges and through tight slots within the larger chimney, beginning to feel certain of the climb and the summit.

A discovery cooled their enthusiasm. "A little pile of rocks on a ledge, and another above, and beyond still others, meant that someone had preceded us," Farquhar wrote. They had been beaten to the climb by some unknown party. All their smug thoughts at the ease of their ascent turned against them now, for if they had found the climbing easy then they could only assume that their predecessors had found no trouble either. Barring an unseen crux above, they had no hope of being the first on top of this peak.

They continued on, somewhat dispirited. Their gulley ended at a hanging notch in the upper ridge, and now empty air tumbled down on both sides. They stuck their heads over the eastern edge and looked down into a cracked and chaotic glacier two thousand feet below. This sight enlivened them. The view was no less breathtaking just because someone else had seen it first. They hurried toward the summit, climbing ridges and channels through the rock, eager for the wider view above. When they reached the topmost point they found a final pile of rocks, killing any last hopes they might have had for a first ascent. And then they had another surprise. "The view was spectacular enough," wrote Farquhar, "but it contained a quite unexpected element . . . there, standing clearly before us only a short distance away to the northeast, was another peak unmistakably higher than the one on which we stood." They were not on the summit of Middle Palisade. They had been snookered by the strange sightlines and the curving summit ridge. The true summit, separated from them by a deep gulf, eclipsed the northern view.

"At first we were chagrined by our mistake," Farquhar wrote, "but presently another thought occurred that somewhat lifted the gloom." If they had arrived at this spire by mistake, then perhaps the other party had as well—and what if that meant that Middle Palisade was still unclimbed? The two men examined the cairn on the summit and found a little can with a note that read: "July 20, 1919.—The undersigned made a first ascent of this peak this day and were disappointed not to find it the highest point of the Middle Palisade. We hereby christen this summit 'Peak Disappointment.'"

◆ ◆ ◆

STARING UP AT Middle Palisade I understood the trick the mountain had played. To my eyes, the top of Disappointment Peak looked no higher or lower than the ambiguous ridgeline to the north. But at least it looked like a summit. It had converging lines and a clearly visible triangular top. It proved the perfect lure to eyes searching for that sort of geometry.

I hung my pack out of marmot reach from a cliff by a patch of soft gravel that I planned to use for my bed. I followed a creek that cut through flower-filled meadows and leapt off shelves of granite. Pink and purple Jeffrey shooting stars, their petals swept back from their pistils, hung over the stream. I found a shallow puddle filled with hundreds of tadpoles. In a normal year, the pool would have been larger, but this year dry flats surrounded a skin of water only a few inches deep. The poor tadpoles, some as long as my fingers, were packed side by side and stacked one above the next. I tried counting them in a square-foot patch and extrapolating, but the best I could figure was that there were more than a thousand squeezed into that puddle—just another symptom of the land panting for water through the drought year. Many had already sprouted arms and legs, but none had nerves hooked up to their new limbs yet, so they floated in place, looking bored with waiting to evolve: striped, crouched, motionless frogs, attached to enormous and vigorously active tails.

I returned to my pack in time to watch the afternoon and evening light slide across the rock. It's a good day when you get to see sunrise and sunset paint opposite sides of the same mountain.

The next morning I slipped out into the gray, headed for Disappointment. I checked in on the tadpole slum, but half of the occupants had buried themselves in the mud at the bottom and the rest were settled into a thick layer above the mud, and the water was still. The grasses and flowers gave up a short distance past. Smooth billows of bare granite led up to a circular lake and above the water the rock turned to jagged talus sloughed off the mountainside.

Up in the cleft I entered a dark world of shelves and chimneys. The walls of the fissure blocked out most of the sky, leaving only a stripe of air behind me. I crawled around in the back of the space where the walls converged, feeling buried between the pages of a huge, barely opened book. Farquhar had been pleased to discover kinder climbing here than he had expected. And it is true that from the look of the exterior the insides could have been a horror show of steep, smooth rock with nothing for a climber to hold. But the climbing was not exactly easy, either. The difficult moves called for technical answers: knee locks and arm bars and other strange wedges that climbers have devised to keep themselves from falling out of body-sized slots. The fact that Farquhar blew off Disappointment Peak says plenty about the state of climbing in the Sierra. Standards were on the rise—climbers were studying the stone and learning techniques both from the mountains and from each other.

I reached the notch and had my first view down into the crevasses of Middle Palisade's eastern glacier. The crevasses queued down the center of the glacier's motion, hungry mouths made for gobbling stones and anything else the mountain might care to toss down at them. No doubt the glacier is smaller now than it was in 1921, but it still made me happy to see a healthy ice river alive and grinding away at the mountainside.

I followed the last ridge up to the local summit. Middle Palisade's upper crest curved away to the north. There was nothing ambiguous about it now— a massive granite stairway running up high through a corridor of air. Middle Palisade is only a hundred, or a hundred-and-fifty feet taller than Disappointment Peak. But the difference seems far greater than that from close up. Middle

Palisade is bigger, higher, more complex and striking; Disappointment Peak is well named.

◆ ◆ ◆

FARQUHAR AND HALL retraced their route down through the chimney and back to the talus below, already talking about making an attempt on the real Middle Palisade now that they knew where to find it. One look had been enough to dissuade them from trying a direct traverse between the two summits—the intervening ridge looked too harrowing and exposed. They would have to begin again from ground level.

When they arrived back at the talus they were surprised to discover that it was only eleven o'clock. They ate the pocket food they had brought with them and lay down on flat boulders. By the time they had finished their lunch they felt reenergized and decided to take their next shot at the mountain right then and there.

They began up another deep cleft parallel to the first but running up toward the higher summit. Right off the talus they found this new route precarious and dangerous. "Almost immediately," Farquhar wrote, "we found that the climbing was much more difficult than before." The inside walls were steeper and smoother. Loose rocks and gravel covered ledges that otherwise would have offered the men at least a measure of security. Instead, they frequently had to climb one at a time while the lower man hung back or hid behind a corner or roof in order to avoid "cascades" of falling rubble.

As they pressed up the chimney the cliff planes on either side pushed back against them. They tiptoed up thin ledges with the rock right in their faces, feeling increasingly strung-out above a long drop and the ugly fate of being chewed up by a gizzard of loose boulders in the bottom of the cleft. Up ahead, a hulking buttress capped their chimney and stared down at them with a forbidding look. They thought about backing off. "Several times we were discouraged and considered abandoning the climb," Farquhar wrote. "But the feeling of discouragement never seemed to attack us both at the same time." One of them always saw a way forward, or at least an unexplored possibility that had to be tried before he could retreat with a clean conscience. So yard by yard they persisted, despite feeling unsure of the wisdom of continuing (and even growing certain it was foolish to go on).

Halfway between the talus and the summit, Farquhar traversed out of the main chimney onto one of the facing walls. Probably he hoped to avoid the miserably loose rock in its center, rock that crumbled into dirt under his hands and boots. But the holds on the cliff face were slick and insecure. He reached a ledge, and paused to search out his next holds. He found he was stuck.

> I had reached the point with difficulty and was now absolutely blocked from further progress upward . . . The more I looked the more impossible seemed a descent, and presently I became unnerved and thoroughly scared. The longer I looked at the enormous depth below the worse I felt . . . This feeling could not have lasted long, but I did a good deal of scared imagining during the time.

Farquhar forced back his fears, focusing only on the solid holds within reach. He ignored the drop below and the consequences of a fall. Giving mind only to his next hold, and then the next, and the next, he traversed back into the main chimney, where he found comparative safety, and Hall, who had just extricated himself from a nasty spot of his own. "We then had a brief consultation," Farquhar wrote, "and . . . concluded that we had had about enough and definitely decided to go down." But then something strange happened. "We looked around for a route for the descent, and then, instead of climbing down, we both began to climb up." Just like Muir on Mount Ritter, the uncontrollable within them grabbed hold and ordered them onward—"let the judgment forbid as it may," as Muir put it.

They traversed left out of the chimney, below the scowling buttress that blocked their way, and out onto the face of the mountain. They snaked a complicated route through cracks and up steep cliffs, traversing back and forth around blind corners. The climbing never eased and the exposure was unrelenting. But it did not matter. Having broken once with judgment, they did not pause to question the sanity of their project again. After the moment of their decision to retreat, Farquhar wrote, "we did not stop until we reached the summit."

The final crest was the airiest place of all, but the angle relaxed and the mountain gave them broad ledges for hands and feet. They scrambled up and down over rectangular teeth sticking out from the ridge, taking care not for lack of holds but because the blocks were perched right on the edge of the eastern drop to the glacier. At the far end of the ridge they reached the highest pinnacle. No mark of any previous human mountaineer intruded on the native stonework. Farquhar felt elated. "With a shout," he wrote, "we greeted the summit as its first visitors."

◆ ◆ ◆

I DESCENDED DISAPPOINTMENT Peak to the talus. Shadows still held the western base of the Palisades, but bright sun lit the boulders further down. I stretched out on a rock and stared up at the peaks.

Nowhere else in nature is there such a singular point as at the summit of a mountain. The whole landscape swells in that direction, all of the lines converging purposefully. I neither know nor care which came first: the symbols of elevation and ascension embedded in human thought, or the first conscious sight of mountains rising above the flatlands that birthed our species. Either way, the gravity that mountaintops exert on our eyes and hands is built right into the architecture of our minds. We like our gods to be above us, for our stories to have ends, for journeys to have destinations, and here is the one place on earth where geography satisfies the abstract symbols of our thoughts and dreams.

A band of solid granite protected the foot of the chimney through which Farquhar and Hall passed to reach the summit. I found a crack cut through it which I climbed to a hanging terrace of talus above. When the talus ended the difficulties began. I entered a mobile world of perched rocks and smooth granite. I still cannot understand how so much loose rubble finds a home there—shouldn't it be flushed off every spring by avalanches and runoff? Gravity alone ought to do the trick, given how lightly the stones hold on to the cliffsides. I avoided the center of the chimney, where I could practically see new debris being spat out from a seam of rotten rock, and climbed the steeper, cleaner faces on either side.

In this lower reach of the cleft, despite my careful handling of the mountain, I knocked loose a foot-wide cubic stone that rocketed down the insides of the chimney. It seemed almost delirious to be free the way it bounced off buttresses and leapt off ledges, enthusiastically pulling along its neighbors wherever it touched down. Pretty soon the narrow airspace in the chimney vibrated with the hollering of scores of rocks sliding and tumbling down below, sounds that lasted for nearly half a minute before they died away.

Where the cliff planes narrowed and steepened I climbed up a poorly developed crop of holds, like shallow eyebrows nicked out of the rock, to the ledge that had briefly paralyzed Farquhar. I followed his traverse back into the main chimney. Here the central seam of decaying rock spewed gravel and dust at the lightest touch. There was no gain to be had from delicacy, now—I grabbed holds on the cliff faces with my hands, and paddled against the disintegrating rock with my feet, and lurched twenty feet higher.

I ran out of chimney to climb; above me the decaying rock reached out and merged with the buttress that had forced Farquhar and Hall out onto the face of the mountain. I traversed left along a narrow ledge. The rock changed. There were still loose chunks all around, but it no longer crumbled under my hands. It was rougher, more crystalline, less polished by runoff. The sun sparkled against the quartz, blasting refracted light back at me that dazzled my eyes as I stepped out from the shadows of the chimney.

Narrow channels ran down the face of the mountain, splitting cliffs and buttresses. I would have to climb one of them though none looked appealing. The first seemed impossibly steep, riding smooth rock up through bulges that would probably toss me off if I tried them. The second looked possible if I squinted at it and forced an optimistic mood. But I wasn't feeling particularly optimistic, and foresight played a dumb show on the screen of my imagination in which I reached an hourglass narrowing in the channel and ran out of cracks for my hands and edges for my feet. My boots scuffed across blank stone; panic built up in my forearms. The footage was hardly confidence inspiring.

I pressed further out along the ledge, hoping for something better, moving cautiously because of the loose chunks at my feet and the long drop below. I peeked behind a corner and found a squeeze chimney between two parallel planes of smooth granite. It would do. I wormed myself inside it, pressing, squeezing, and cranking with my ankles to lock my toes against one wall of the slot and my heels against the other. Where the crack widened I pushed with my knees and palms and my back, shuffling up toward the chimney's opening. Loose rocks fringed its top. I swam over them with my legs split wide against the spreading planes of stone, my hands grasping for solid holds amid the rubble.

That chimney set the tone for the last thousand feet of the mountain. No casual stretches of mellow climbing were offered, and I kept a tight grip on the holds the rock did provide. Many times, looking up above, I thought I would be blocked by dead ends and blank stone. But then I would find a thin crack in a corner that gained me fifty feet, or a ladder of finger slots in a wall that had at first looked bare. The mountain always allowed me a way forward, though I might not see it until the exact moment I needed it, as if the rock required a certain amount of faith from the mountaineer.

One blank sheet of granite, peppered with scintillating crystals, particularly worried me. It floated above, steep and sheer, and every turn I took back and forth across the pleated granite seemed to carry me toward it. I reached its base and it still looked like a wall designed to keep away undesired guests. But when I brushed my hands against the rock I found marvelous, deep, incut holds. The closer I looked, the more holds appeared, until the whole brilliant wall revealed a water-carved mosaic of handles. I climbed straight up the near-vertical face, sinking my fingers into deep curves in the granite, pausing to look down past my boot heels, which hung out from the wall and above two thousand feet of air. I thought of Farquhar and Hall up here, not even knowing whether their route would prove possible, but climbing along anyway on the faith that the mountain would give them just enough and that their hands would not let them fall. For a bookish accountant with a tendency to wear some paunch around his middle, Farquhar put together one hell of a hard climb.

When I arrived at the summit crest the first thing I saw was a Clark's nutcracker perched on the ridge. She looked strange there, ruffling her crisp black-and-white feathers against the backdrop of hushed and outwardly lifeless stone. When she saw me, she dove off the east face, dropping fifteen hundred feet before extending her wings and gliding away into the valley below. I have said that summits hold no thrill for birds, but even they must feel a rush from a plunge like that.

Steep rock and deep holds on the Farquhar route

I traversed along the final ridge, reveling in the tremendous exposure down both faces of the mountain. Lakes filled the land on one side, ice on the other, with the narrow crest of Middle Palisade dividing the two worlds from each other. At the far end of the ridge I found the true summit, a pillar of rock with a flat seat on top. I installed myself there, balancing against a breeze, glad to be made to enjoy such places.

◆ ◆ ◆

FARQUHAR CALLED MIDDLE Palisade about as hard as North Palisade. Whether he fashioned this comparison out of modesty or poor memory, I do not know, but Middle Palisade is a different beast—devious, dangerous, unnerving, and technical. It combines the loose rock of Black Kaweah with the vertical cliffs of Mount Humphreys. Be that as it may, Farquhar probably took more pleasure from the historic value of the mountain than from the difficulty of the gymnastics involved. Middle Palisade had held out against sixty years of climbers even while catching the eye of some of the best mountaineers who had wandered the Sierra. Shortly after returning home from the climb, Farquhar wrote a letter to Hall, his words warmed by a satisfied glow.

> Colby told me that Jim Hutchinson was very much worried when he heard that we had gone off into the Kings River region for fear that we would run away with his hoped for first ascent of Middle Palisade. But when he heard the news he gave us his most cordial congratulations. I am to take dinner at the LeContes' this evening and Hutchinson is to be there too.

That fall, Farquhar dove headlong into the past tales of his mountains. He gathered all of the material he could find about the early years of exploration and climbing. He struck up correspondence with men like Theodore Solomons and Lilbourne Winchell, men who had traveled the Sierra before LeConte's map, when the passes and rivers and canyons had not yet been fixed on paper. Farquhar hoped the men would donate photographs, letters, trail journals, and maps; he wanted to put together an all-encompassing collection that could be used by future generations no matter where their interests might lie.

When Farquhar put his mind to a project, good results tended to happen and happen quickly. By the end of 1922 he wrote again to Winchell.

> I already have a very fine nucleus of material ready to deposit with the University and have the assurance of much more. The object is to make this collection as complete a record as possible of everything pertaining to the Yosemite and the rest of the scenic regions of the Yosemite and all the other National Parks in the country.

The University, of course, was U.C. Berkeley. Farquhar planned to add his material to the Bancroft Collection, an amassment of the literature of the West assembled by Hubert Howe Bancroft (with dozens of assistants) and gifted to the university library in 1905. This was the same Bancroft for whom Farquhar had gone to work as an advertiser for his first job in California.

Farquhar also expanded his own library. In another letter to Winchell, a year and a half later, he wrote, "I am constantly adding to my collection, books, papers, and maps of the Sierra Nevada and am rapidly getting the most complete collection of such material that has been gathered in any one place." Eventually, his private collection would make its way to the university's libraries as well; he always thought of himself as a "trustee" for the material, with a genuine desire for it to be made accessible to all who wanted to study the mountains.

Farquhar's presence has always hovered over my own research. When I go to the Bancroft Library now, I find his notes and letters scattered throughout the archives, reaching far beyond the boxes and cartons of his own files. He compiled the letters of William Brewer. He tracked down E. C. Andrews to learn the story of the first ascent of Mount Darwin. His reference books and histories sit well thumbed on my shelves. I have become pleasantly acquainted with his slanted, looping handwriting, and with the many tones of voice he could work into a printed sentence—from the chummy exclamations in his letters to Hall to the dry crackle of his professional speech. Empty minutes must not have overburdened Farquhar. As if his full-time accounting practice, his library collections, his histories of the early explorers, and his own mountaineering pursuits were not enough, he took on the editorship of the *Sierra Club Bulletin*. For twenty-one years he turned out beautiful volumes capturing the past, present, and future of his mountains.

Farquhar handed off the editorship of the *Bulletin* in 1946. The succession indicated changing times; David Brower, a fountainhead of new ideas and radical politics, became the new editor, and he would go on to reshape the Sierra Club and lead it through dark days and triumphs. Though Brower was an expert climber, and though the Sierra Club had always worked for conservation, the priorities were about to shift; environmental causes and political activism would now become primary while mountaineering and exploration would be left to other organizations.

Farquhar, who had always been politically conservative, never seemed to muster much enthusiasm for the spirit of the 1960s. He was proud of the successes of the new Sierra Club, and he saw a continuity of purpose reaching back to its founders, but he found the new methods and attitudes unsettling. He believed in decorum, was well-known for his gentlemanly manner, insisted on being photographed in a suit and tie at home, and those qualities were going out of style. During the last decade of his life he was occasionally asked probing questions about feminism and environmentalism in the early years of the Sierra Club. He tended to reply with scrupulously polite, and scrupulously noncommittal, answers—even though he had championed the expansion and protection of Sequoia National Park in the 1920s and often took care of his kids at home while his wife went on ski trips in the Sierra. Perhaps he didn't wish to be associated with radical movements. Perhaps he simply didn't care to play the role of a historic relic questioned about the quaint origins of an organization that had opened his eyes to the mountains but which he didn't quite recognize anymore.

◆ ◆ ◆

THE REELS OF the tape recorder continued turning in Farquhar's famous library. The two friends bantered back and forth, and Hall's story came out in pieces, the way a bear rambles through the woods, pausing at the scents that interest him most. Outside the room it may have been 1958, with a new generation of climbers dreaming up adventures and facing a new set of problems in the wilderness, but inside the library it was 1917 and Hall and Farquhar were the new generation—young men smitten with the mountains, eager for wildness, freedom, and beauty.

Hall continued the tale of his first summer as a park ranger. The park superintendent had asked him to build a cabin for himself and future rangers. There was no lumber, but he had a sledgehammer and wedges, a couple of axes, a froe for cutting shingles, and an eight-foot crosscut saw. He found a sequoia log that had been downed by some calamity a hundred or a thousand years previously (it was hard to judge the age of the wood because sequoias barely rot, alive or dead). The log was ten feet through, which gave him some trouble with his eight-foot saw, but when he did succeed in opening it up he found straight-grained wood perfect for his needs. Like Robinson Crusoe on his island, Hall set to work, describing the construction piece by piece for Farquhar. He built his entire cabin from about a third of that downed sequoia trunk.

He paused and Farquhar asked him whether the cabin still existed.

"I don't know," he said. "I'd certainly like to go back and see."

"I think we'd better go up and have a look some day," Farquhar replied.

"Wouldn't that be fun?"

"That's forty years ago."

"Is it?" Hall said. "My heavens. We must go up there sometime while we can still hike!"

◆ ◆ ◆

FROM MY SEAT on the summit I looked down into the valleys on either side of Middle Palisade. The granite seemed to roll away, running down off the mountainsides, through the canyons, spilling out into the forests, suggesting all the movement of a river without the stone so much as quivering. There may be a special point where the mountain ends and the sky takes hold, but picking a definitive spot where the mountain begins is not so easy. The curve between land and mountain is not built for subdivision. Should you start where a climber starts using his hands? Or where the glacier ends? Or begins? Or where the grade of

Camera propped on a rock, author propped on the summit block of Middle Palisade

the land eases toward horizontal? Before long the mountain has extended down into the desert and has rolled up into the Inyo Range on the other side.

History also resists subdivision. It does not like to be cut in pieces. So where to begin? When Hall and Farquhar first fingered the holds in the back of the rotten chimney below the summit? Probably not. The story would look as hollow as a cliff with nothing beneath it; either would collapse without the ground below. Maybe when Farquhar first saw the mountain and began to dream of it? Further back? When his brother told him stories of the Alps? When Muir taught Colby to love the mountains, so that Colby could pass that inspiration to Farquhar? The story of a climb does not even confine itself to the life of a single climber.

The lines of the land swell up toward the mountaintop, and so do the lines of history. They converge where the stone stops and the sky begins. It is a between place, after the end of one story and before the beginning of the next. When the sky is friendly the sun warms a seat on the summit that seems held apart from the regular chain of events. Time passes strangely; a minute can stretch or flutter by as easily as a bird diving off the crest. Only after stepping off the summit do gravity and history seem to grab hold again, pulling me on to the next day and the next climb.

·12·
Charles Michael + Michael Minaret
[OCTOBER 1923]

Michael Minaret (12,240 feet), west face

W ITH OCTOBER SLIDING into November, I had hopes for one more climb
before the season changed for good and the snow locked up the mountains for another winter. At the entry station to the Ansel Adams Wilderness, a
white-haired ranger gave me a stern lecture.

"You know, it dropped two foot of snow in there last weekend," she said.

"Yes ma'am."

"If you drive in there, and it snows again, we won't come get you out. Your
truck'll be there till next June."

"Sure," I said. "I'll keep an eye to the west." This talk of snow was alarming—not so much for the next few days, as the forecast was clear, but for the
amount of snow already covering the stone I planned to climb.

The ranger shook her head and let me through. "It will be beautiful back
there," she said. "Certainly will be."

Back in 1866, when Clarence King climbed Mount Clark with James
Gardiner, King saw, for the first time, a mile-long row of nail-sharp peaks to
the southeast. If Mount Clark had stood a little farther north, King would have
seen nothing but a brown ridge, the way a saw blade, sighted end-on, loses its
serrations and looks like a solid disk. But from his angle, each peak cut its profile
into the sky with sharp, steep lines. On the spot, he named them the Minarets, an
inspired choice, capturing both their geometry and otherworldly appearance.

The Minarets are not the most elevated peaks in the Sierra, the tallest of the
group topping out at just over twelve thousand feet. Nor are they aesthetically
attractive, like Cathedral Peak or Mount Clark—peaks made of gleaming granite
that invite descriptive poetic phrases and meditative reveries by nearby lakes. No,
they are ugly mountains that look dangerous and inhospitable, and sixty years
would pass before the first of the Minarets was climbed by Charles Michael.

Michael was Yosemite's assistant postmaster, a position that entitled him to a year-round residence on the valley floor without overburdening him with responsibilities. He spent his time and freedom exploring the cliffs and peaks that together composed the vast canyon walls of his home. By 1923, the year he and his wife Enid made their expedition to the Minarets, the Michaels had already become well-known to the Yosemite connoisseurs of their era. Their hiking partners included Donald Tresidder and Ansel and Virginia Adams, among others. Word spread that an outing with the Michaels was not only the best way to see Yosemite, but also promised a good chance for an adventure along the way.

The relationship Charles Michael developed with Yosemite can hardly be separated from his relationship with Enid. Investigating their mountain world was a shared passion—or, perhaps, their alpine studies became an extension of their affection for each other. Theirs was an easy companionship and the days passed for them in an idyllic sort of way. They'd have a swim in a local lake, or scramble up to examine the multicolored cliff lichens high above the valley floor, or light a lunchtime bonfire in a cave behind the Yosemite Falls curtain. He specialized in birds, she in wildflowers—he even had the tall, gaunt, skin-stretched look of a heron and she the round face and cheerful grin of a California poppy. They both climbed and hiked with robust appetites for steep topography. It seemed they needed nothing more than each other and Yosemite to be quite happy.

Enid captured her husband well when she wrote, "He will not walk across the street to see a fire; he climbs over dangerous places on the cliffs without a sensation of excitement; those happenings that move most men leave him cold, yet let a beautiful bird come within his vision and suddenly he is on fire." Their personalities complemented one another. Enid had the more effervescent spirit, blown along by enthusiasms and delight, while Charles trod a steady path. His descriptions of his climbs disguise their seriousness. Even modern climbers, with all their training and equipment, tend to find more to thrill them than the birds when they venture out on the Michaels' old routes in Yosemite.

One trait is missing from Enid's description of her husband. She does not mention the compulsion that gripped Charles when the climbing became difficult. He was a stubborn man who did not retreat easily. An unclimbed cliff called to him and he would not allow himself to quit until all of the upward possibilities had been exhausted. Enid recalled one occasion when Charles, still recovering from a broken leg suffered in a fall, insisted on attempting to climb difficult new rock on Mount Starr King. She wrote that she "became extremely anxious and commenced to ask him to return." (Charles, it seems, was not the only specialist in understatement.) Outwardly, Charles may have been calm, but some internal passion forced him up into high, dangerous places.

Ediza Lake encourages thoughts like these. To me it seems to be a brooding place, a steel-colored surface that falls into the afternoon shadow of the Minarets. The Michaels camped here the day before they climbed their Minaret, and so did I. Perhaps those who come to catch trout and devour the views are unaffected by the history of this place, but I feel ill at ease here. A far sadder spirit than Charles and Enid makes Ediza Lake his home. Walter Starr Jr., a young, strong, Stanford-educated lawyer with a practice in San Francisco and a love for the Sierra, died alone on Michael Minaret in 1933, trying to climb a new route. His body is still on the mountain, but his camp was here, and the last picture taken in his camera was of the lake with the mountains in the background. To me, the place feels haunted.

I had a book, but I did not want to read. So I sat with my back against a rock and stared at the strange silhouette the Minarets cut from the setting sun. If the Michaels were so obviously happy, then what were they doing here by these grotesque spires? Why risk what they had for peaks and cliffs? Neither of them was an adrenaline junkie, in the modern sense of the term, nor did they attach the kind of romantic heroism to their exploits that Clarence King would have. I feel like I should have an answer to these questions, because my wife and I often climb together unroped. Some couples go for afternoon strolls to talk over the day and visit their neighborhood. Ashley and I go for afternoon climbs that take us to high places. Sometimes we chat, sometimes we move in silence, one right above the other, footholds becoming handholds. At the top we always feel refreshed and relaxed. Why do we need the air under our heels? I still don't know.

Nights are cold at October's end in the High Sierra. By early evening I had burrowed deeply into my sleeping bag. With nothing to do but conserve body warmth, the time passed slowly. Wind rushed over the top of my bag, discouraging exposed skin. It was an uncomfortable womb and a long gestation till dawn.

I rose with relief at the first blueing of the eastern sky. Early morning is the coldest time, and the wind rattled through my body. But light—even those dim, blind, first few minutes of the day—marked the end of the nighttime stasis, and the possibility of a warmer future. Best of all, the morning meant that all my loose thoughts could finally be subdued by the day's work. I was eager to dislodge the vague fears that had spent the night pacing my brain, leaving their muddy tracks where I wanted them least. So I pulled off my sleeping bag, put on my boots, ate a hurried breakfast, and pushed my stiff joints into motion.

Less than an hour passed before the sun touched the meadows above Ediza Lake, warming away the frost that had cased every blade of grass. Red-and-black grasshoppers exploded from beneath my footsteps, three, five, eight at a time. There could have been a hundred thousand in a few acres. A hatching? A mating ritual? It seemed dangerously late in the season for either, but they know their business better than I do. Judging by the number that escaped, I must have crushed many. I could never see them until they moved. The land swelled up toward the Minarets and the meadows ventured no farther, giving way to great piles of brown rock shed from the sides of the peaks.

As the years passed after the Michaels' expedition, and as climbers returned to the Minarets with ropes and pitons, each spire, nineteen in all, was climbed and named. But the Michaels considered the mass of rock holistically, and hoped to reach the highest point on what they called the "Minaret Crest." The eastern face of the Minarets held little hope for such a project, however, as it dropped most precipitously at the very point along the crest where the tallest spires were located. So the Michaels decided to try their luck on the west side, and pioneered a route through a high pass above Ediza Lake that has come to be called North Notch.

I left the meadows far below me but seemed to gain little on the pass. At over eleven thousand feet, North Notch is not that much lower than some of the shorter spires. The notch passes right through the Minaret chain, two-thirds of the way along its length. It looks like the place where a twentieth pinnacle has been yanked out, leaving a toothless gap behind. Just as the lower meadows had given way to boulders, the boulders yielded to snow, a solid, steep blanket covering the last eight hundred feet to the notch. Leaning against my rock at Ediza Lake, I had wondered what I would do here. The Michaels carried no equipment

The Minarets from the east

for snow-climbing, no ice axes or crampons, so I, in faithful imitation, carried none either.

One step onto the snowfield suggested that matters were more serious than the soggy boots and numb hands I had imagined at the lakeshore. The heavy precipitation that held sway over the Sierra the previous winter and spring had dropped snow in such quantities that it never fully melted during the summer. Instead, the cycle of thaw and freeze had only consolidated and condensed what was there, withering the soft young powder down to hard old ice. The recent storm, the first salvo from the advancing winter that had so concerned the park ranger, had draped six inches of loose, new snow on top of the previous season's ice. My first kicked step collapsed as soon as I weighted it—the snow broke free from under my boot and I slid right back onto the rock I had stepped off.

So I clawed my way up, digging down through the upper layer to find hand- and toeholds directly in the ice. I gained a hundred feet, then two hundred. When I had the breath, I cursed the Michaels for not bringing ice axes, and cursed myself for following them so slavishly. But mostly I talked to my fingers about gloves and wool-lined pockets and hot cups of chocolate and all the other soft, warm things that I would give them when we returned to the outside world, if they would just hold on. I couldn't see or feel the chinks in the ice which held my boot-edges, so it was left to my imagination, which proposed fragile ripples and crusts that would crumble or melt and send me on a toboggan ride into the boulders.

I emerged at the notch thirty or forty minutes later, damp, cold, somewhat shaken, and feeling foolish for having let myself be abused by the first part of the *approach* to my intended climb. The one luxury I had brought was a change of socks, and I took my time wringing the meltwater from my first pair, while sitting in the gap between the spires. To the east and west, air spilled down toward the stone-bound lakes far below; to the north and south, twisted pillars and sharp points queued to the horizon. The Minarets are ancient metamorphic remnants, geologic dinosaurs hoisted skyward by the uplift of the younger granite. The way they stick up seems violent, as if the spires are the rusty claws of some fabulous beast trying to tear its way out of the earth.

A shift occurred in the history of Sierra mountaineering when climbers turned their eyes toward objectives like the Minarets. When people first began to climb the mountains, they looked for the high peaks, from which they could survey the range and claim status by sheer numbers of vertical feet. And they were drawn to the pretty mountains, which are abundant in the Sierra, because they made them think of God and Eden and Byron. If challenge, in terms of pure climbing difficulty and objective hazard, was found on the way to the summit of these high and beautiful peaks, then the early mountaineers chewed their beards and dealt with the difficult climbing as best they could. But they generally did not pursue difficulty for its own sake, a sane choice in the days before ropes rewarded a falling climber with a second chance.

Priorities have largely been reversed now. Most modern rock climbers do not even think of summits, pursuing instead purely gymnastic, extremely difficult routes that may be no more than a hundred or fifty or fifteen feet long. Our equipment has become so good that risk has been largely eliminated from the typical climbing outing. There are still mountaineers, to be sure, but they have become something of a fringe group compared to the vast numbers of rock climbers traveling the country to test the limits of their forearms on cliffs and boulders.

In the Californian branch of the evolution of climbing, Charles Michael might well be the link between mountaineers and rock climbers, with one boot on the way to the summit and one hand feeling for holds in the vertical. The peak tops mattered to him. He visited nearly every rocky summit around the Yosemite Valley at one time or another, and some he returned to many times. But he was not content to take the easiest scramble to their tops. He looked for difficult, thrilling variations. ("Thrilling" was a word used frequently by Enid.) Even on rambles through the meadows and by the rivers, there were swallows' nests built up in the rocks, and cliffside flora requiring investigation, so he always had an excuse for a climb. He showed all of the compulsions of the rock climber: the need to test his strength and physical cleverness against blank stone, the willful persistence to hang on and search for that last handhold needed to convert the unclimbed to the climbed.

And he was willing to tangle with an ugly mountain. In fact, the dangerous appearance of the Minarets called to him. His description of them contains both the foreboding visuals and perverse allure that certain mountains inspire. "When seen from the distance they wear a black and sinister look," he wrote. "There are no gentle slopes to beckon one to the summit; rather does the scowling sheerness warn one off. The spirit of the mountain is the spirit of defiance, and in every aspect there is a challenge to the climber." This last phrase can be read two ways and Michael surely intended both. In a practical sense, there are no easy routes among the Minarets. But the rock is also challenging him, daring him, to come test his hands and guts.

Call it coincidence, but the transition from mountaineer to rock climber and the campaign against the Sierra's ugly peaks began shortly after the First World War. While the soldiers were killing God in the trenches, the romantic quest was going out of fashion in the Sierra. John Muir, Clarence King, James Hutchinson, all communed with God on the summits of their mountains, but Charles Michael never mentioned a deity and prayer is unusual among his successors. The Minarets are appropriate to a postwar world: a troublesome place, not necessarily built for human pleasure, and evidence, perhaps, that humans were not built with pleasure in mind either. At the very least, the Minarets could not have been made by the same God who made Cathedral Peak.

From North Notch, the Michaels worked their way south, parallel to the row of spires. They explored the joints between the Minarets, looking for a route to the skyline, but steep cliffs and dangerous climbing turned them back each time. Eventually they came upon a narrow groove that ran up immediately to the north of what appeared to be the highest peak. They entered this deep chimney and found no immediate obstacle blocking their way, so they began to climb. "The crack was so steep," Michael wrote, "that but little loose material found lodgment, and often the walls came so close together that we were able to brace ourselves between them." Enclosed by smooth, water-worn rock on three sides, with a thin slice of sky at their backs, they pulled and braced and pushed themselves higher and deeper.

In two places, car-sized boulders wedged in their crack forced Charles and Enid out onto one wall or the other, where holds appeared each time and allowed passage. Halfway up the chimney their way was blocked by an even larger fixed stone. "This third boulder," Charles wrote, "was as large as a good-sized building, at least thirty feet high . . . Once more we must climb out; but this was to be a longer climb, and the walls were sickening in their smooth sheerness." Charles first explored a tantalizing line of holds that rose up to and then around the lower right margin of the boulder. He named this section "the ladder with the lower rungs missing," and though he tried several times, he was never able to reach those upper bars.

Abandoning the ladder, he looked for other options and found a subtle series of holds farther down the right-hand wall of the chimney. Here the way would be longer, but the cliffside was not quite so steep. With little in the way of commentary, he ascended this line to a ledge that took him to the top of the boulder. But he found the climb risky and "just a little too thrilling," so he requested that Enid stay where she was, and she agreed.

I asked Ashley whether she would have stayed put under that boulder if I had asked her to. She told me not to be an ass; if I had climbed it she would have as well. Under no circumstances would she have sat under a rock and waited.

This can't be rational. She has spent the last four years in medical school and I have spent that time teaching rock-climbing classes, so at least at the moment I am stronger. And yet, how much wisdom is there really in letting your companion climb off alone? What would Enid have done if Charles had not returned? How long would she have waited? Rational or not, I do not doubt Ashley's sincerity. On a winter's day in Joshua Tree that we spent soloing easy climbs together, I blundered onto a more difficult variation of one route and thrashed my way up out of pigheadedness, then spent a queasy five minutes watching her follow me, even though I had shown her from above exactly where the correct line ran. I keep that episode bright and dustless in my memory. Knowing that I am climbing for two people makes me more sensible and that is, no doubt, Ashley's point.

From above the boulder, Michael continued up a shallow gulley, the route less steep now that he had exited the chimney. But pleasure was hard for him to find up there, even though the difficulties had eased. "I missed the steadying influence of my climbing partner," he wrote. He emerged at a notch an arm-span wide that joined the shoulder of his Minaret to the next spire north. The notch was capped by another boulder to form a portal of rock set into the crest of the ridgeline. Through the portal, the eastern vista rushed up to meet him, as though he had perched himself on a windowsill. Below his feet he could see the entire Shadow Lakes chain, from Ediza to Iceberg to Cecile, and in the distance the great eastern desert spread its shades of orange and tan and sage throughout the Sierra rain shadow. Enid remained beneath her rock, though, so he did not linger.

Only a few hundred feet separated Michael from the summit. He traversed out along a narrow ledge fronted by a sheer wall that hung across the eastern face of the final pyramid of the mountain. There was no chimney to hide in now—fifteen hundred feet of empty air stroked his boots. Back and forth, and once all the way around his Minaret, he connected precarious ledges that brought him closer to the summit. "I had a feeling," he wrote, "that the wall might give me a little shove on the shoulder and tip me into nothingness." But the rock stayed its hand and allowed him to pass and he found himself with no more Minaret to climb. There he received the mountaineer's rewards: the view, the free air, the sense of space above with nothing solid to obstruct the sky, the "billowy sea of mountains" stretching to the far southern horizon.

He had marked his ledges with small cairns, so his retreat was orderly. He passed back through the portal and down through the gulley to return to the boulder and an unpleasant dilemma. Downclimbing is far worse than ascending; the balance is all wrong and boots lack eyes. Should he go down the way he came? Or tackle the unknown way down the shorter, steeper wall? He found his route up so unnerving that he opted against it and arranged for Enid to point out the likeliest toeholds for him on the "ladder with the lower rungs missing." Down he climbed with direction from Enid, and from the last rung he let go and dropped down to the floor of the chute, unharmed. They quit the peak at once, stopped only for some photographs, then pressed on back to North Notch and their camp at Ediza Lake, which they reached at three o'clock that afternoon.

When I regained sensation in my hands and feet, I too descended North Notch, but headed west, following the Michaels' outbound tracks toward their Minaret. There was no snow on this side of the pass. In the Sierra, snow lingers on the eastern and northern sides of the mountains, where it is protected by colder temperatures during the morning and by the shade lee of the peaks in the afternoon. Meanwhile, the western and southern fronts melt early, leaving the rock bare and dry.

The land below the western half of the Minarets was pleated like an accordion. Deep ravines cut downhill from the peaks, crosswise to my own direction of travel. Angular rocks of all sizes made piles upon piles of orange and brown. Forward progress came slowly. I felt child-sized, my limbs too short for this landscape.

When at last I reached the base of Michael Minaret, I could not mistake it even though I had neither picture nor route description with me. A warty finger of rock jutted up from the ground with no intermediate buttresses or peaks to hide its full height. To the north, the chiseled groove of the Michaels' chimney dropped straight down to a little fan of snow tucked up in its shadows.

After the approach, which had felt positively endless, the sight of the peak gave my spirit the lift I had been hoping for all morning. I entered the chimney and my arms and legs felt the right size again. No more crimping up snow-buried ice, no more wandering a wasteland made for demons or giants or god-knows-what-else. Here, finally, was uninterrupted, vertical rock. I knew how to climb this. My joints found a satisfying rhythm and I pushed and pulled and braced, just as the Michaels had, and gained height rapidly.

Large holds set in solid rock allowed me to bypass the first and second chockstones and I soon found myself within sight of the third. Here the chimney angled down toward horizontal for a hundred feet, and the back of the crack became an uneven floor that could be walked on. At the far end of this amphitheatre the walls tapered in, and there the giant rock had wedged itself and blocked passage. Between the floor and the lowest point of the rock, a gap of fifteen or twenty feet collected shadows and oozy drips. Above this damp, unpleasant cave squatted the main portion of the boulder and another twenty-five or so feet to the easier gulley above.

I made directly for Michael's ladder. Though I was curious to know what had scared him so badly on his path of ascent that he had chosen to come down another way, I had no interest in experiencing it for myself. I had no one to point out my footholds. I needed to know the moves and holds before I tried to reverse them. Besides, years of pull-ups made me confident that if there were ladder rungs to be had, I would be able to yank my way up no matter what else might be there. I was sure that anything a postman from the 1920s had climbed down, I could climb up.

Half an hour later I had not emerged from under the boulder. Ladder with the lower rungs missing? I found no upper rungs either. Instead I found a cryptic puzzle of tiny edges that pointed in all the wrong directions above an uneven landing made of sharp rock. I cannot even guess which hold Charles might have jumped from, or where he could have touched down without breaking his ankles or worse on the rocks and trenches below.

Though I tried any number of different sequences to solve the mosaic above me, my right hand always ended up on the same fragile-looking flake that offered a half-pad grip for the tips of three of my fingers. I spent long moments staring at this hold, trying to guess what it held in store for me. Under its lower margin ran a thin but conspicuous fracture line, and though I wanted to go up, I could not bring myself to trust that scab of rock to stay attached to the mountain.

With persistence taking me nowhere but toward a newfound awe of Charles Michael, I took a break and walked back down the chimney floor, just to see what he had climbed up instead. Once I began to look for it, it wasn't that hard to spot. I could see the line of holds clearly enough. It began from ledges that I could stand up on, and then there were a few thin edges, then a damp little finger slot hidden under a roof, then more edges and a vertically oriented fissure that I

303

torqued my fingers into, and a big foot move that brought my boot up below my hands and allowed me to reach another edge. The climbing was tricky, but the holds were there. I looked down. The wall was blank. Blank? I checked again. Blank. From above, every hold was concealed, camouflaged. It looked like there was nothing down there.

Twenty-five feet up, the trap had sprung; the only option now was up. Eighty years after Michael's ascent, the mountain played the same trick on me. Lulled up a path that I would not dream of downclimbing, my only option would be to climb down a section I had already discounted as too difficult. Without meaning to—specifically intending not to—I had followed Michael's path *exactly*.

Why did I go up? I went up because the holds were there. I climbed because I knew that I *could* do it, and to back down would allow the mountain to prove me wrong. The mistakes I have made in the mountains usually come about like this, times when I have reduced climbing to a pissing match that the mountain can't lose and I can only hope to pull through. The mountain isn't even properly involved in the competition; it's just me against my own head. But now I'm probably being unfair to Michael and myself and all the others who have been in similar spots. The gains made in places like this have their value. Courage needs exercise too, just like fingers and biceps.

At the time, standing above the boulder, there was not much use worrying, not right then anyway. The descent would wait until after I had been to the summit. It could hardly change for the worse while I was gone. I scrambled up the easier terrain of the open gulley and gained the ridgeline.

The portal is like a floating picture frame: look to the east and your snapshot is of gunmetal lakes and craggy peaklets; look to the west to bracket distant rolling carpets of green forest. I passed through the portal, and stepped into another world.

I could not have been more unpleasantly surprised had I leapt from summer to winter in the distance of a single step. For hours that had felt like days, I had been scrambling and climbing through the dry, western aspect of the Minarets. Now, across a distance of ten feet, I had returned to the east, and the snow. Great streaks of sparkling white slashed the mountain's face on this side. It had collected most of all in niches and on ledges and everywhere else that a mountaineer might put hand or foot. The snow! The ranger had warned me, North Notch had tried to dissuade me, but now I had entered its domain, and the snow would get its way at last. I made an attempt. I couldn't give up without trying. I teetered out above the east face, fighting for footholds under the white, fighting to keep suddenly wet boots in contact with slick stone. I managed thirty or forty feet out the ledge, far enough to find that giddy feeling that dwells above long drops, and to see for myself that the ledges were entirely covered and the snow was just as deep and slippery and real as it looked from the portal.

Here is the beauty and folly of mountaineering: after the risks have been run and the effort spent, the mountain still can shut you down just below its summit with something so slight as a little leftover deposit of snow. People who speak of conquering mountains know nothing. We are children slipping our hands into the cookie jar while the indifferent nanny slumbers.

There was nothing to be done about it, so I recrossed the portal and headed back down the gulley. I was dawdling—no, I was delaying—studying the rocks instead of hurrying back to the ladder-without-any-rungs-at-all under the boulder, when high above something metal and brassy caught the sun. In the back of my mind, I knew at once what it had to be, hidden up in the middle of nowhere, but I was in no rush, so I climbed up to it. The flash had come from a crumbling buttress far up the left-hand wall of the gulley. It was a plaque dedicated to Walter Starr Jr., and I realized that the height I had gained put me level with the spot across the gulley and on the mountainside where his body had come to rest and then been interred by Norman Clyde and Jules Eichorn. Bad luck? Too much courage? His plaque reads:

Walter "Pete" Starr Jr.

May 29, 1903 – August 30, 1933

A bold and passionate mountaineer of the Sierra Nevada, and a Stanford alumnus, Pete Starr died while attempting to solo a new route upon these flanks. He now stands in the grand company of those who have not returned. His name continues to live in the hearts of the young men and women that follow in his footsteps today, tomorrow, and forever . . . "Defiant mountains beckon me to glory and dream in their paradise."

Grand company, perhaps, but not the kind of company one wants to keep. The immortality offered by the plaque never looked less appealing than from my stance on the crumbling buttress in sight of Starr's grave.

I descended back to the top of the chimney. I sat on top of the boulder and spent some time inside my own head. The cliff was hidden from view below me, but I had stared at it for so long from the bottom that I had a detailed map of the forty feet of rock in my mind. I looked up and down this picture and picked my holds. I visualized every individual move until I knew my sequence. I wanted the whole forty feet to happen automatically—my mind would press "go" and my body would do the rest. There would be no jumping for me. I did not trust the jagged floor to treat me kindly. I would climb every move from first to last.

I slithered a few feet down the groove between the boulder and the wall. Where the boulder curved in toward the mountain I stopped and my right hand latched onto its first hold. From there I began. I remember the forty feet only in

snatches. The sequence was utterly bizarre. None of the holds had a simple upward orientation, and I leaned my body far to the left and far to the right in order
to stay attached to edges rotated ninety degrees off axis. My feet forced clumsy
boots onto precise nicks set in the wall. My conscious faculties complained and
worried and pled for time to think, but my body followed the program I had
given it. I stepped on—I tromped on—the little flake that had given me so much
worry before, and used it again for my fingers, because it was necessary and it
would hold. And then I was down, and my instincts relaxed the walls that had
kept my thinking parts suppressed, and they flooded back in to retake control.

Visually, the amphitheatre was the same, of course, but the filters were different. On the way up, the boulder and Michael's ladder had been shaded by desire
and hope and fear. If I had reached the summit I might have looked out through
colors of triumph or elation. But I mostly felt confused and hollowed out, and
the rock looked simply like rock, gray and shadowed and cold. I climbed back
down the chimney and headed back north toward the pass.

At some point in the years before we were married, Ashley asked me whether
I thought that I could live a purely happy life: no highs, no lows, just a steady
state of pleasant existence. I pretended to think about it for a moment, but I
knew my answer right away. I would be bored. I would feel soft in the spirit.
I can't remember if she said anything in return; she may have only nodded.
But I recognized in her expression the same restless need of contrast, for joy
won through hardship, and another bond between us was secured. For better
or worse, we both know how it feels to have hands built by the likes of Michael
Minaret, to carry these places in our fingers.

·13·

Norman Clyde + Mount Russell

[AUGUST 1926]

Mount Russell (14,086 feet), south face

O N AN AUGUST day in 1920, Francis Farquhar set out to climb North
Palisade with a few companions from the larger group on that year's Sierra
Club High Trip. They had reached the snow chimney on the original LeConte
route, when they heard a noise from below. A single climber, moving fast, caught
up to them. None of them had seen the man before. He wore a broad-brimmed
campaign hat over a pair of ice-blue eyes and a chin like a granite prow. He introduced himself as Norman Clyde. He was, wrote Farquhar many years later,
"his usual extraordinary self, carrying a pack and a cartridge belt and a revolver.
What the latter two were for is hard to conceive." Soon everyone—at least in the
expanding clan of California mountaineers—would know his name.

When climbers describe the arrival of Norman Clyde in the Sierra they often
sound like they're talking about a force of nature, like an avalanche or earthquake. His shoulders might as well have been made of stone; his temper could
flare up as quickly as an afternoon thunderstorm. The legends bluster around
him, sometimes revealing and sometimes concealing his character. The bare
truth is that in his lifetime in the mountains he saw more of the Sierra—more
lakes and woods and summits and storms—than any person before or since. The
Sierra was his home, and Clyde became one of its features, like the sequoias or
North Palisade.

Like John Muir and Bolton Brown, Clyde also had a minister father. But
theological questions do not seem to have clouded Clyde's mental sky—or if
they did, he did not write about them or discuss them with his friends. His
father shaped him in other ways. He began teaching Norman Greek and Latin
around the time Norman first started talking, and he moved his growing family
(Norman was the firstborn of nine) among the farms and forests of rural Ohio
without ever stopping for long in any one place.

During Clyde's teenage years, they settled into Glengarry County near Ottawa. Here Clyde learned his way around an axe and a crosscut saw, taught by the Highland Scots who had settled there, and he hunted and fished, which he could do just outside his backdoor. In those dense, shadowed, Canadian forests Clyde spent much time alone. As he put it later in life, with his customary brevity, he enjoyed "going it alone because that was the way I liked it." He also must have acclimated himself to the forty-below northern winters because in the Sierra he had a tendency to cheerfully weather blizzards in his shirtsleeves.

When Norman's father died young of pneumonia, the Clydes moved back across the border and down to Pennsylvania. Clyde enrolled at Geneva College and took a degree in Classic Literature, cultivating the words and stories his father had planted in his mind as a boy. Diploma settled, he took teaching jobs as they became available. Each position carried him west, through Wisconsin, North Dakota, and Utah. Norman had read Muir's *The Mountains of California*, and his map tilted down toward California as a result; he rolled in that direction when one commitment ended and the time came to move on to the next.

He landed at Berkeley in 1911, at the age of twenty-six, and entered the university, thinking a master's degree would further his teaching career. He invested two years in the degree, and finished nearly all his coursework, but, according to one friend, "he could see no sense in struggling with a thesis which no one would ever read," so he broke with the university, continuing to follow the path of his own inclinations. The next summer he immersed himself in the high peaks; "1914," he wrote, "was the first year that I did any climbing of any account in the Sierra."

Then he fell in love—but not with the mountains, with a woman, named Winnie Bolster. She worked as a nurse at the Alta Bates Sanitarium in Berkeley.

Norman and Winnie married in the middle of June 1915, and apparently had a happy and passionate union. But they had little more than one good year together. Tuberculosis found its way from the hospital wards into Winnie's lungs, and she began a two-year decline that ended in February 1919. Clyde cared for her as long as he could, but she lived her final months in a sanitarium near Pasadena. Clyde's heart never healed. Winnie was his last romantic relationship. He refused to speak of her. Many of his later friends and climbing partners never even knew he had been married.

During his years with Winnie, Clyde did not return to the Sierra. Photographs show the couple by the sea, with the rocks and breakers of California's northern coast their backdrop. But with Winnie gone, Clyde flung himself back into the mountains as if he hoped to close his wound by force, a psychological cauterization performed with cold air and granite. Or perhaps his map simply remained tilted in that direction and when his mooring line was cut he gravitated to his natural place.

His appetite for mountaintops was voracious. During one stretch in the summer of 1923 he climbed thirty-six peaks in thirty-six days; during his first years in the Sierra he climbed hundreds of mountains in all—more summits than most see in a lifetime. Clyde climbed in winter and summer, on rock and snow, up historic routes and untried peaks; he used skis, snowshoes, hobnailed boots, and rubber-soled shoes; there was no time of year or type of climbing he avoided. He sought out the mountains in all their moods.

Stories began to spread of a gruff loner who could climb, carry, and eat more than any other mountaineer—man or bear. Clyde strenuously denied the latter charge, particularly in the face of the oft-repeated tale featuring him consuming forty flapjacks. (He insisted that the pancakes in question were small and that they multiplied with each retelling.) But he had a sly sense of irony, and it's hard to know if he actually disliked the story or whether it was even untrue.

For all the talk of Clyde's physical qualities, he was a medium-sized man. He stood five-foot-nine and weighed between 140 and 160 pounds, depending on the season and the person doing the estimating. Still, he could freight a load that would cripple most mountaineers of any era. In the summer of 1920—the season he first met Farquhar on North Palisade—Clyde hiked out of Yosemite planning to catch up with the Sierra Club group. He didn't know exactly where he would find them, so he provisioned accordingly; on his way out of the Valley he passed a platform scale used by mule packers, and found that his kit weighed in at seventy-five pounds. On his first night on the trail he camped with a survey crew he had met along the way, and the men were astonished by the size of his pack and the casual way he carried it. They decided to test him. They professed concern that he might not find the club's party, and would starve. They offered to give him food from their stores.

Clyde did not like going hungry. In the stiff tones of his printed voice, he offered this advice: "lack of adequate sleeping facilities and insufficient food or of enough cooking utensils with which to prepare food properly is bound to tell upon a person, however strong he may be." So he freely accepted the crew's food. They offered him more, and he did not turn them down. Of course, backcountry food in those days generally came out of a tin can, so each new gift added a pound or two to his kitchen. By the time the men gave up their game, Clyde's pack had gained twenty pounds. He walked out of their camp the next morning with an undiminished stride and close to a hundred pounds on his back. Asked once why he did not use pack animals, he explained, "I can carry a damn mule faster than he can carry me."

◆◆◆

MOUNT WHITNEY—SIGHTED AND named by King and Cotter on their first expedition through the high peaks in 1864—is the highest mountain in the United States outside of Alaska. It is also an easy hike. By 1884 a trail led to its top and mules had walked the summit. In 1904 another, better, trail was built from the east. Thousands of people made (and continue to make) the summit march. For a time in the teens and twenties there was even a scientific research station on top.

Mount Russell unwinds the curving blades of its ridgelines immediately to the north of Mount Whitney. Its summit is only a mile away and a few hundred feet lower than the highest rock of its famous neighbor. Anyone basking in the view on the summit of Mount Whitney cannot help but see the blank drop of Mount Russell's south face, the sharp cap of its summit blocks, the swoop and slice of its long ridges. And yet, in 1926, after fifty-five years of visitors to Mount Whitney's summit, and thousands of eyes pointed north, Mount Russell had never been climbed. That year Farquhar called it America's last unclimbed fourteen-thousand-foot mountain.

What was the mountaineering clan waiting for? Despite the proximity to Mount Whitney, Mount Russell was guarded on all sides by wild canyons and cliffs which the Whitney trail bent away from and avoided. And once past the labyrinths of granite and brush there were still those steep ridges. At least from the short distance between the mountains, they looked sharp enough to split a climber in two if he attempted to balance out along their edges.

At the end of the eastern labyrinth (somewhat tamer now after many years and footsteps), I put down my pack and looked for a place to pass the night.

In the lower reaches of the approach canyon I had tunneled through willow jungles, but here, dwarfed pines and meadows made their last attempts to grip the soil before quitting altogether a short distance higher. Above the northern canyon wall, Mount Russell's long east ridge unfurled across the sky; above the south wall, Mount Whitney's east face shouldered up into a gathering of clouds. Mount Whitney may be an easy hike from the south, but to the east, where the Sierra breaks up out of the continental fault, it presents a half-mile-long row of white granite towers never much less than two thousand feet high. Huge boulders filled the canyon bottom; I could imagine them rolling and crashing down in shuddering impacts while I stood there in the peaceful aftermath. This is one of the world's best places to feel tiny. I wandered through the resting stones hoping for a place to sleep.

◆ ◆ ◆

WHEN I WAS twenty-one I finished my philosophy degree a quarter early so that I could move to Yosemite and climb full-time for the spring and summer. I came back to campus for graduation weekend amid a sea of black robes and proud parents. The philosophy program was small compared to most others, so during the departmental ceremony each of the graduates was presented individually and at length. I remember impressive litanies of awards won, papers published, and offers from graduate programs. As I sat there in my robe waiting for my name to be announced it dawned on me that in my time away I had missed a call for resumés (and even if I had been around to reply, mine had little to recommend itself). When my turn came, my adviser got up and said something along the lines of: "Daniel Arnold has told us nothing about himself. But I spoke to him briefly yesterday and learned that he has spent the last several months in Yosemite, living in a cave." Laughter and smiles all around, I got my paper and ran back to the mountains.

It was true, I had been living in a cave. I had neither the funds nor the disposition to pay for a campsite. And I liked melting away into the boulder fields, away from the smoke and noise and regulations. Back in my granite home, I could hear the laughter when I settled in at night—and it had a kindly sound. These were parents who had accepted that their children were not going to be doctors or lawyers, and maybe to them a philosophy degree seemed like the appropriate preparation for a season spent living under a rock.

Granite doesn't make dim black caverns like limestone. Its caves are not dank holes. Caves in the Sierra are more like stone lean-tos, and this makes them airy and light with good roofs overhead but wide outlooks on three sides. A tilted boulder is best, one that's been planted in the ground with one side at an angle. Down in the canyon between Mounts Russell and Whitney, the stones seemed to have landed with my needs in mind—every boulder seemed to shelter a hollow space ready-made for a tired climber.

The Sierra is filled with good places to spend a night. The land is clean, the surface materials are choice; flat granite shelves offer fine sofas and bed frames while the flood-gravel and pine needles provide the cushions and mattresses. Clyde had hundreds of first-rate spots marked in his mental atlas of the Sierra, and he returned to them when he found himself nearby, like favorite rooms in a rambling old mansion. As one friend put it: "Norman was not just visiting the mountains or passing through the peaks. He lived there!" Certain prime locations received special names. The "Palace Hotel" overlooked North Palisade and its glacier, and Clyde liked to say that the view alone was worth fifty dollars.

Another spot, in a sunny gap by a clear running creek in the hills above the town of Bishop, he called the "Hospital." Apparently, three weeks of dozing there on the warm ground, listening to the creek and the songbirds, could cure any ailment that he carried up to it.

Back among the boulders in the canyon below Mount Russell, the weather closed in and I moved into my latest home. Soon, rain splashed and ricocheted off the stones and pines, and I watched the show from inside my snug cave. Night closed in but the clouds continued hosing down the mountains, filling the air with a damp, mellow smell as if the land were exhaling after a long breathless moment. I put myself to bed, and, except for a mouse who shared my shelter and scuttled across my nose in the night, I slept solidly beneath the sound of the rain.

◆ ◆ ◆

IN 1924 CLYDE became the principal of Independence High. He took the job to be close to the mountains—Independence was just a few houses and streets in the Owens Valley, but the Sierra crest filled the sky to the west and he could hightail it to the peaks every weekend and whenever he had a day or two free. In fact, this habit of Clyde's made for an uneasy relationship with his patrons. The citizens of Independence seemed to think that their principal should be a man of the community, attending church and Friday night functions at the schoolhouse, not vanishing into the hills to play lumberjack or mountain climber or whatever it was he did up there.

Around this time, Clyde and Farquhar struck up a regular correspondence. Though they walked the Sierra via different paths—Farquhar through his papers and libraries, Clyde by spending every unfilled minute hoisting his boots up toward another summit—they shared the same consuming fascination with both the spirit and substance of the mountains. Along with his letters Clyde provided Farquhar with articles for the *Sierra Club Bulletin*, while Farquhar occasionally sent Clyde a backpack or an ice axe or some other necessity because Clyde rarely had any money.

Clyde climbed all summer after his first year at the job in Independence. He summitted forty-eight peaks during those months, half of which had never been climbed before. Afterward he wrote to Farquhar, "I sometimes think I climbed enough peaks this summer to render me a candidate for a padded cell—at least some people look at the matter in that way." And then, with his typical dry understatement, he added: "However, I get a lot of enjoyment from this . . . form of diversion."

The next year followed the same rhythm. Clyde spent nine months attempting to corral and educate his rowdy students and then plunged back into the mountains as soon as the spring semester ended. He hiked up over Kearsarge Pass (the closest pass to Independence) and worked south, climbing the peaks that took his fancy along the way. He camped for a week or so just below Wallace Lake, one of his "hotels" and a particular favorite for trout fishing. The lake was high and his views spectacular—out over the headwaters of the Kern River and across to the Kaweahs and the Great Western Divide. The mornings were clear and great masses of cottony clouds puffed up over the western mountains each afternoon. The camp itself was comfortably situated in a grove of foxtail pines. He spent his days climbing and fishing and staring at the giant peaks and tiny flowers and at all the colors and creatures in between.

Clyde spoke with several different voices. On a climb, when he had a partner, he had a notoriously short fuse which could be lit by a minor infraction against his personal code of efficiency and proper mountain craft. He could also be encouraging when guiding novices—though he might complain bitterly about their shortcomings later, particularly if they were female. I suspect he never forgave Winnie her weakness for dying and leaving him alone, even as he continued to love her. He seems to have projected his inner expectation of disappointment onto women in general. Around a campfire, after a plentiful dinner, particularly in his later years, he could be a superb storyteller and liked to claim that he was nine hundred years old and had been born in the Eocene. He was a gruff, cantankerous, irascible wit who could spin a comic yarn, or read aloud *The Odyssey* in the original Greek, or let loose a "blast" of "loud and pithy profanity" when circumstances demanded it.

In his written work he has another voice entirely. Sometimes he seems to be self-consciously channeling Muir's most prosaic passages of blank landscape description, except that Clyde's mountains tend to hide behind words like "striking" and "beautiful" and "interesting." He often wrote about himself in a distant third person, as if the very idea of a human perspective would be distasteful to his pen. Many of his early essays are formulaic, with the concluding paragraph mirroring the first, and the interior following an order like a checklist. For a man who was so deeply human, it may seem strange that he purposefully stripped his personality from his words. But on this score he diagnosed himself: "I seem to write well, but do not get enough of the dramatic and human interest 'stuff.' This may be partly because I am very much afraid of exaggeration and am primarily interested in the mountains themselves." He mistrusted himself to stand between his reader and the summits.

Back at the camp below Wallace Lake in the summer of 1926, Clyde had other projects in mind besides fishing and staring at the peaks. He had chosen the spot because it brought him within striking distance of Mount Russell. He had crept around the mountain the previous fall, studying its faces and ridges, looking for a climbing route. On his reconnaissance trip, from the top of Mount Carillon, he had concluded that Russell's long eastern ridge offered the most hopeful route to the summit. Still, he hardly seemed optimistic about his chances. Examining the ridgeline, he noted that it was "too deeply gashed to permit one to follow its crest"; not only was it a narrow knife-edge, there were gaps where the rock simply fell away. But he thought he saw a skinny ledge winding along the northern front of the mountain, just below the ridgeline, and his hopes followed this shelf even though he could not see its entire length or even where it ended.

On the morning of June 24, he left his camp and hiked up through bare-rock basins high above the tree line. Norman understood the plan of this topography; he could read the round excavation tracks of a glacier as easily as he could a page of Virgil or Cicero. In all his years Clyde never stopped being a student, despite his uneasy relationship with universities. With his attention devoted so closely to the Sierra he came to know its geology—and its birds, flowers, trees, and other habitants—with an easy and neighborly intimacy.

The final basin, an austere expanse of gray rock and snow, was circled round by four shark-fin-shaped peaks. The largest of these, nearly a mile from end to end, was Mount Russell. Below the mountains, Tulainyo Lake pooled its waters on the basin floor. Its shores had no wood for fires—and its waters had no trout for dinner—but still the lake put a hook in Clyde and he returned to it many times. Something about the thin air, and the wide expanse of metal-gray water and gray talus and jagged, circling mountains, makes the scene otherworldly, like a place you might find in an old adventure story about the moon. "Lying in a shallow basin," he wrote about Tulainyo, "scooped out by a long since vanished

Tulainyo Lake (12,802 feet)

glacier . . . it is the highest lake of its magnitude in the entire United States." It "possesses," he continued, "an air of remoteness and isolation not often encountered." Still, Clyde found life on its talus beaches. On the occasions he returned to Tulainyo he saw tracks and scat and sometimes a glimpse of a little herd of bighorn sheep—one of the shyest of all Sierra travelers—who roamed the area in the summers. Clyde liked the mountain sheep because they climbed the peaks (he found their droppings on the mountains around Tulainyo), and since he could not imagine what they would be eating up among the bare peak-top rocks, he concluded that they must feel the same kind of attraction to the summits that he did.

Above the lake, Clyde scrambled up to the col between Mounts Russell and Carillon, and lumbered through the talus toward his mountain. After a short distance the solid blade of Mount Russell's east ridge rose up out of the piled blocks on which Clyde stood. "The route ahead looked formidable—at times, impossible," he wrote. "To the south the wall dropped abruptly; to the north, after descending at a steep angle for a few feet, it fell away sheer." Between these twin drops snaked the ledge, and he had no choice but to follow it wherever it led.

He climbed out along the shelf, and it gained altitude parallel with the ridgeline above, while the empty air piled up below him. Short cliffs and blind corners blocked his way, but each time the ledge threatened to end, a good handhold or hidden traverse allowed Clyde to carry on, and the ledge never quit him altogether. "The way opened up as I progressed," he wrote. "There were always enough protuberances and crevices to afford secure handholds and footholds." In fact, the route unfolded so smoothly that the mountain seemed more welcoming than fierce, as if all Clyde had had to do was knock on the peak's forbidding-looking door in order to be greeted and led up to the summit.

It makes for tidy history that Clyde should have climbed this peak, the last fourteen-thousand-foot mountain of the era. Why had no one done it before him? The mountain simply looked too improbable. But Clyde never seemed to be intimidated by a mountain. So long as he had a good hold for a few fingers it did not trouble him to have a stomach-fluttering drop below and an uncertain way forward. At a time when climbers gravitated toward chimneys and gullies because they offered a certain kind of enclosed security, Clyde pushed routes up proud faces and ridges, windy haunts that others had not dreamed to try. He once said, with his usual straightforward logic, "If you are certain you can make it without difficulty, it shouldn't disturb you whether it's ten feet down or ten thousand." His words could be the credo of a modern soloist. In his own era, the attitude led him up steep rock and ice that had looked impossible through the eyes of his predecessors.

Clyde rambled on along his ledge, enjoying the views and the solid stone the mountain offered him. "Now and then I came to a gash in the ridge through which I looked with a thrill down vertical cliffs, hundreds of feet in height, to the basin below, and beyond to the flanks of Mount Whitney." The mountain had proved willing, but that hardly made the topography benign. The edge was very near on all sides. "In case of an inadvertent slip," he wrote, "the mountaineer runs the risk of having free and rather expeditious transportation down over the cliff."

Clyde's ledge brought him to the eastern summit. A few hundred yards farther on, a second summit stood slightly higher, with another narrow blade of rock stretched between the two. "The whole summit, in fact, is nothing more than a knife-edge with a high point at either end," Clyde wrote. He traversed the final ridge between the summits and then heaved himself up onto the highest rock.

He might have celebrated—after all, he had just wrapped up the first ascent of the highest and wildest unclimbed mountain left in the Sierra—but he made no mention of any shouting or happy gesticulations. Given his personality he probably did nothing of the sort, but even if he had, he would have been disinclined to share it in print. The mountains always came first and last. Many years later he recounted a conversation with editors who had approached him about writing an autobiography: "I told them plainly that I did not know of any subject on which I was less interested in writing than on myself." So, when Clyde described reaching the summit of Mount Russell, he faded away, letting the summit, and the mountains, take all the glory.

It was just such an eyrie as delights the heart of the mountaineer. Only a few feet in diameter, the summit drops away vertically to the south and west and at a very steep angle to the north. The view was superb. To the south across a narrow cirque rose the precipitous eastern front and northern flank of Mount Whitney . . . Beyond, to the southeast, was an array of craggy mountains, and westward across the wide basin of the Kern were the stately and imposing Kaweahs . . . To the north the eye followed the crest of the Sierra as far as the Palisades, with Goddard, Darwin, and Humphreys looming hazy in the distance.

◆ ◆ ◆

DARK CLOUDS HAD already swallowed the horizon, and were gnawing on the mountains to the west by the time I reached the col between Mount Russell and Mount Carillon. It was an eerie, monochromatic day. The lake, the stone, the clouds, the invisible air itself, all bled shades of gray that mingled together. When I developed my photographs later, the mountain seemed to be dissolving in the sky. The sharpest color in view lived inside the black clouds stalking the peaks, and I knew I would be racing them before long.

Up on the ridge, I watched through the gashes, like windows, as the clouds wrapped themselves around Mount Whitney and the mountain disappeared. But I still had a little time; a column of lighter gray held out above me, and my summit had not yet been snuffed out. The granite in my hands felt superb— clean, compact rock with true edges that hardly noticed my weight. I rushed on. I could feel the storm flexing its muscles above me. I'd like to think I was invigorated by the atmospheric tension—but probably I was just afraid of getting squashed.

When I reached the top, my time was already about up. I took a moment to look around, mostly at black clouds and gray air. Enormous square stones pushed their heads up out of the mountain around the summit. From the distance, Mount Russell's ridges had looked razor-sharp, but up close the geometry ran more rectangular, the mountain constructed with outsized blocks of articulated rock. The sky fell, a black layer pushing down on top of me, though not yet within striking distance, and it was time to go.

◆ ◆ ◆

THE MOUNTAINS BREWED up a storm for Clyde as well. Those cottony clouds that had puffed up in the west every afternoon during his stay at Wallace Lake? While he sat on his summit watching the peaks, the clouds turned the color of charcoal, and individual clots detached themselves from the mass and tumbled by his summit. Soon, the whole front began to advance on him.

He had a decision to make. He could descend the way he had come, knowing the climbing would give him no trouble but that the time it would take to follow the ridge might be enough for the storm to catch him. Or he could attempt a rib of rock running directly down the north face of the mountain—a new route, which he knew nothing about, except that it was far steeper than what he had already seen. He stood on the eastern summit, staring down the upper portion of the unknown way, imagining what he would find down there. If he misjudged it, if he met a holdless stretch or a drop he could not skirt, he would have to climb all the way back to the summit in order to regain the east ridge, and by then the storm might be in full blow. But he chose the north rib anyway, because it would take him down out of lightning range, and, more likely, because it would be more interesting—and therefore more to Clyde's taste—to throw open another door on another side of the mountain.

Right away he found himself wrestling stone of a strange new disposition. Instead of traversing along his ledge, going with the grain of the mountain, he had to lower himself from shelf to shelf, sometimes leaping down past blank cuts of granite. "The joint-planes of the rock were rather far apart," he wrote, "and it was sometimes necessary to make a rather long drop in getting down from some huge block." He must have known that each drop threw up another barrier behind him if he were forced to backtrack. But he hardly seemed to worry—in fact, he seemed to enjoy himself and the sensation of dangling his body over the edge. Meanwhile, the clouds broke around the mountain: "the storm passed harmlessly by, with only a momentary gust of snow." The snow did nothing to slow him down; Clyde did not recognize a little wind-driven frost as a reason to stop climbing.

Eventually the mountain did make Clyde pause, at least for a moment, by doing exactly what he had feared it would. "A rather formidable wall appeared to bar farther progress," he wrote. "On one side was a vertical cliff, on the other a steeply shelving slope." He could not slip around it, and he certainly did not want to retreat back up to the summit, whether or not the storm had declared itself innocent. So he took the cliff straight on, "by an assortment of gymnastic maneuvers familiar to every rock-climber." I'd like to have been there to watch his gymnastics, to see his square body—an "animated block of granite," Jules Eichorn called him—stretched out between planes of stone, fingers grasping holds, heavy rucksack denting his shoulders without weighing him down, ubiquitous Stetson campaign hat jammed on his head.

Back on the ground he galloped home—that is, back to the Lake Wallace room of his Sierra home, a place far more home-like for him than any building he inhabited down in Independence. "I sped down a snow-slope," he wrote, "hurried onward along a stream, past a lake, and safely reached my camp in the grove of foxtail pines near the base of Mount Barnard."

◆ ◆ ◆

LOOKING DOWN OFF Mount Russell's eastern summit, down the scales of steep rock jutting endwise out of the north rib, I had to admit that the idea of descending this way would not have occurred to me. Clyde's most impressive quality as a mountaineer may well have been his perfect comfort among the mountains. He possessed a degree of confidence in his hands and his judgment that could be taken as a sign of insanity but for the fact that he was always right. Instead, he simply seems to have seen more than the rest of us, piloting himself through wild rockscapes with an innate sense of what the mountain would offer to one who looked in the right places.

I dropped off the summit ridge and followed Clyde down through the overlapping shelves and gaps of the rib. I ricocheted from rock to rock and swung down off square cliff tops, losing height fast while the storm fell down on the mountain. I know just why Clyde called the climbing gymnastic. Hanging from rails in the granite, I'd kick a foot out to find the next shelf, rocking through the motion to free one hand and reach down to join my toes, then repeat the whole sequence again to pass the next gap, finding huge shelves for hands and feet always just within reach. While the east ridge had been almost genteel—the

The genteel east ridge of Mount Russell unfurling across the sky

classic "sidewalk in the sky"—the north rib belonged in a monkey cage for the entertainment of the primates.

The ground came too soon. I had forgotten my destination and forgotten the storm; I was too busy playing on the rocks. But down on the talus floor of the basin I saw that clouds had swallowed the summit, and I raced on toward the shores of Tulainyo, where the moon-lake rippled against the stones in the wind. Lightning touched a nearby mountain and a fountain of thunder spilled down off the rock and rolled around the basin. I dashed up to the col east of Mount Russell as more lightning whizzed and popped through the heavy air, and then I was down below the ridge and out of range.

I churned down talus and scree, enjoying the sounds of the clamor above and behind me. All at once water filled the sky, rain slapping down with force. The rain streaked the air with vapor trails—or maybe they were only the afterimages of the flying drops. Either way, the view out across the canyon looked suddenly submerged, as if I had walked into a lake. I was soaked, but it didn't matter. In fifteen minutes I was back in my cave, and I spent the afternoon warming up, drying out, and watching the rain.

◆ ◆ ◆

So WHAT WAS Clyde doing with that pistol and cartridge belt on North Palisade? In fact, he owned close to twenty handguns, in a range of sizes and calibers, carefully packed away in metal boxes when not in use. "Of my few possessions," he wrote, "among my most cherished are a considerable number of pistols and revolvers." The small ones were for plinking, varmint killing, and small-game hunting. In the Sierra foothills his favorite gun was a Colt Woodsman .22, which he wrote about often and with considerable affection—probably this was the gun that Farquhar saw strapped to his hip on North Palisade.

At least as a general principle, he followed the rules forbidding shooting inside national parks, though this did not prevent him from carrying his pistol, at least in his interpretation of the law. Outside of the parks was another matter entirely, and Clyde was a very good shot. One episode, recorded in his typical scrawl of green ink, illustrates both the steadiness of his hand and the contours of his mind. It was a sunny June day and Clyde found himself "lounging" in a shady stand of aspens on the east side of the Sierra above the Owens Valley. The woods and a nearby meadow were filled with birds. "Among others," he wrote, "the jubilant notes and songs of wren, grosbeak, orioles, meadowlark and robin could be heard and from the nearby mountain slope came the flute-like call of the plumed quail." Norman lay there for a time, letting the birdsong flitter around him. Then a Cooper's hawk flashed past and landed in one of the aspens. Clyde reached for his pistol, took a couple of steps to open up a clear line, and shot the hawk out of the tree. "As a result of this shot"—he concluded with satisfaction in his essay titled "Revolvers and Pistols are Sometimes Useful"—"there will be more robins in the meadow, orioles in the tree and quail in the mountains."

Clyde reported it as a fifty-yard shot, and he was not one to exaggerate. He chided some for believing that handguns could not be used for hunting and instructed them to practice. He also conceded that killing carnivores would upset the natural balance of an ecosystem—he was not unaware of the new ideas of environmental stewardship emerging at the time. But he brushed the worry aside. "As soon as man enters a region the balance of nature is disturbed," was his answer, and his meaning is clear enough. Since human presence will disturb the land anyway, why not disturb it in a way that makes it better? For Norman Clyde that meant more songbirds and fewer hawks. He simply shot a pest that upset his preferred order of things, and that was all the justification necessary. Despite his time spent in Muir's Sierra, man was still at the center of Clyde's conception of nature and the universe.

Norman's firearms have some grim stories, made more so by the offhand manner of the telling. He kept his heavier guns for self-defense, arming himself against the empty roads of eastern California and Nevada. In the event of a "hold-up," he explained, "a reckoning would probably have to be made with a blazing .45 . . . In case of need I do not want a pop gun." Another story—frustratingly brief—comes tumbling out as an aside in an essay on another subject. Using the same tone with which he dispatched the hawk, he wrote about the one time he fired his guns in self-defense. He mentioned a lonely desert and necessity and then: "There was no law officer to resort to in the affair. I had nothing to depend on to protect two defenseless women, but a handgun in either hand, and when the menacing party began to shoot I did likewise, with the result that the former was silenced, in very summary fashion."

Clyde had sharp edges that were never smoothed away. He needed a lot of space around him, even if just for the purpose of reading Goethe in German with a pistol in reach and a mountain at his back. But the frontier had long since left California behind, and Clyde often seemed disappointed with the people and towns left by its passing.

The Halloween incident of 1928—two years after his ascent of Mount Russell—yanked out the last few pegs holding Clyde to the routines of city life. The story has been repeated by so many people in so many ways that the details can be hard to make out now. What is clear is that Clyde got wind of the project of some local teenagers to vandalize the school as a prank, so he stationed himself there to wait for them. Sometime after dark they arrived in a car, and Clyde shot at them. No one was hurt, only scared, and the kids fled the school. Whether Clyde warned them off first, how many shots were fired, and whether a shot actually struck the car, all change with the teller of the story. Clyde said he fired only to drive them away; one of the girls in the car, in an interview many years later, claimed that a bullet went all the way through both sides of the passenger space.

The people of Independence rose up against Clyde. His habits had never pleased them in the first place, and now they had righteous anger on their side.

Some simply wanted him ousted, others wanted him arrested. In the end, he was offered a choice: resign his position at the school, or stay and have legal action brought against him.

Clyde thought about fighting the school board in court. But with so much ill-will built up against him, he did not see how he could win, and he thought his defense might cost four or five hundred dollars, which he did not have. So he resigned. Clyde had always been critical of the locals in the Owens Valley—now he felt angry and wronged, and it must have galled him to have been shown the door by those whom he considered small-minded and uneducated. "I have little but a feeling of bitter contempt for the people of Independence," he wrote to Farquhar a week after the shooting. "All the thanks which I get for protecting the high school from vandalism was to be threatened with a suit for shooting within town limits and charges of unprofessional conduct." In another letter to Farquhar, several months later, he continued in the same vein: "A considerable portion of the people there are beyond the pale of civilization. As I look at my own case with some perspective and some inquiry into the law—California not Owens Valley law—it was little more than a disgusting frame up by a bunch of ignorant rubes."

A brief time of stability for Clyde had ended. With his position at the school had come a pattern of living—every year, nine months of work in a town with a home, followed by climbing in the summer months. Now the future was entirely unclear again.

For a certain distance, Clyde's story cuts a parallel track to William Brewer's. Brewer also took refuge in the mountains after the death of his wife. But Brewer, after his four years in the wilderness, returned to his former life, pulled back by the friends and family he missed and the academic calling he had never questioned.

Clyde had no similar ties. He felt burnt out—and burned—by his experience with schools. "I do not care particularly whether I ever teach again, if I can find something else congenial to me," he reported to Farquhar. But what would be congenial? He was forty-three years old, and his callings—cutting wood, climbing mountains, reading the literature of past generations—hardly amounted to much in California in the Roaring Twenties. Besides, if he wanted to do those things he could just as well lodge himself at Third Lake and glance up at Temple Crag every time he turned a page.

Clyde was not yet quite ready to abandon the world below the mountains. He would make one more effort to find his place in it. "I shall probably remain here several weeks," he wrote Farquhar from Independence at the end of November 1928, "and then go to Los Angeles to look for another position." But if he thought that a city like Los Angeles would be the right place to discover congeniality after three years spent in sight of the Sierra, he was mistaken. Some part of him already knew this. The very next sentence of the letter reads: "I do dislike to leave these mountains."

·14·

Norman Clyde + Norman Clyde Peak

[JUNE 1930]

Norman Clyde Peak (13,855 feet) and Middle Palisade

CLYDE WENT TO Los Angeles in the spring of 1929. At the University of Southern California he began, tentatively, to work toward a principals' credential. Misgivings about his location and purpose troubled him right from the start. "Whether it is wise or not I don't know," he wrote Francis Farquhar that March, "as I dislike to spend further time and money in more preparation for a profession which I may abandon." Farquhar suggested that he look into Park Service work and offered to introduce Clyde to his friends in Sequoia, Kings Canyon, and Yosemite. But Clyde balked at any work—no matter how ideal the location—that would occupy his summer and constrict his freedom to climb. By the middle of June he had left Los Angeles and was already trying to return to the Owens Valley, this time with an eye on a position starting in the fall at the high school in Bishop, a town forty miles north of Independence. This job failed to materialize—at least for him—and he left California for the Canadian Rockies on a climbing expedition later in the summer.

When he returned from Canada, he found himself with no work and no money. "Matters," he wrote to Farquhar, "have come to a crisis." He returned to Los Angeles, ostensibly to hunt for a position, but spent his days writing and waiting for something to turn up. He used Dawson's Bookshop as his address. The owner, Ernest Dawson, was a friend of Clyde's (the two had climbed the Grand Teton together in 1926, a few weeks after Clyde's ascent of Mount Russell), and Dawson often helped him out in the years that followed. Dawson's son Glen summarized their relationship this way: "Norman Clyde used Dawson's bookshop—my father's shop—as his mail office and his storage shed and his library and his bank account." Clyde would "admire a book in German or French or something and my father would say, 'Oh, take it along with you,' you know . . . and probably gave him a ten-dollar bill when he was down." Clyde remained hopeful in his letters—in fact he was often incredulous at his difficulty in finding means to live by—but the Roaring Twenties were sputtering to a halt. And then the crashing markets of October 1929 announced the beginning of the Great Depression and the scarcity of work became a permanent state of affairs.

Here, Clyde's story splits wide from William Brewer's. The Sierra was not just a place for Clyde to recuperate and reflect on his life, as Brewer had done in the forests below Mount Shasta. Each step along Clyde's path—Winnie's death, the school shooting, his own unease at academic institutions, the economic collapse of the country—pushed him farther from cities and deeper into the mountains. As an older man, tracing the route he had taken, he once said, "I sort of went off on a tangent from society and never came back."

In the coming years he began to find caretaking work at the lodges built above the winter snow line at the peripheral edges of the Sierra. He returned to one in particular, Glacier Lodge, just down from the Palisades, winter after winter. The owners paid him to live there in the months when the snow was deep and the buildings shuttered and no tourists came to fish or hike or breathe the mountain air. The winters were long—five or six months of dark, cold seclusion. "Like a bear, I went into hibernation, along in autumn, the precise time varying," he said. Occasionally he would make the trip down to Big Pine for mail and groceries, but once the snow set in he had to haul his supplies up on skis. One friend, Smoke Blanchard, who knew Clyde well in the latter half of his life, tells a story of how he went to visit Clyde at the edge of spring one year, when the snow was beginning to melt, and Clyde "complained of almost losing his power of speech" from having been alone so long.

During the dark months, Clyde wrote feverishly, often by kerosene lamp, sometimes with the snow piled above the windows of his cabin. More and more he hoped to make a living as a writer, and he filled boxes and cartons with hand-written essays about the mountains. He liked to call writing "scribbling," an apt description of his penmanship, which is so cramped and indistinct that I had to use a magnifying glass and a forensic mentality to decipher many of his sentences. Probably he also used the word as a belittlement to mask his disappointments.

When the snow did melt, Clyde had to move out of his cabin at Glacier Lodge to make way for the tourists and workers who came for the summer. Most years the owners turned Clyde out early because he had made such a mess of his cabin and it took days to put it right. It wasn't dirty so much as disorganized—decades' worth of tattered mountain gear and clothes mixed haphazardly with notebooks, photographs, and manuscripts. Poverty and personality had made Clyde a pack-rat and he was rarely willing to throw away anything that might have future use. The nest he made of a living space was a considerable embarrassment to him. Apparently tidiness was a virtue he esteemed even if he could not manage it himself. Despite his temper and manner, he was not at all a crude man. Smoke Blanchard's wife described him as "a thorough and complete gentleman— honest, reliable, dependable, kind, with an old-world courtesy."

In the summers, between his own excursions, he worked occasionally as a guide and a woodcutter for climbing parties. He also filled a singular niche; as the popularity of mountaineering surged in the late 1920s and '30s, the number of climbers who went missing increased as well, and then people turned to Clyde because no one knew the Sierra as well as he did. He had an uncanny ability to find bodies. Somehow, upon learning a little about the climber, Clyde could put himself into the missing man's thoughts, and then deduce what the mountains had done with him. Other climbers of the era took a rather ghoulish interest in Clyde's process. One described it like this:

He would lie down with his head on a rock and study the face of the mountain where the man went up, and he would study the character of the climbing surface, and he would pick out the place where a climber of this kind would fall off. Then he would go up there and find the corpse. This was a service that Norman Clyde rendered to society, because people were very anxious to find their sons.

Clyde's essays about his searches read like mysteries. Clyde is the clear-eyed detective leading his reader through a briar patch of clues that he alone can navigate: the angle of a boot print, a stained handkerchief, a cryptic note in a summit register. He always called his searches "quests."

As befit his character, Clyde could be scathing toward climbers who had made mistakes; and he tended to be brusque about dead mountaineers in general (he once described to *Time* magazine the trail left behind by a tumbling climber: "First you throw your hat. Then your knapsack. Then your clothing"). But he also spoke with a mixture of compassion and matter-of-factness that could be a comfort to devastated parents, and when he put himself on the case of a disappeared climber he stuck with the search to the end. In all, he only once failed to return either a live climber or the location of the remains.

Pete Starr, the young lawyer who died on Michael Minaret and is still entombed on the mountain, was Clyde's most famous find. A gathering of twenty experienced mountaineers began the search, but after several days obligations in the outside world called the climbers away a few at a time. The apparent hopelessness of the pursuit in such rough country drove away the rest, until only Clyde continued on, running methodically through the conclusions he could generate from the traces Starr had left behind. After Clyde found the body, many of the climbers reassembled in the Minarets with Starr's father, Walter. While the others watched from Michael's chimney, Clyde and Jules Eichorn climbed up to the ledge on which Starr had landed in order to wall off his body with rocks.

Walter Starr wrote Clyde a substantial check in thanks. (He also gave Eichorn, who was only twenty at the time, a scholarship to attend the University of California.) Clyde felt uneasy about the gift, though he needed the money badly, and he wrote to Farquhar to unburden his conscience. "Had I a good income," he explained, "I would not have accepted it, but as matters have been, I thought that it would not be out of order to do so."

• ◆ •

WHEN CLYDE WAS pressed to choose favorites, he would admit that North Palisade stood out to him above all the other mountains in the Sierra. So in spite of the meager pay and his frequent clashes with the owners, he returned each season to Glacier Lodge, which was tucked right into the past diggings of the Palisade glaciers. On any day, as long as a storm wasn't barreling along so violently that even Clyde was housebound, he could ski off his doorstep and up a canyon onto the glacier below his favorite peak.

But there was another mountain, also in the Palisades, which enjoyed at least as much of Clyde's affection. North Palisade was hidden from view by a bend in the canyon; in fact, the best views of North Palisade can really only be had from right up near the snout of its glacier. The other mountain, which did not even have a name in those days, looked straight down a parallel canyon to the south and towered over Clyde's cabin at Glacier Lodge. Blanchard sets the scene: "The cabin in the canyon was deep in a grove of big trees, but one window— the one by his bed—offered a day-and-night view of the most spectacular peak standing boldly at the head of the canyon." For half of Clyde's year, this one mountain watched over him and kept him company. Blanchard wrote that a surprising share of Clyde's photographs (and Clyde took thousands of beautiful photographs) were of this mountain, many taken from his porch or framed by the surrounding pines.

The mountain grew up out of the ridge running northwest from Middle Palisade; Clyde, in fact, called it the west peak of Middle Palisade, though it had nearly fourteen thousand feet of elevation of its own and from the cabin it looked to be the taller of the two. Its sharp summit point seemed to poke into the belly of the sky. A long ridge slicing down toward the canyon divided the mountain in two triangular halves; its faces on either side were complex and steep, and in the winter they tended to be streaked with snow and frozen waterfalls—dark rock overlaid with bright whites and pale blues. Because of the photographs and the cabin and an overall sense of ownership, the mountain was officially named Norman Clyde Peak just after Clyde's death, though climbers by then had been using the name for more than thirty years. Blanchard offered a few words he felt described both Clyde and his mountain: "*wild, aloof, dignified, difficult.*"

◆ ◆ ◆

AN ELECTRICAL FIRE burned down the main lodge in 1999, though small outlying cabins still exist for the use of visiting hikers and fishers. The view is unchanged. The north and south forks of Big Pine Creek tumble down their canyons and converge with a rush of sound and spray. Troops of pines and aspens march up alongside the creeks, alternating to fill their preferred altitudes. Clyde's mountain still sharpens its summit against the sky at the head of its canyon, while the other strange shapes of the Palisades—the fins, horns, and spires of dark granite—grip each other shoulder-to-shoulder in an unbroken chain to the left and right.

I followed the braids of Big Pine Creek's south fork past islands of talus and thickets of willow on up toward the mountain. I was a week later than I had intended. At the end of May, a strange east-moving storm had swallowed the Sierra, dumping feet of new snow on the mountains. When I arrived it still looked like winter on the high peaks; the mountains all wore clean white lace. I hiked up through cliffs next to a long cascade where the creek funneled through a crease between hills of stone. At the top of a buttress the mountains erupted on the horizon, much closer than I had expected, ice twinkling on steep, dark rock shot through with veins of quartz.

Would I trade human company in order to see these mountains every day? To watch morning light become evening light and January light become February light? I see Clyde in his cabin hunched over his writing table in the dark, trying to make his words stick to the mountains while forgetting how those same words sound in his own mouth. After a day of fighting to squeeze granite out of a pen, I've opened my mouth and been surprised to find a senseless mumble roll out. The weight of half a year alone in the mountains could be enough to squash my voice like a stone on a snail. Clyde practically invited creatures into his cabin in order to have contact with other live things. He allowed, for instance, a ring-tail—a raccoon relative that looks like a hairless cat with a bottlebrush tail—to inhabit his attic, even though (or perhaps because) the little beast took a liking to hissing and thrashing around in the dark at four in the morning. The pleasures of deep loneliness seem to come with the risk of drowning in it.

And yet the idea of a life with the mountains, with nothing to come between the granite, my eyes, and that brimming rush of awe and joy that stands my hair on end, remains seductive. I think (or maybe I fear) that if I were to become unanchored like Clyde I might drift into the mountains as he did. To me, the strongest warning against Clyde's path is the simple fact that Clyde himself, who seems to have been better equipped than anyone to handle solitude and the unrelenting pressure of raw beauty, struggled so hard to find his place in the borderland between the mountains and civilization—and only surrendered to the peaks after exhausting the possibilities in between.

I walked through benches of forest and meadow watched over by the Palisades. Sometimes I could see nothing but the immediate pines and cliffs; other times gaps offered glimpses of the mountains shooting up into the sky. From inside the forest, the peaks hardly looked real. The wood showed the compromises of a living creature bending to circumstance. The mountains looked razor-sharp and aloof in comparison.

I turned south toward Clyde's mountain and walked through a meadow walled in by talus at the bottom of a canyon left by the mountain's northern glacier. Higher, cliffs with broad ledges circled the grasses and flowers. The mountain's lowest snowfield stuck its foot through a talus chute between the cliffs. A young creek melting right out of the snow tripped and crashed down over the bare rocks. I clambered up the cliffs, past impromptu waterfalls and bunches of purple Jeffrey shooting stars, looking for a flat place to sleep with a view of the mountain.

I found a bench above the snow guarded by an ancient foxtail pine. I filled my bottle from a waterfall and settled in. Stray clouds washed over Clyde's mountain from the west and the summit pushed through them as easily as a spear through cotton. Every few minutes, rocks tumbled off cliffs to the north, making cracking and growling noises as they slammed past their downstairs neighbors. Fresh avalanche tracks marked the glacier. In tight places the falling debris had gathered and worn grooves through the permanent ice. Lower down, two slabs of snow, a third-mile-long each, had slipped loose from a lower layer, slid a few hundred yards, and then stopped in formation. The mountain looked grumpy and ill-tempered, and I thought of Clyde emerging from his cabin in the spring.

◆

CLYDE LIKED THE snow. "Two things," he wrote, "greatly enhance the beauty of the mountains—snow and clouds. The Sierra Nevada is much more impressive in winter, spring, and early summer, when the range is set off by an abundance of snow." After all, he had grown up on Canadian winters, and in the Sierra he could have clean, beautiful snow with temperatures that rarely even managed zero, instead of the mind-dimming squeeze of forty-below.

The climbers who preceded Clyde in the Sierra avoided snow as much as possible. Most of their routes stuck to dry rock. No doubt this was sensible since the Sierra holds an embarrassing tonnage of the most wonderful stone on the planet. But climbers who confined themselves to granite lost seven or eight months of the year, and Clyde had too many mountains to visit to operate on that schedule. Besides, even in the summer he found interesting snow formations to explore, particularly in steep chutes, called couloirs, where narrow tongues of snow were shielded from the sun. On the higher Sierra peaks, couloirs that face north or east—and therefore shade their snow in the heat of the afternoon—will keep snow year-round. But the snow still warms during the day, and partially melts, before refreezing at night. Day by day as spring turns to summer, the snow consolidates into what climbers call alpine ice: hardened snow varying in consistency from Styrofoam to glass.

Clyde had relatively few close calls in the mountains—far fewer than one might expect given his record of hard climbs and first ascents. But his occasional near-accidents generally involved snow. Clyde liked to expound upon prudent mountain practice, and he freely pilloried those who made mistakes, but he was not himself particularly cautious, or at least he had so much faith in his own physical power that he put himself into some extraordinary situations.

On a day in May, while descending a peak above the headwaters of the Kaweah River, he found himself trudging down through deep snow. He discovered that if he sat down hard enough against the top layer of fresh snowfall he could induce it to slide, and this seemed to him to be a method of free transport. "Weary of forcing my way through the snow into which I sank knee-deep," he wrote, "I decided to start a slide and ride it down the mountainside." His plan worked perfectly well, until, in the middle of his second manufactured avalanche, an enormous rolling snowball sped up from behind him and knocked him flying forward and under the river of snow he had been floating atop. "As I was shoved along," he wrote, "the sucking action of the snow, half sliding, half rolling, was very pronounced, but the speeding volume of snow was not sufficiently deep to do any harm except to half smother me." He swam up through the snow-current, righted himself, and stayed with the slide long enough to catch up with his hat, which "had gone gaily bobbing up and down" below him. Hat retrieved, he exited his avalanche and decided against any further "freewheeling" descents.

Another time, on the Palisade Glacier, Clyde was descending toward camp when he slipped. This should have been the moment when he rolled toward the pick of his ice axe, dug it into the snow, and arrested his fall. But he lost control of the axe and dropped it, so that he had nothing to use to stop his plunging slide. Up ahead he saw a rapidly approaching crevasse which he could not hope to avoid. So he leaned back and sped up, and just before the lip of the crevasse he leapt up in the air, hoping his momentum would carry him beyond a likely fatal fall into the guts of the crack. His plan nearly worked. He sailed over the gap—twenty-five feet through the air, by his estimate—but one crampon caught in the lip on the far side and his ankle twisted underneath him. He spent the next month and a half recuperating at the Palace Hotel, camping, cooking, and doing his other chores on his hands and knees. "I'm a rather stubborn individual," he said when asked about the recovery, "and I decided I wasn't going to walk until the ligaments had a chance to heal. And I didn't, and the result is that the ankle— except for a slight weather twinge once in a while—is the same as it ever was."

It's easy to dwell on Clyde's reckless side—the stories are just so good. But most winter days did not involve an avalanche or hair-raising fall. On most days he'd ski up from his cabin to a view of the mountains, take some pictures, and then swoop down the open snowfields on his sticks, enjoying the pillowed curves of snow and the cold, clean air flying past. One of his favorite stories from his winter backyard came from a day he saw a hummingbird. "It was so surprising," he wrote, "as to be almost startling to see this tiny bird, preeminently the bird of flowers, fly past, the nearest flower miles away and several thousand feet lower, in an area where not a single one would spring into bloom for weeks to come." Though Clyde liked hummingbirds under any circumstance, the contrast of the vast white cold with this little flashing jewel of life thrilled him. Clyde was especially fond of animals that went up into the mountains for no apparent reason but to be there.

◆ ◆ ◆

WHEN CLYDE FIRST started climbing Sierra couloirs in the mid-1920s, no one had ever taught him "proper" ice-climbing technique. He simply carried a woodsman's hatchet and chopped steps and handholds for himself in the hard surface of the refrozen snow. On his trips to the Canadian Rockies in 1928 and '29 he learned how to handle a mountaineer's ice axe from the Swiss guides who operated there. This tool was a vast improvement over Clyde's hatchet, but the basic procedure was essentially the same. Unlike a hatchet, an ice axe could also be used for self-arrest—that rolling stab of the pick into the snow which Clyde would have executed on his way toward the crevasse below North Palisade if he hadn't dropped his axe.

Step-cutting was the high art form of the era, though its heyday had already passed by the time Clyde picked up his first ice axe. Experienced mountaineers developed a steady rhythm: a few measured strokes with the axe made a space for one hobnailed boot, and then, without a pause in the beat, the next step would already be taking shape, and the next, and the next. The technique carried climbers across glaciers and up steep ice from California to the Himalaya. Whether cutting wood or ice, Clyde was a formidable machine with an axe in his hand.

It comes as no surprise that Clyde had particular opinions about what sorts of nails should be used on a mountaineering boot. A lumberjack's screw caulks, for example, were a menace to the life of a mountaineer, and though Clyde grudgingly admitted that Hungarian cone heads would do, he thought they were too soft and tended to "skate" on rock. Instead, he championed tricounis, a Swiss nail made from steel that looked like a section of a thick, serrated knife, attached blade-down on the boot sole. He developed a preferred pattern for attaching the nails which he diagrammed and distributed to his friends. A rumor circulated in the Sierra Club, particularly among the younger set who were developing their own ideas about fast-and-light mountaineering, that Clyde carried an anvil with him on the trail to repair his shoes. Clyde always denied this, though he did admit to a shoe repair kit and he clearly enjoyed his reputation as a man with a bit of mule in his blood. Blanchard wrote a gentle parody of Clyde on the

Norman Clyde (Photo courtesy of Bancroft Library)

subject: "It's not true that I carry an anvil in my pack. Only this little piece of iron to put in the heel for replacing tricounis. That's something these go-lightly boys never think about . . . And anyway, if I want to carry a rock in my pack to keep me steady down the trail, that's my business."

Around this same time, probably on the 1928 trip to Canada, Clyde also had his first opportunity to use crampons: paired sets of spikes on metal frames lashed to the boots for steep snow and ice. These spikes were what caught in the snow and twisted Clyde's ankle beneath him at the end of his flying leap across the crevasse. As crampons improved, the days of step-cutting waned; now climbers kicked their crampon points directly into the ice without needing to cut a step first. Clyde used crampons in the Sierra at least as early as 1928, though he had a natural affinity for hobnails and never entirely gave them up.

Muir might have brought Clyde to the Sierra, but Clyde did not intend to travel the mountains with a pocketknife and a sack of bread crusts. Clyde believed that the right choices of equipment could mean the difference between walking out alive and ending up head-down in a snow hole or broken up on the rocks. He was "convinced," wrote Blanchard, "that there was at least one right and proper piece of equipment for every conceivable situation that might happen to a man in the mountains, and he believed in having it ready to hand—if possible in duplicate." So he had three different lengths of skis, and he carried several pairs of boots for different conditions on any given climb. Clyde lashed his entire kit to an enormous Trapper Nelson wooden packboard, though in the 1950s, he switched to the new aluminum-frame backpack manufactured by Kelty. He enjoyed specifying that he used the same size and model as the one chosen by the American Mount Everest expedition; mind you, when the Americans took their Kelty packs up Everest in 1963, Clyde was then seventy-eight years old.

Clyde had one foot in the past and one in the future. He liked an old book, a nailed shoe, and a heavy axe to chop wood or ice. But he was also ready to experiment with equipment and learn new methods. Change was on its way. The future of climbing—the ropes, pitons, and belay techniques developed in Europe—had reached Canada, Colorado, and Wyoming. The future was closing in on California. Clyde and Farquhar and a few others who had traveled to other mountain ranges had already seen hints of what was coming. But until it actually arrived, climbers in the Sierra, though their numbers had multiplied over the years, kept on pretty much as they had since the days of King and Muir. For Clyde, in 1930, that meant his first full year of living at elevation in the Sierra during all twelve months and all four seasons and uninterrupted by teaching obligations or frustrations in Los Angeles; a full year of rock, ice, snow, summits, trout, and solitude.

◆ ◆ ◆

I DIALED THE fifth number on my list, but the conversation was no different than the first four.

"Hello, Nevada Custom Leather."

"Hi, uh, I'm looking for boot hobnails—do you carry any?"

"You want what?"

"Hobnails. For the bottom of boots. The old mountaineers used them—like cleats, only for ice and snow."

The voice on the other end of the line disappeared for a moment. My list of leather and boot shops crisscrossed the western states, but I wasn't having any luck. The voice returned.

"Well, we have hobnails, but people mostly use 'em to dress up German tank boots."

Hmmm. Somehow, I didn't think those would be up to Norman's specifications. I thanked the voice and rang off.

Then I found a Canadian company catering to high-end lumberjacks who actually carried tricounis. Fantastic! I said. How much would they cost? Five dollars per nail? Not including installation? I consulted Clyde's diagram, did the math, and realized I was looking at a three-hundred-dollar bill just to get started. Poverty spoke up, I kicked the bald tires of my truck, and decided I would have to make do without. Unfortunately, Clyde isn't the only insolvent climber in this story.

◆ ◆ ◆

IN EARLY MAY 1930, Clyde returned to the Palisades. He still entertained vague thoughts of returning to the U.C. system to finish his credentials, but he attached no definite timeline to the idea. In his letters, the future becomes increasingly distant and blurred. He climbed Temple Crag five times in a fortnight, then moved up the south fork of Big Pine Creek to a lake in the talus below Middle Palisade's glacier.

On June 9, he woke early and crossed the same forested benchland that I walked eighty-five years later to reach my camp below his mountain. The morning had still barely begun when he turned up the canyon excavated by the resident glacier, which now hid itself higher in a granite pocket, sheltered by the stone it had once shaped. The mountain, unclimbed and nameless, "stood in magnificent perspective, a massive, sheer-faced peak with its lower portion in deep shadow

North Couloir, Norman Clyde Peak, in late summer

but with summit glowing in bright morning sunshine." He did not hope to climb straight up the steep rock above. It "was obviously so sheer," he wrote, "that a direct escalade was out of the question." Instead he turned his attention to a couloir on the right edge of the north face. He thought that if he climbed the snow to the top of this chute he might then be able to traverse the crest of the mountain to its summit. He reached the snout of the glacier, which was frozen hard, and

352

clanked up the ice in his hobnailed shoes, cutting a few steps where the angle pushed back enough that his nails would not hold on their own.

Above him, the glacier steepened, and dark rock fogged in by dark shadows shot up out of the ice. The couloir climbed up through the one weakness between the cliffs; to the left and right a curving wall of mountain wrapped around Clyde and the glacier. The dragon-backed summit ridge ran atop that wall, and though Clyde could see a half-mile length of it, he could not see the summit itself, which was even farther east. At the joint between the couloir and glacier, Clyde reached the lower lip of the bergschrund, a large crevasse split open where the body of the glacier pulled away from the stationary cliffs and snow above. He found a snow bridge spanning the gap, and pounded it with the spike of his axe to test whether it would hold his weight before crossing it to gain the foot of the couloir.

The snow in the couloir was softer than what he had found below, even though it was steeper. He rarely needed to cut steps now, "being able—in most places—to 'kick-in' sufficiently to avoid using the ice-axe except as a staff." For a thousand feet he kicked a line of steps up the couloir. The cliffs turned in toward him and held a narrowing alley between their walls. When he reached the notch at the head of the couloir he had already climbed most of the height of the mountain. But the summit was still far to the east, a distant point hidden by a chain of spires like thorns on a branch. He had hoped to climb directly there along the crest of the ridge, but one look from the top of the snow told him otherwise. "To my surprise and chagrin," he wrote, "I discovered that it is so cut up by deep gashes with sheer walls below them that to follow it to the summit, then little more than five hundred feet vertically above me, would be impracticable."

◆ ◆ ◆

TWILIGHT SMOTHERED THE peaks and my camp below the mountain. The temperature dropped. The previous night had been cold, and tonight, at eleven thousand feet, with a level view of the glacier, I expected the drop to be much steeper. The wind ramped up until it roared. It was not a howl; there was nothing plaintive about the noise. It felt like an enormous engine in the sky rubbing down the rocks and trees. The foxtail pine guarding my ledge had a rough night, its branches pinned back with hardly a lull to straighten itself, though I suppose it had seen worse. Down among its roots, with a stone wall shielding one side, I was protected from all but a few gusts that reached through to fluff my beard and let it be known that I could hide all I wanted but the wind would still find me. I stretched out on my back and peeked up through the quivering tree branches at the stars—the only part of the night holding steady against the wind.

A few minutes before four in the morning, I leapt out of my sleeping bag, dripping wet. The air had become thick and warm and the wind had stopped. I had gone to sleep cold around the edges, but now I was covered in sweat. The temperature had jumped; it felt like it was fifteen degrees warmer than when I had drifted off in the rumbling wind. Maybe a new front had come through, or maybe summer had just decided to arrive all at once. In any case, I did not welcome the change; climbing unstable slush is nerve-wracking and slow. I fumbled with my boots in the dark and stumbled off toward the mountain as a thin blue line opened on the eastern horizon.

My boots had no nails, but I did have a wood-handled ice axe which was probably twice as old as me and seemed to weigh twenty pounds. I felt a little guilty, like I had kidnapped a museum piece and was pressing it into service, but it seemed solid enough once I got used to the extra weight and length. On the way through the Owens Valley I had stopped by the Eastern California Museum in Independence where they have a few of Clyde's things on display behind glass: a crusty, battered Stetson campaign hat, a pistol, some books, and an ice axe. The old axe I'd brought along was virtually identical to the one in their display case. Its stainless steel head held the top of the shaft with a pair of flanges; the bottom of the shaft was split and the spike rammed directly into the wood with an outer collar to hold it in place; it looked like it should be relaxing on someone's mantelpiece.

The snowfields below the glacier were firm but not frozen—either it had never hit freezing in the night, or the warm air had come through early enough that the snow had softened. Still, I needed to chop steps in the steeper places, particularly since my boots had nothing sharp on the soles to grip the snow. I had decided I would chop steps for as long as I could stand it. My step-cutting was clumsy; admittedly, I haven't had much practice. I'm sure Clyde would shake his head or worse. I blasted away with my lumbering axe, shards of ice flying in all directions, making progress through luck and violence rather than through any semblance of measured technique.

The glacier lifted up its head and the surface snow became granular and icy. A long, steep slope ran away beneath me. My footing became less solid and my steps shrank as the ice turned hard. Balanced on slippery nicks, I tried not to pop my boots loose with the recoil of my axe stroke. Visions of a wild slide began to press urgently into my imagination. I could hear Clyde growling out a posthumous critique of my equipment and method. I cut a larger step and slipped on a pair of old, rudimentary hinged crampons. As Clyde put it: "For secure footing—rubber on rock, steel on ice." I did not want to become one of his "quests." My crampons were purposefully old and dull (though not as old as what Clyde would have used in the late 1920s), and I still had to chop steps sometimes in order to make them stick, but at least I no longer had that fluttery feeling every time my boots squirmed on the ice.

I passed the piled-up remains of the slab avalanches I had seen from below. They were even more impressive up close, long corrugated fields of snow blocks piled waist high. Three feet of the stuff would be plenty to drown in if it buried you—there was nothing soft and fluffy about those piled-up blocks; they looked more like an acre of fast-drying concrete poured down the mountainside. I thought of Clyde riding his avalanches. Underneath his gruff, old-man-of-the-mountain airs hid a boy still enamored with big, crashing things and a young man with too much spirit and too little fear to remain on the sidelines and watch.

I reached the bergschrund but found it narrow and inconsequential. The Clyde Glacier is dying along with so many of the Sierra glaciers. It has too little mass anymore to bulldoze down the mountainside and open up its crevasses. I passed the bergschrund and it was still early and the cliffs held on to thick layers of shadow, but lines of sunlight snuck through gaps up higher and streaked across the upper reaches of the couloir. I hurried on, not knowing what would be released by the sun. A nice thick skin of stiff snow does wonders for holding a mountain together, but when that skin thaws, rocks and blocks of ice slip loose. This is why alpinists wake up in the middle of the night, and I began to think that four o'clock hadn't been quite early enough.

The snow inside the couloir was a strange collage of different species of snow and ice patched together without any clear pattern. One moment I would be scratching out a hold in a crust of rotten, granular ice; the next I'd swing my boot to kick a step and have my whole foot disappear into slushy powder that barely held my weight. In the soft sections I pushed the entire shaft of my axe into the snow and held on by the head, using the axe as an anchor against the chance of my steps collapsing. Then the shaft, being wood last varnished before I was born, would freeze in place and I would have to wiggle it round and yank it back out. It particularly enjoyed sticking hard and then coming free all at once, leaving me fighting not to topple over backward out of my steps. A few corners of my mind found this all very amusing, but I was breathing hard and trying to gain height quickly because small ice chunks kept zinging by with a sound like tearing fabric and I had no faith they would stay small forever.

The couloir bent a few degrees to the right around a buttress of rock, and when I turned the corner I could see its top, a floating gap in the mountain wall. I kicked my last hundred feet of steps and had a seat on a rock ledge in the gap— the only bit of flat ground in a jagged world of rock and ice. To my left, the couloir spilled down the mountainside; to my right, cliffs alternated with snow down another chute to the south. In that direction, the interior of the Sierra opened up for the first time, a land made all of mountains still covered in snow by the recent storm. In front and behind me cliffs shot up to the ridgeline. The air had been still all morning, but the wind hadn't died; it had only been pushed up to a higher stratum of atmosphere. Now it tore through the gap, plucking my breath away and chilling me down.

Where had Clyde brought us? It was certainly an unlikely place from which to climb a mountain. Teetering cliffs plastered with snow hemmed me in on all sides. None of them looked appealing to touch, let alone climb. I couldn't see the summit, though I knew pretty well where it was, and there seemed to be an inordinate bulk of mountain between me and it. I ate some chocolate and raisins for a much delayed breakfast, but it was too cold in the wind to stay for long and I had to move.

◆◆◆

CLYDE PROCEEDED BASED largely on elimination. Going back down the couloir would not take him any nearer to the summit, so that was out. The mountain's north face was "obviously impossible"; he could see it plainly and it consisted of dark, ledgeless sweeps of sheer rock. The ridgeline itself was also out, being too jagged and broken to offer much hope. So that left the chute to the south, which looked wholly unlikely, and wasn't really going in the right direction, but at least it wasn't pointed away from the summit and that was good enough for Clyde under the circumstances. So he climbed down in that direction past piled snow, perched boulders, and cliffs, which required, as he put it, "careful maneuvering."

In his description, Clyde makes the climbing from the top of the couloir to the summit seem so simple and straightforward that it comes across as a short jaunt of a half-hour with time to stop and admire the polemonium. He climbed down a few hundred feet, then he traversed eastward along the south face of the mountain to a broad gulley. He climbed up the gulley until he reached a rightward branch and then, with a wave of his ice axe, he was on the summit ridge. The only indication he gave that all was not quite so easily done was to admit that by then the afternoon "was already well-advanced." I did not take this to be a good sign given Clyde's early start and the speed he liked to move in the mountains.

In fact, Clyde's route zigzags across the entire southern face of the mountain. All in all, with the start up the couloir, it is the most circuitous route to a summit I have ever followed. Which is not to say it doesn't abide a certain logic. The mountain has barricaded itself behind long ridges and twisted spires, so

Clyde worked with the spaces in between to piece together his route. He acted like a water droplet rolling back and forth through cracks in the rock on its way toward the center of the earth, only he traveled in the opposite direction, pulled along by the gravity of the summit.

I climbed down two hundred feet and prepared to make the prescribed eastward traverse. Of course, I was buried inside a narrow chute and a wall of snow-caked rock blocked the entire eastern tack to my left, so it was hard to see how that was going to be possible. Ever the optimist, I assumed that the cliffs would dutifully kneel down somewhere as they must've to offer Clyde his traverse. They did not. Above and below they looked the same: steep and snowy, with loose, evil-looking blocks bulging out through the snow. I was going to have to climb directly up and over the cliff wall, so it seemed pointless to descend any further. I stopped and eyed my options. A string of ledges in a corner seemed less likely to drop a block on my head than elsewhere, and a snow fan at its base offered a boost to the first hold. I kicked steps up the fan until it felt likely to collapse, and from there I reached up, brushed three inches of snow off the first hand-sized ledge, latched it with my fingers, undid my crampons with my other hand, and eased my boots off the snow and onto the rock.

With the recent storm I had been sure that the north face would be snow-covered, and it was—which was fine, since on that side of the mountain I planned to climb snow in the couloir anyway. But I had thought that the south face, the sunny side of the mountain, would have melted out and been bare. The same principle had worked against me in the Minarets. There I had climbed up the dry southwest side of the mountain only to be surprised and turned away by lingering snow on the last few hundred feet of the northeast face. So it seemed only fair that today I would climb snow on the snowy side and rock on the sunny side.

But the mountain had some other priority in mind besides fairness or my personal druthers and in its wisdom decided that half of the snow accumulated on the south face should stay and the other half should be turned to ice. Probably I am being ungrateful. No doubt it was beautiful, the kind of place a painter would willingly follow a madman to reach. (At least that's the state of mind I imagine for the painters who followed Muir into the mountains on his way to Mount Ritter.) The new snow on dark rock, the glittering streaks of black ice pouring off the cliffs—the effect was almost hypnotic. But the fingers-and-toes reality meant scrappy climbing that unnerved me enough to want to thoroughly damn art and beauty and the idea of following madmen.

For twenty feet I wrestled with the corner, locking off one arm in order to use the opposite hand to brush away snow, boots finding fragile edges to scuff against between my excavated handholds. At the top of the corner I pulled myself onto the first full-sized ledge, which was a mixed relief since it gave me a stance but was covered in a pool of ice. Apparently, any flat surface large enough to stand on here also had the tendency to collect afternoon melt that puddled and froze overnight. I shuffled along a system of ledges, struggling for handholds good enough to protect against the inevitable moments when my feet shot out from under me.

Above the iced ledges I reached a bank of angled snow leading to the top of the cliff wall. I waded through it until the snow became too steep and loose to hold my weight. For the last few feet I climbed blocks jutting out through the surface—stones which I could only hope were firmly attached to the mountain. They held, as they usually do, but I was much happier to be above rather than below them.

Up on top, the cliff revealed itself to be a narrow ridge with another cliff dropping down the opposite side. Below the ridge, ledges led into a gulley which headed up toward the summit crest. I tried climbing down off the ridge in three or four different places, only to be blocked by holdless bands of steep rock. Giving up, I pushed down through the snow on the ridge crest, losing another five hundred feet before finding a ladder of shattered blocks that provided escape. I had lost almost as much elevation as I had gained climbing the couloir, and the sun was outpacing me, the morning slipping away.

Crumbling ledges cut across smaller ridges and funneled into the central gulley. The ledges thinned when they passed the blade-ends of the intermediate ridges, making for touchy moves around corners where protruding jags of rock seemed intent on toppling me backward. The skeletons of last year's polemonium carpeted the stone, hooking their roots into the most unlikely-looking chinks. Many had a few green fronds growing close to the rock below the dried husks of their other limbs, a first sign of the sun waking them from their winter sleep. Each plant must represent a stroke of luck. I saw one flower perched right on the edge of a cliff and another growing horizontally out of a seam in a block and it was hard to imagine how their seeds found their way in the first place. In a month there would be hanging fields of polemonium on Clyde's mountain, and then in two months they would lose their color and tatter in the wind. Clyde was particularly fond of polemonium—they were his most reliable companions on the high peaks. And the flowers seem to like Clyde, too. Right next door, Middle Palisade hosts healthy bouquets of polemonium here and there, but in high summer Clyde's mountain grows them so thickly the air stiffens with their scent.

Iced slabs ran up the bottom of the gulley, the ice making a quarter-inch veneer of glass above the granite. I tested the ice only once to see if my boots would hold it, and ended up sprawled out on my hands and knees. The ice felt more than frictionless; it felt as if an invisible hand had grabbed my heel and pulled the moment my foot made contact. I traversed back and forth to find dry rock, jumping ice runnels when they were too wide to clear with a normal step. The slabs themselves were polished smooth, and I imagined huge avalanches blowing through the gulley during the spring melt.

By the time I regained the height of the couloir the mountain steepened and I branched right. For a thousand feet, Clyde traversed above the south face and below the summit ridge, connecting ledges and plowing through snow banks. I followed along behind him, nosing out the throughways and occasionally being turned back by dead ends. The mountain began to run out of rock and I could sense the summit coming even though I still could not see it. Above me, stone had been replaced by sky, and I could feel the air moving with the light freeness it acquires in its own domain. I turned a corner and the mountain's highest spire pushed itself up from a small saddle covered in snow.

The snow had been in the sun all morning and I sank through it to my hips while meltwater trickled through my pants and my boots fell through gaps between unseen boulders below the surface. For the first time since leaving the couloir I could look back to the north and east, at the lacework of creeks falling out of the mountains and into the desert beyond. The north face of Clyde's mountain fell down and down, the threshold between rock and air a square edge just a few feet away from the trench which I was cutting through the snow. The last length of ridge emerged from the snow and raised a narrow stairway to the summit. It was steep without being hard, but a fall would put a climber right back on the East Clyde Glacier a half-mile below. Clyde called it "an interesting, strenuous but short scramble."

The summit was a small island of rock in an ocean of air. The wind continued to blow hard to the south though the sun had become bright and strong.

Middle Palisade looked, from this angle, like the front tooth of a giant shark. To the west a vast congregation of snow peaks lifted their gleaming white heads into the sun. Clyde stopped at last for a rest. "I sat down," he wrote, "to eat luncheon on the brink of the northern precipice." Rosy finches played around him, gregarious little birds which often joined him on summits. I had a seat, too, and ate a little food, though I felt unusually worn-out and hypoxic. No finches came to join me. (Maybe I didn't have the right kind of lunch.) But that was all right—I could see Clyde sprawled out on the summit rocks, his Stetson tilted low over his eyes, and I could see his birds fluttering close by him to retrieve the crumbs of lunch he poked their way.

◆ ◆ ◆

CLYDE CLIMBED MOUNTAINS until the end of September, but eventually the season had to end, even for him. In October he emerged into the Owens Valley and began prodding at the future again, only to find that it remained impenetrable. In a letter to Farquhar he summarized his thoughts: "I am in a 'don't know where I am going but am on my way' frame of mind." He took the caretaking position at Glacier Lodge at the beginning of November and set to work "getting in a huge wood pile." In fact, for a month, he seems to have done little else than chop wood and lay in supplies.

The months turned dark and cold and Clyde retreated into his cabin where he turned his attention to setting down words. "I have gotten down to doing a considerable amount of writing," he told Farquhar in early January, "and have placed a considerable amount of non-pay stuff." Still, he sounded anything but optimistic. "I do not know," he continued, "whether I shall be able to write for the moraes of the general public. I am afraid, in fact, that I am in danger of becoming a cynic, both from experience and observation."

Over the years Clyde filled boxes and boxes with manuscripts—hundreds of thousands of words about the mountains and mountaineering. For many essays he wrote a dozen or more drafts. But only a slight fraction of his work ever saw the inside of a book or magazine. He never gave up, but the response to his work frustrated him immensely. He blamed editors first and foremost. "Most editors don't seem to have done anything but look out over city roofs," he wrote to one friend. "Judging from the junk that some of them publish as written material it looks as if one's chance of having them accept any of his work is in inverse ratio to his knowledge of what he is writing about." But the deeper wound seems to have been his inability to make general readers connect with his vision of the mountains. He wanted to present the mountains *his* way: no drama, no hyperbole, no people at all, if he could avoid them, and certainly not "a hopped up personal story," as he described the wants of one editor.

Unfortunately, by self-consciously stripping so much from his writing, he flattened his voice until little remained; he wrote with so many constraints that he wound up trying to squeeze his mountains into tiny prose boxes. However, in his letters and in essays on small subjects he was more relaxed. The humor he brought to a trout chase, the wind he piloted through a meadow, the shrewd aspersions he tossed at those who aggrieved him (he once described the owner of Glacier Lodge trying to "crayfish" out of a deal they had made), all reveal his eye and wit more than many of his essays about peaks and summits.

Clyde did have some successes in his writing career, though never enough to please him. An editor at a magazine called *Touring Topics* published a series of his essays, which, decades later, were put together in a collection called *Close*

Ups of the High Sierra. At the end of Clyde's life another slim volume of his work appeared with the title *Norman Clyde of the Sierra Nevada: Rambles Through the Range of Light.* The editor of that collection, Dave Bohn, figured that Clyde had waited ten years for the book to be published. That was the amount of time passed since Clyde reneged on a contract with Prentice Hall because he decided the publisher wanted to include too much autobiographic foolishness in a book Clyde thought should be about the mountains. In truth, Clyde had probably been waiting three or four decades for the book he had in his mind to finally become real.

In those long dark hours with a lamp, pen, and piece of paper, Clyde must have thought of Winnie a great deal, even as an older man. When *Close Ups of the High Sierra* was published in 1962, Clyde, then seventy-seven, asked that it be dedicated to her, a request finally honored in a reprint years later. Winnie died before he had the chance to do much more than feel the potential of their future, but apparently she remained with him all his life.

Is it better to have the company of ghosts during lonely hours, months, years? I'm not sure whether the visitations of a wife who died much too young would be a comfort or a source of pain, and Clyde never bared this part of his inner world. When Brewer wrote about his wife and their home during his lonely times in California, his words suggested longing and sadness and the sense of a sequestered exorcism in the wilderness. But Clyde returned to the cabin in the snow year after year, where the silence and solitude could only have encouraged Winnie's appearances, and he didn't go mad or tunnel into despair. I like to think that she provided him with some warmth in the cold.

◆ ◆ ◆

I CLIMBED DOWN off the summit, through the snow, past the iced slabs, past the brittle husks of the polemonium. The ladder of shattered blocks carried me back up to the ridge where the snow had been turned to deep fluff by the sun. The moves down off the ridge—over the pools and drips of ice, which were still shadowed and frozen, and down the steep corner—gave me the creeps, but my hands stayed attached to their handholds and my boots never slipped. I returned to the gap at the head of the couloir with my body relaxed and only my mind wound tight.

I had hoped to be back down the couloir early in the day before the sun had worked on it for too long, but the sun had finished its own ascent and was on the descent by the time I caught up to it. The outer skin of the couloir was a sloppy mess, the next layer down was still brittle ice, and each step sent gooey snow sloughing and skittering away down the chute below. I envied the falling snow its speed in racing down the couloir, and I thought for a moment of Clyde and his avalanches, but the slope was too steep and the underlying ice too brittle for me to have a chance of stopping myself once I got started. So I kept my face turned inward to the mountain and kicked collapsing steps, moving off them as quickly as possible, sometimes surfing a small slide for the distance of a single rabbity heart thump when both my steps gave way at once.

When I think of Muir I see him by Yosemite Falls, in the Valley, the land of water and stone shaped by his glacier-angels; Muir lived there in the sawyer's cabin with his bread and books at a time when Yosemite was still mostly empty. Clyde is in the Palisades, where the snow meets the rock and the summits meet the sky. The two of them are the wellsprings of the era—one at each edge, beginning and end. Muir was the first to understand the rare beauty of these mountains, to bring them to life, to give them their true name, the Range of Light. Clyde could be called a disciple, I suppose, though he needed only the invitation from Muir, in the form of Muir's books; Clyde discovered the mountains, and his place in them, for himself. In the end, Clyde lived the life more fully even than Muir. He spent more months and more seasons in close contact with the peaks; he saw more summits and sunrises. Perhaps he was more single-minded. Perhaps he simply had nowhere else to go. When Muir sent his words out into the world, a chorus of voices—Emerson's, William Keith's, Jeanne Carr's—shouted back at him: *Come out of those hills, mad mountain genius! Share your gifts with the world! You owe your voice to literature, philosophy, religion. Don't squander it on rocks that cannot hear what you have to say.* When Clyde sent his own words down he was met with a silence that said, *Stay where you are.*

It's hard to see another John Muir or Norman Clyde on the horizon. There are no more unknown mountains awaiting a prophet—there's too little unknown left in the world in general for a mind like Muir's to breathe life into stone. And where will the next mountain-climbing hermit come from? We're too mobile. We reach the mountains so fast and return home so quickly that we have no reason, or place, to stay in the in-between times. We crave too much stimulus to be happy staring at the snow for a day.

I kicked my way down through the slop, following the sun-corroded steps I had left from the morning. The couloir opened up and lost its shape. I reached the faint line of the dormant bergschrund and the angle eased just enough for me to turn around and put my backside in the snow. Lifting my heels, I shot down the glacier, gravity finally claiming me. I careened along a half-mile glissade, bouncing and rolling where choppy snow unhorsed me, while the mountain rose up behind and the rocks and trees multiplied below. It felt almost unfair to head home to Ashley and leave Clyde to his mountain, knowing that he must often have wanted to return to Winnie.

◆

IN THE LATE 1960s and early '70s, big changes barreled through the larger world, but nothing much changed in Norman Clyde's. He still lived without electricity, chopping his own wood and hauling his water. In his later years, he inhabited an abandoned ranch house on Baker Creek, still within sight of the Palisades though not quite so far above the winter snow line. He kept rambling his mountains in the summers all through his eighties, until his heart put him in a rest home in Big Pine.

Blanchard saw him frequently in the last few years of his life. After one visit in 1971, when Clyde was having trouble with one of his legs, Blanchard recorded Clyde's reading list: Goethe in German, the New Testament in Portuguese, and a biography of Napoleon in French. Clyde's heart gave out on him in the end, and he died in 1972, at the age of eighty-eight.

Jules Eichorn, Nort Benner, and Blanchard and his son took charge of Clyde's ashes. They hiked up the south fork of Big Pine Creek, up to Clyde's mountain, and climbed its north face. Blanchard ported Clyde in a paper bag in his backpack. They put the ashes on the wind from the summit. "We tossed the ashes," wrote Blanchard, "over the Northeast Face, because that was Norman's side of the mountain." Then Eichorn reminded them that "all sides of the mountain belonged to Norman," so they spread the last of the dust to the west and south.

Blanchard called himself a "firm believer in immortality" even though he considered heaven and reincarnation to both be "powered by the same wishful thinking." In Clyde's case, immortality passed through Blanchard and his son and the other mountaineers of the next generation. "His spiritual self," Blanchard wrote, "lives on in his ideas, which some of us will treasure; in the memories his friends will keep and pass on, by mountain stories, to new generations; and in his contribution to mountain lore, which may live as long as men tromp the Sierra." All of that is true, and Clyde's name is never far from a conversation about the Sierra even today. He is the ideal climber and wanderer, possessed of a devotion to the mountains that is about as close to a pure quality as a person might hope to achieve and still be human. Still, I'm not sure how Clyde would feel about this

Polemonium on Norman Clyde Peak

brand of immortality. After all, this was the man who spent decades scratching his way toward authorship but broke a book contract because his editors wanted him to write about himself. He always put the mountains first and his own voice a distant second. When I think of Clyde in the Sierra he is a surprisingly physical presence; he is there in the holds he touched, the stones he slept on, the waterfalls and birds and flowers he admired.

If a polemonium seed on the wind can find a thumbnail crack in a block of granite at fourteen thousand feet, I have to think that Clyde's ashes could do the same. To me this means that at least a few of the flowers on Clyde's mountain have little specks of him in their stems and fronds and purple petals. I think this small notion of physical immortality would give Clyde pleasure. His idea of a summit celebration was rolling crumbs to the finches who came to greet him; now his body nourishes the flowers that kept him company on the high peaks.

·15·

Thunderbolt Peak: The End of the Era

[AUGUST 1931]

Thunderbolt Peak (14,003 feet) from the Palisade Glacier

NORTH PALISADE'S GLACIER fills the mile-wide amphitheatre at the mountain's feet. The ice is ancient, cracked and seamed with years of sun and storms, covered with rocks thrown off the mountains from above. Its volume is still enormous—it's the largest glacier in the Sierra—but there was a time not so long ago when it was vastly larger, a powerhouse built for muscling rocks down off the mountain and gouging up bedrock. In its prime it plowed up enough rubble to leave a massive moraine running parallel to the mountains, like a barrier reef made of boulders and loose stones.

The snout of the glacier now melts into a round lake at the base of the inner wall of the moraine. Bits at the edge calve off into the water and there are always a few small icebergs drifting back and forth. Nothing grows here. On one side, the glacier runs up toward the wall of jagged mountains. On the other, the piled boulders of the moraine mound up to the sky. The lake has no visible outlet; it drains straight down through the rocks, following hundreds of capillary pathways under the moraine to feed the creeks and meadows on the other side.

The climbers gathered here to learn the future of climbing. Both generations, young and old, were present. Norman Clyde and Francis Farquhar had already invested decades in the mountains; Jules Eichorn and Glen Dawson were both nineteen, but climbing far beyond their years; Lewis Clark and Bestor Robinson, two future Sierra Club presidents, added their apparently inexhaustible eagerness for peak tops and difficult rock-work. They all came to learn from Robert Underhill, their visitor from the East, who had climbed in the Alps and the Tetons and the Canadian Rockies and carried with him the collective experience and knowledge of mountaineers from around the world.

Dawson recalled the scene by the lake under North Palisade: they sat among the raw boulders and Underhill taught them butterfly knots and bowlines and the mechanics of belaying. Dawson knew that everything was about to change; he knew they were "pioneering," as he put it. The possibilities were about to break wide open again; the mountains they were looking at over Underhill's shoulders as they watched his hands work the rope were about to reveal a multitude of new routes up stone that had once looked simply blank and unclimbable.

◆ ◆ ◆

FOR THE SEVENTY years prior to the summer of Underhill's visit, men and women sought out summits in the Sierra. Some traveled singly, others in close pairs or companionable bunches; occasionally immense groups from the Sierra Club traced ant-lines up easier peaks. And yet, no matter how many people surrounded them, no matter what bonds connected them to their companions, each one of them climbed alone. Encouragement might be offered back and forth, descriptions of routes or specific moves given from one to the next, but each individual climbed his own mountain, trusting only his hands and physical cleverness to keep attached to stone and snow. A fall in the company of twenty friends, or with no one around for twenty miles, ended equally badly.

Put a rope between two climbers and they are no longer alone. The individuals transmute into a team, bound together by the cord into which they tie their knots and trust their lives. The rope offers immediate resurrection from a fall, a kind of salvation made to suit the needs of the skeptics and freethinkers who seem drawn to climbing in the first place. Well-matched climbing partners share a marriage of trust that is hard to find in the flatlands, and the rope is the physical manifestation of their partnership. When I tie in with Ashley I can feel her reaching right through the line between us and wrapping her fingers around my waist. We can speak to each other through nothing more than the feel of the rope at either end. Nowadays, a rope strung between two climbers is such a natural image that without it, the climbers look naked and vulnerable. The climbing rope is one of those simple technologies that arrives and changes everything.

◆ ◆ ◆

THE CHANGE HAPPENED suddenly because of California's isolation from the rest of the mountainous world. Before interstates and easy air travel, California was a long way to come for a mountaineering holiday, so visitors were rare. Within the state, other mountain ranges received slight attention for much the same reason. A few Californians had gone north to the Cascades in order to climb Mount Rainier or Mount Hood, but for the most part locals found they had their hands full with the hundreds of peaks in the Sierra.

As 1929 became 1930, no one in California was thinking too much about the future of climbing. Clyde was stuck in Los Angeles, fretting about work and money. Farquhar was focused on the early history of exploration in the Sierra; his contributions to the *Sierra Club Bulletin* around that time looked backward to the beginning, when mapmakers and adventurers were simply trying to understand the geography of the state. But then sometime early in 1930, Farquhar received a letter from the Harvard Mountaineering Club announcing an expedition to the Selkirk Range in British Columbia. Farquhar was a Harvard alum, and as editor of the *Sierra Club Bulletin* and historian of all things great and small in North American mountaineering, he did keep track of climbing excursions all around the continent despite the currents of his own research. On this occasion he found that he wanted more than merely being in the know, so he wrote back to ask if he could join the expedition. Just like Clyde, Farquhar turned to Canada for broadened horizons.

When he arrived in the Selkirks that summer he found himself in elite company. There were twenty college boys led by three men Farquhar's age. Of those three, two had been on Mount Everest expeditions. The third was Underhill, a philosophy professor at Harvard and editor of *Appalachia* (the East Coast version of the *Sierra Club Bulletin*). Clyde himself described the man as "one of the most expert rock climbers in the United States." Most importantly, the Harvard climbers had brought ropes and their working knowledge of the European belay techniques invented to safeguard mountaineers on difficult climbs.

Farquhar was thrilled. Right away he could see the blossoming possibilities for hard new climbs if ropes appeared in the Sierra. He returned home and began making plans. He had always enjoyed guiding others up peaks; now he had the chance to lead Sierra mountaineers, en masse, into the modern age of climbing. He invited Underhill to California as an instructor and gathered as many of the top California climbers as were available. They planned to meet in the summer of 1931 at Garnet Lake. They would start in the Ritter Range and work their way south through the Sierra, learning the new methods and climbing new routes as they went.

The Underhill Camp was set to begin at the end of July, but Farquhar couldn't wait. He had learned enough in Canada to tackle a simple climb using roped belays himself. So, just before Underhill arrived, Farquhar led a small party up a new route on Unicorn Peak in Tuolumne. At the difficult sections they stopped and climbed one at a time with the rope tied around their waists while Farquhar belayed from above, ready to catch a fall should anyone come off. Harnesses were still far in the future. To belay, he wrapped the rope around a spike of rock or around his own body.

In truth, the event had more personal meaning for Farquhar than historic significance. For several years, a lively redhead named Marjory Bridge had been coming on Sierra Club trips and signing on to the climbing parties led by Farquhar. She admired him for his intelligence and gentle command over a mountaineering party. Apparently, he never seemed to notice her, but tied to the same rope on Unicorn Peak in July of 1931 he certainly did. From that day on they climbed together—except on occasions when Marjory wanted to climb something beyond Farquhar's abilities. As it turned out, she had a talent for vertical rock. Farquhar had very happily met his match in a woman who could climb harder, ski faster, and hike longer than he could, a woman who would become one of the new faces of climbing in the coming decade, making hard first ascents in Yosemite right alongside her male counterparts.

◆ ◆ ◆

EICHORN AND DAWSON also met up with Farquhar in Tuolumne for the Unicorn Peak climb. They were young, but both had already been climbing Sierra peaks for years. Dawson had been introduced to the mountains as a boy by his father who, along with being Clyde's benefactor, had a long and enthusiastic association with the Sierra Club and would be made its president in 1933. Eichorn was brought to the mountains by Ansel Adams. In the late '20s Adams was still making a living playing the piano, even as he crossed the threshold to his lifework as a virtuoso photographer. Eichorn was one of his piano students—one of his prodigies—but Eichorn had no money, so they struck a deal in which Adams gave piano lessons and Eichorn helped him wash prints in the bathtub in Adams' makeshift darkroom. They got along so well that Adams encouraged Eichorn to come along on the 1927 Sierra Club High Trip. Up in the Sierra, Eichorn discovered the second great passion of his life, and he was fond of saying: "Music and the mountains; they're the greatest!"

Eichorn and Dawson met for the first time on that 1927 summer excursion, and they quickly formed an alliance. In the coming years they established many hard climbs together, first without ropes then with, as the new decade brought the roped revolution to the Sierra and the boys into their twenties. They approached mountaineering with an appealing kind of brash self-assuredness. After all, they were teenagers when they started. They were strong, gymnastic, light on their feet, and surrounded by older men who must have seemed a little dusty.

A few days after climbing Unicorn Peak, Farquhar left to collect Underhill, while Dawson, Eichorn, and another friend set out on foot for the Ritter Range where the Underhill Camp would initially convene. The young men wanted to arrive early in order to solve a minor controversy in the Minarets. When Charles Michael climbed his minaret in 1923 he believed he had climbed the highest spire in the chain. Four years later, Norman Clyde came to the Minarets, also intending to climb the highest spire. But when the descriptions of their two climbs were compared, it was discovered that they had climbed two different peaks. Neither Michael nor Clyde cared which of the two was actually higher (they were interested in the climbing, not the numbers on the map), but everyone else wanted an official coronation of the highest Minaret. So Dawson and Eichorn brought a hand level up to the top of both Clyde Minaret and Michael Minaret and confirmed that Clyde's minaret was, in fact, a few feet taller. They also climbed a third spire which, following the pattern, became Eichorn Minaret

(Dawson Minaret came a few years later). Then they hurried on to Garnet Lake to meet Farquhar and Underhill.

Glen Dawson is now ninety-five years old. He's the only member of the Underhill Camp still alive, the only voice left from the ropeless era of Sierra climbing. I arranged to meet him at his retirement apartment in Pasadena. After so much time spent reading old letters and staring at black-and-white photographs, I felt a bit strange and tongue-tied talking with a living, breathing mountaineer over salads in the Villa Gardens cafeteria. I asked him how he was holding up, and he said, "I sometimes tell people, the most interesting thing about Glen Dawson is that he's still here." Joking aside, he's in outstanding shape, moving with the ease of a man thirty years younger. His small frame is still spare. Back as a high school kid when he first started climbing he was downright skinny, a look emphasized in photographs when he stood next to Clyde, who appeared to be about twice as wide and a head taller than he was.

Dawson's memory is as sound as his body. The mountains, his climbs, and his partners were all remarkably present in his mind, especially considering that the stories we were reliving happened more than seventy-five years ago. He still speaks with the pluck and pride of someone from a younger generation taking over from an older one. I asked him about Norman Clyde, expecting the usual hyperboles about Clyde's physical strength and appetite for mountains. Instead I got an answer through the eyes of an impatient teenager. "From my standpoint he was slow-moving and cantankerous," Dawson said. "He carried a terrible lot of what I considered junk." Later, Farquhar came up. "He was not a very agile climber himself," Dawson reported, almost apologetically. "But," he added, "he had great enthusiasm." He said these things without any unfriendliness. Dawson's father had trained him to be a fine-book dealer (a profession

Dawson embraced wholeheartedly), and I could imagine Dawson appraising books in a similar way.

Back at Garnet Lake, Dawson and Eichorn returned to the larger group convened to meet Underhill. That summer's Sierra Club High Trip was in the area, so the assembled climbers made quite a crowd. Underhill led teaching sessions around the camp, and then climbing parties went up to practice their lessons on Mounts Ritter and Banner. The two mountains—called by some the King and Queen for their visibility up and down the Sierra and the way they seem enthroned side by side—had been climbed before, of course. The more adventurous of the students attempted new routes up the steepest sides of the peaks. Underhill and Eichorn climbed a particularly hard new route on Mount Banner, turning overhangs and solving a succession of puzzles through blank rock up the mountain's thousand-foot-high east face. The Sierra climbers had plenty to learn from Underhill, but they had surprises for him, too. In the isolation of the Sierra, surrounded by so many vertical miles of beautiful stone, they had developed into bold, able climbers. Underhill had landed among a band of expert rock gymnasts who made up for their lack of mountaineering tools by becoming confident on steep rock whether or not they had ropes. Underhill was particularly impressed by Dawson and Eichorn—he called them "young natural-born rock-climbers of the first water."

Clyde arrived at Garnet Lake a few days after Underhill. Like Farquhar, he sensed the future that ropes would unloose in the Sierra. He knew all too well that there were not many unclimbed peaks of any kind left among his mountains; after all, he had been the one to climb most of the ones that remained. The Sierra's exploratory phase was nearly at an end. Now climbers would focus on the harder, steeper faces of known peaks, pursuing physical and technical difficulty as much as the summit. Clyde understood the progression even as it was happening—the new way climbers would see the peaks and imagine their possibilities. "Among mountaineers," he wrote a few months after the Underhill Camp, "second in fascination to the making of first ascents is the finding of new routes up mountains already climbed, especially if these be difficult." Climbers, he continued, will "turn their attention to new, more arduous ways of attaining the summits of mountains . . . They are forever seeking new problems of ascent against which they may match their skill and strength, puny as these may be compared with the forces of lofty mountains."

Still, there were a few prominent summits in the Sierra that no mountaineer had touched. Farquhar, who had become personally invested in the success of the Underhill Camp, wanted to tackle something high and dramatic that would showcase the new equipment and methods. So he asked Clyde whether he knew of any unclimbed peaks that would prove the worth of Underhill's teachings. Clyde replied with a tantalizing letter a few weeks before Underhill's arrival: "There is a spire on the North Palisade as yet unclimbed which possibly a group of good climbers with an alpine rope might be able to negotiate." That was good enough for Farquhar. With Clyde as their native guide, he made the Palisades the next stop on the Underhill Camp's itinerary.

◆ ◆ ◆

I HAD ALREADY been in the mountains for ten days when Matt and Joe met me at Third Lake, below Temple Crag. I had been on the run, climbing peaks, pushing hard, and felt unreasonably glad to see them. I hadn't seen or talked to anyone in five days, and though I like solitude, my own company was wearing thin earlier than I had expected. Better still, they brought in loads of food, including onions and peppers, while I was down to the dregs of my ten-day supply. It was evening and we got right down to cooking big batches of hot, good-smelling dinner. Between the food and the conversation my brain and tongue began a rapid thaw.

The next day we hiked up to the lake at the end of the glacier. It didn't take long from Third Lake, but we might as well have strolled onto another planet. Layer by layer—through lodgepole pines and scarlet gilia, over creek-side meadows of grass and shooting stars, up past whitebark pines, columbine, rock fringe—we left all the green growing things behind. By the time we topped the moraine and lurched down through the boulders to the lake, we had passed into a place made all of rock and ice except for some shivery lichens and a few brown threads of grass. We put down our baggage by a flat bit of packed dirt surrounded by stones. Mountaineers have camped on this patch of ground for decades. Clyde, I'm sure, slept here. It is the only flat spot worth inhabiting in the entire basin between the mountains and the moraine.

The glacier tilted down at us from on high. The compressed snow of millennia—striped through with blue ice, cracked by crevasses, sparkled by surface crystals—crept imperceptibly toward our camp. Up above, North Palisade and its brethren stood side by side, joined at the hips in a wall of stone. Each peak dressed itself in dark granite and wore a crown of spires. Fingers of ice crawled up the joints between the mountains. All of the summits seemed to stare down at the lake as if it were the focus where their eyes converged.

We convened our own miniature version of an Underhill teaching session. I had brought Underhill's comprehensive article on the state of the art, published in the *Sierra Club Bulletin* the winter before he came to California. The article covered it all, from the appropriate make and length of the rope to team dynamics and the correct position for a body-belay.

Everything that climbers do now has its seed in those pages. Then and now, the system works like this: Joe and I stand at the base of a mountain, tied to opposite ends of a rope. I begin to climb while Joe belays me. When I have climbed up for most of the length of the rope, I stop, and anchor myself. Now Joe climbs while I belay him from above. When the follower reaches the leader, the process repeats itself, or the two climbers swap roles. If Joe falls while he is following, it matters little; belayed from above, he will only fall a few inches. If I come off while I'm leading, with Joe belaying me from below, I will fall a distance great or small (and therefore serious or not), depending on whether and how I have placed gear to protect myself along the way. The devil is in the details. Two years ago Joe took a sixty-foot fall off Temple Crag. Using modern gear, he walked away (continued to climb, actually) with a cut lip and a mind-warping adrenaline high. In 1931 he would have been hauled out in pieces and added to the "grand company" with Pete Starr and the other Sierra ghosts.

On easier ground, Joe and I might climb at the same time, with the rope stretched between us—what is now called simul-climbing. Underhill emphasized this arrangement, a standard practice of guides in the Alps. In his conception of the system there was no running gear between the two climbers, so if it was 1931 and I was to slip, Joe would be expected to brace against the rock and catch me simply by holding on. "Owing to the character of the terrain the question is only one of *checking a slip*, not of breaking an abrupt fall," Underhill wrote. "A leader," he added, "carrying a little spare rope may be able to throw a quick belay over a rock beside him." When I read this to Joe he shook his head because he saw the implications. If I slip and he does not respond quickly enough, I'll drag him off the mountain right along with me—an accident which did in fact occur in the Alps and elsewhere during Underhill's time in the mountains.

Since the Underhill Camp, climbers have taken the basic roped system and innovated every detail so fervently that the mental aspects of climbing have been completely transformed. When a modern leader anchors herself, she places a collection of high-tech, removable pieces which she equalizes and ties herself to with the rope. When Underhill wrote about an anchored climber he simply meant one with a secure stance, or perhaps with a turn of the rope looped around a horn

Matt Farrell on the reading rock

of rock. Our ropes, now, are nylon, made to stretch under load—not nearly as much as a bungee cord, but following the same principle. The stretch of the rope absorbs the shock of a fall (which is why Joe survived his whipper on Temple Crag). Underhill used a manila rope, and it did not stretch. Instead belayers were taught to catch a lead-fall with a dynamic belay. They held the rope wrapped around their hips or over one shoulder, and if a fall came, they were supposed to let the rope slip at first and then slowly clamp down with their hands and bring the rope to a stop. This spread out the force of a fall instead of concentrating the shock into a single jerk likely to break the rope. For even a short fall, the belayer would end up with shredded clothes and bloodied hands, and the leader would consider himself lucky to be alive.

Underhill knew the limits of his equipment, and so in his article he devoted almost as much time to team dynamics as he did to ropes and the belay, with the idea that a smoothly functioning team will not find itself butting up against the breaking point of its gear. To a modern ear, his exhortations sound wonderfully earnest and anachronistic, and we enjoyed ourselves reading bits back and forth. About a second-man named *B* in a three-man party he wrote:

> Nothing could be more erroneous than to suppose that he is momentarily off-duty, free to contemplate the landscape, indulge in a smoke or a bite to eat, or enter into casual and airy conversation with C . . . Any such attitude of carelessness would operate seriously to impair A's morale . . . A leader, struggling alone with difficulties, must have nourished in him the feeling that he is the center of his party's tense interest; that he is every moment, it is scarcely too much to say, carrying with him their hopes and fears. Leave him morally, as he is necessarily physically, alone, and you cut the nerve of his inspiration and enterprise.

Since this was my foolish notion (we three would be climbing with an eighty-foot manila rope I had found at a hardware store), I would be doing the leading. Matt and Joe promised not to indulge in any smoke breaks and to nourish my ego with their tensest interest.

Further down toward the lake we colonized a huge flat rock where we spent the afternoon with our books. The sun was bright and the sky like glass, but the air had too little weight to hold any warmth. When the sun grew too strong on top of the rock we settled into the shadows under its eaves; when we got cold in the shade we put ourselves back atop the rock. The ice floated back and forth across the lake. Stones tumbled down from an unstable bank of the moraine and hit the water with a sound like laughter. We called our roost the "reading rock" but we actually got very little reading done there. It was too easy to stare at the mountains and let our thoughts drift and our tongues wag.

◆ ◆ ◆

FARQUHAR CALLED THE trip to the Palisades their "postgraduate course." The Sierra Club High Trip had ended and most of the Sierra Clubbers had gone home. The group that hiked up to the lake under the glacier was much smaller and more ambitious.

I asked Dawson what it was like to learn from Underhill and climb with him. He said he was a good teacher, "a modest, quiet-spoken person." He must have shown quite a contrast to Clyde's gruffness and loosely bottled exasperation. But Underhill also had a cutting side and a fine sense of irony. As editor of *Appalachia*, he compiled the accident and death reports for skiers and hikers in the White Mountains, and, apparently, he shared Clyde's opinion of those who suffered

such accidents. Underhill's wife Miriam described his attitude: "The people involved were invariably fools. By persisting in the face of bad weather, not having
proper equipment and clothing . . . they richly deserved whatever fate they got."

Of course, Clyde admitted that he was himself "not over-endowed with precaution," and Underhill seems also to have indulged the double standard that
while fools might have accidents in the mountains, he was not a fool, and could
therefore race thunderstorms and shrug off blizzards. In the Palisades, the climbers met ugly weather. They climbed Temple Crag and North Palisade, and each
day the sky grew dark and hail traded off with rain—but no matter; they weren't
fools so they had nothing to fear, and they reached their summits under close
and threatening skies.

North Palisade rises from the center of its glacier. To its left, a ridge curves
down and then back up to Mount Sill, which is built like a ship's prow headed
east. To the right, the west, North Palisade has a twin summit only a few feet
lower in elevation called Starlight Peak. From Starlight Peak, a snaggle-toothed
ridge drops down into a deep notch. Clean sweeps of stone run back up from
the notch on the other side to join a square-shouldered mountain built like a
flying castle. Parapets and towers spike through its roofline, a jumble of granite that's hard for the eye to organize. But from the center a single pinnacle
juts up above all the others. This was the spire Clyde had eyed from the top
of North Palisade and Starlight Peak, the unclimbed summit he had offered to
Farquhar in his letter. It was high and wild, over fourteen thousand feet tall,
just what Farquhar wanted. When he had congratulated Clyde back in 1926 for
having climbed America's last fourteen-thousand-foot mountain, Farquhar had
lumped in Starlight Peak and the western spire with North Palisade. But climbers' eyes were changing along with their equipment, and mile-long complexes

of rock and ice, once treated monolithically, were becoming disentangled into their constituent mountain parts.

On August 13, the seven climbers left their camp to attempt the spire Clyde had brought them to climb. The morning sky was blue, but they had little faith in the good intentions of the afternoon. They crossed the glacier—Clyde wrote that "its upper half was rent by a large number of open crevasses," but that "none of these were of any great width"—and reached the cliffs at the base of the mountain wall where the stone shot up out of the ice. Already a number of white clouds had puffed up over the summits, cottony fluff that looked innocuous enough on its own but which signaled gathering forces in the air above. A rockslide had filled the bergschrund at the head of the glacier, and the men crossed over on the freshly piled stones.

They had decided to climb the joint between Starlight Peak and their intended mountain. They roped together in three teams. Loose rubble filled their channel, and the teams all took slightly different paths in order to avoid knocking rocks on each other. Over the easier ground they simul-climbed, but where the joint necked down and its walls steepened they would have paused for belays.

High above the glacier the teams converged at a gap in the ridge, what Clyde called the "great notch" between the two peaks. Ice to the north, lakes to the south, granite rising up to the summits on the left and right—the climbers occupied the crossroads of the landscape. Their mountain claimed the west. "The one which we contemplated climbing," Clyde wrote, "rose in a great granite blade apparently almost sheer." Long, straight cracks, like claw marks through the skin of the rock, reached up along the blade, and the climbers used these for their hands and feet while their ridge narrowed and the free air encroached on both sides and piled up below.

The storm gathered force. "The sky had become overcast and masses of dark, threatening clouds were approaching from the southwest," Clyde added. They hurried on. They had raced so many storms in the past few days, why would they stop now? A buttress blocked their way—the lowest wall of the castle complex barring passage forward along the ridge. Two of the roped teams "swung around the buttress" on an "exposed face with few rounded holds." The rock vanished beneath them, cliffs giving way under their boots, the lakes and stone of the southern quarter laid out like a map below. The third team traversed to a split in the stone walls and climbed up through a narrow gulley. The clouds turned black and pressed down on them from above. They could feel the electricity building in the air all around. The teams converged on the upper summit ridge and threaded along it between spires and jagged outcrops. "The storm," Clyde wrote, "was almost upon us." They hurried to the summit block. Twenty more feet would land them atop the last fourteen-thousand-foot mountain to be climbed in California—and the only one to have ropes used on its first ascent.

But what good would their ropes be for the summit monolith? It was only twenty feet tall, but smooth and sheer on all sides, and tapered to a rounded point at the top. There was nothing magic about the ropes; the climbing still had to be done by hand, and, as it turned out, with their backs and shoulders, too. Underhill called up another trick he had learned in Europe, a *courte échelle*— a shoulder stand. One of the seven—I assume it was Underhill because it was his idea—leaned against the final spire, and one at a time Dawson and Eichorn each had a turn climbing up over his back to get their boots on his shoulders. Balanced there, they reached up to a few small edges set in the stone. With most of their weight on their fingers, they stepped off his shoulders and onto the granite, trusting friction and finger strength, pawing up the edges of the spire until they ran out of stone and perched on the topmost point.

If the sky had been blue and the day unlimited, they would have found a way for all the climbers to visit the true summit. But as it was, they had already waited too long. "Static electricity began to hum and thunder began to crash," Clyde wrote. They dashed east along the ridgeline, looking for shelter. Eichorn was the last in line. "Within five minutes it seemed the storm moved north and enveloped the whole peak," he said, recalling the climb later in life. "There was an unbelievable force of electrical energy around the area." Sparks snapped off the rocks and the climbers. "Jules," Dawson told me, "had an ice axe with him and there were little blue flames coming off it."

"I had never experienced this before," Eichorn recalled. "Clyde felt strongly that we should get off the damn thing immediately." But it was already too late; Eichorn had overstayed his welcome. "I was about twenty-five yards from the pinnacle when suddenly there was a tremendous explosion right in my face. The electric blast immobilized me for a moment." With that stroke from the clouds the mountain earned its name—Thunderbolt Peak.

The bolt had not hit Eichorn directly—it had only "whizzed by" his ear—and he quickly regained his senses. The climbers followed Clyde down the south side of the mountain against a heavy fall of fat snowflakes. The wind came up and hosed the climbers down with the wet snow. Clyde found an overhang large enough to provide shelter from the worst of it, and they all huddled together under the shelf, while the lightning poured through the sky back and forth from summit to clouds. Clyde observed that they were "a rather bedraggled-looking group."

The storm paused and the climbers crossed back over the summit ridge to look for a descent. Snow covered the rock now, and they chose a snow chute on the north side of the mountain which Clyde had examined from below the previous year. Their respite was brief. The storm came back to life and dumped snow and hail into the violent wind. Clyde could hardly see as he felt his way down through the rocks to the top of the couloir. In the confusion an ice axe was dropped and went spinning and bouncing down over the rocks below. A thick layer of fog settled over the mountain as they reached the permanent snow in the couloir, and now the snow underfoot and the mist in the air were the same color and visibility became very poor as more snow dropped out of the sky. Clyde retrieved the runaway axe but found that most of its shaft had snapped off. He began cutting steps down the chute with the axe head, but the mountain warned him back. "A rock," he wrote, "came ricocheting down the ice and was presently followed by another. The storm had loosened the rocks higher up." Muffled by the fog, the stones had burst out on him without a sound. Clyde retreated to the edge of the couloir, out of the blind bowling alley he had unwittingly entered.

The climbers picked their way down through steps of rock next to the ice, but before too long their route cliffed-out above the glacier. Underhill found a granite horn that would hold a loop of rope, and he threaded one of their climbing ropes to set up a rappel. Rappelling, as taught by Underhill, was a serious business. The rope went through the crotch, over one shoulder and around the chest, an uncomfortable but effective arrangement for generating enough friction to control the downward slide of a climber's body—though now their ropes would be slick and stiff with snow. One at a time, the climbers descended the line while Clyde, who had followed Underhill as the first to go, was busy below cutting steps into the steep ice under the cliff wall.

One obstacle remained. On this side of the mountain a wide bergschrund cracked the glacier. Clyde cut steps to its edge, but he still could not see its full depth. "I tossed rocks into the bergschrund," he wrote, "which seemed to strike bottom within a reasonable time." Trusting to the sound of his rocks to tell him the depth of the crack, he looped one of their ropes around a stone sticking up through the ice. Their ropes were not much more than a hundred feet each—which meant that, with his rope doubled over the rock, Clyde had only fifty feet to find the bottom of the bergschrund. He backed down into the crack, "going down the upper steeply-shelving portion gradually, so as to be able to cut a few steps to assist those following . . . or myself, should I be obliged to come back." Thirty feet down, the ice cut away in an overhang. Once he passed beyond the lip he would be hanging free and committed; an upward retreat would be an act of desperation from a body-rappel with iced ropes. But the remaining distance seemed to be only twenty feet, exactly the amount of rope he had left, and the floor appeared solid, so he "swung over the brink and glided down the rope to the bottom."

Luck was on Clyde's side, just as it always had been for him within the confines of the mountains. ("Luck" may only be another word for "intuition.") The up-mountain side of the bergschrund had been fifty feet tall, but the lower lip was only six feet from the floor, and the climbers would be able to scramble out easily. The floor itself was solid where he landed, filled in by rocks and snow from above. But the floor was not uniform. Clyde wrote, "Only a few rods to one side it dropped away indefinitely."

Clyde relaxed in the bottom of the bergschrund and waited for the others. The rest of the glacier was a gentle trudge, and the sky was clearing, though night had fallen. "All real danger past," he wrote, "it was rather amusing to watch one after another as they came over the wall and shot down into the crevasse." When they had all assembled on the flat surface of the glacier, they pulled their rope and coiled the others, and stumbled down off the snow and through the moraine maze, guided by flashlights and the stars, tired through but elated.

Underhill had brought the ropes and the knowledge to make the climb possible. Eichorn and Dawson had provided the raw climbing talent to reach the final summit. Clyde had led them all through the storm. In the following decades, Eichorn and Clyde partnered up on many excursions through the Sierra; but when Eichorn wrote about Clyde near the end of Clyde's life, he thought back to Thunderbolt Peak.

> All of us almost lost our lives . . . Norman proved to be the most remarkable of mountaineers. In weather conditions which included lightning, snow, hail, sleet and rain, plus zero visibility, he got us safely off the peak and down the east face of the crest, where we roped into the bergschrund in total darkness. Then across the heavily crevassed Palisade Glacier to camp, arriving around midnight. This tour de force made me realize how great Norman's mountaineering ability was.

◆ ◆ ◆

MATT, JOE, AND I had no adventures with the weather. Each morning dawned clear and blue with the hypnotic regularity that gives climbers the illusion that storms never touch the Sierra. On one such morning we woke and hiked up toward Thunderbolt Peak with an eighty-foot coil of manila rope and some food in our pockets.

The glacier was frozen and quiet except for a few creeks running down the ice which had not been entirely shut off in the night. I found two preserved dragonflies sparkling in the snow. When we returned later in the day the whole top layer of the glacier was slush underlain by veins of moving water and the creeks had become torrents. Then I found a foaming waterfall tunneling straight down a yard-wide borehole. The lakes down the canyon were flooding despite the drought. The glacier was bleeding—one of Muir's angels looking inescapably mortal.

Where the glacier met the mountain, the retreating ice had exposed freshly chewed granite, a pile of steep rubble covered with pulverized rock dust. We zigzagged back and forth, searching out the least bad rock, keeping out from under each other's fall-lines to avoid getting brained by loose stones. Up higher, the debris thinned out and the mountain's substance came to the surface. The joint between Starlight and Thunderbolt sharpened. Planes of solid stone stretched out to the right and left with us in the angle in between. We bridged up through chimneys, grabbed fingerlocks on the edges of giant chockstones, and picked our way up delicate faces polished by the yearly passage of meltwater and snow.

On our way up and down Thunderbolt we stopped occasionally for belays. Underhill's article featured several pictures showing right and wrong belay positions, which we had examined at the reading rock. In one of the "correct" panels, a gent in a wool jacket and ivy cap, with his knickers tucked into knee-high socks, stands on the edge of a cliff with the rope passed under his right armpit, around his neck, and over his left shoulder, a so-called Forward Shoulder Belay. He leans back from the edge, by perhaps five degrees. He looks steady enough to handle a solid wind-gust in the neighborhood of ten miles an hour. So long as his partner weighs no more than twenty pounds I reckon he'll do fine. Myself, I took a more conservative approach to the belay stance. I looked for ledges with concavities, like bucket seats in the stone, and something solid to put my heels against. Once I had myself wedged in place, I wrapped our manila line around my hips. Matt and Joe climbed with the other end tied in a bowline around the waist. By the time we were done my hips and palms were filled with manila slivers.

Climbers are marvelously immune to good sense. A rope tied around the waist could be used in a dungeon for torturing prisoners. There are stories from the era of broken ribs and suffocations (which I made sure to relate at length while Matt and Joe were climbing). And yet the seat-harness didn't come into wide use until the early 1980s, just as Californians didn't think to use a roped belay for seventy years until it was shown to them.

A rope, even one as rudimentary as ours, does change the entire feel of climbing a mountain. Tied together, we moved as a unit, never more than eighty feet apart, fully dependent on each other's weaknesses and strengths. Underhill understood the change of thought and practice he expected from climbers, and he expounded upon its virtues at some length (he was, after all, a philosophy professor).

> The rope, in its final meaning, is the symbol which transforms an individualistic into a higher social enterprise. A bevy of unroped climbers, attacking a peak each for himself, will enjoy the pleasures of independence and self-sufficiency . . . With the roped party an entirely new set of attitudes and values supervenes . . . The opportunity is fully given for developing comradeship and the consciousness of standing solidly together, under stress, for a common cause. This is one of the finest experiences that mountaineering can afford.

Dawson and Eichorn embraced the new spirit prescribed by Underhill. They developed into close partners as young men, the beginning of a lifelong friendship. "We considered ourselves coleaders," Dawson told me. They alternated leads, sharing the dangers and satisfactions of a difficult climb. At cramped belays where space was limited, the second-man would simply climb right over the top of the one belaying in order to start the next pitch.

Dawson and I talked for a time about Pete Starr. I wondered aloud if the great tragedy of Starr's story was that he died just as he climbed, alone—while others around him found partnerships in the mountains. "Jules and I ended up feeling that we didn't want to climb alone," Dawson replied. "For reasons of safety and companionship, we wanted to do things together."

Gains come with losses. The qualities Underhill attached to the unroped climber—independence, self-sufficiency—can hardly be discarded lightly. Whether he intended it or not, Underhill's tribute to the rope carries the same tune as the question asked by so many of the founding myths of the West: Is the good life to be found in communities pursuing the spirit of mutual purpose and fellowship? Or is it out in the open lands where each individual runs a kingdom of one? Do you picture yourself in the hubbub of a town with storefronts and a main street? Or are you the lone figure on the horse barely visible on a distant hill? This pattern, mythic or not, maps the human landscape of the West, where large cities filled with concentrated humanity are separated by open spaces dotted with determined outsiders. Of course, the spaces in between the cities are not so large as they once were. The mountains offer one of the last refuges to experience aloneness—not just physical, spatial aloneness, but the deep psychological solitude that comes from relying, for a time, on nothing more than the granite and your own hands. Given the rare opportunity the peaks provide, I do not think it wise to spend all of one's time in the mountains tied down.

In the 1930s, Dawson and Eichorn had an ideal climbing partnership, meeting each summer to explore the future of mountaineering, using the new technology to unite their individual strength. For most of his life, Clyde wandered alone, first in the woods of his childhood, then in the mountains, following no compass or calendar but his own will. They are the models, the test cases. I find I need them both—the camaraderie of partnership and the independence of space and silence, the two poles of western existence. In each season I hope for a full life: pleasant conversational days, like the one spent with Matt and Joe on Thunderbolt, laughing at stories of our forebears and ourselves; still, silent days in the company of the mountains, when the world feels empty and enormous; hard days with Ashley moving fast on a difficult climb, barely needing to speak, communicating through motion and shared understanding.

Matt, Joe, and I reached the great notch between Starlight and Thunderbolt, and had our first views of the lakes puddled on the surface of the immense stone basin to the south. Rising to the west, a red-golden ramp of perfect rock led up to the gates of the mountain, where cliffs slammed down to bar the way and pinnacles sprouted above from the upper ridge. We climbed shallow grooves in the golden rock, crawling toward the mountain castle, looking down to the right at ice and down to the left at blue lakes and bare granite.

We passed a tower to the left and found a body-sized chimney to squirm through, popping out on a terrace above the gates and below the spires. We traversed on a ledge high above sharp black ridges which sliced down toward the lakes and channeled updrafts back at us. A shoulder-high wall floated above the drop at the end of the ledge. One shelf on its top edge had been worn smooth by seventy-five years of passing climbers all pressing their hands on the same spot dictated by the geometry of the stone. Hands on the shelf, I drove it down until my hips floated up and my arms went straight; I threw one foot over the top of the wall, and rolled and pressed until another five feet of air had been added to the pile of it below me.

Pinnacles of all shapes and sizes stuck through the mountain's roofline. We passed square ones and jagged ones and some leaning at angles suggesting lightning turned to stone. But none looked quite like the central monolith, a surprisingly round spike of granite ten feet in diameter and twenty feet above the ridgeline, looking like a bishop's hat or a strange flower just beginning to

The author climbing out of the "great notch" between Thunderbolt and Starlight Peaks (Photo by Matt Farrell)

bud. All of those hands and more besides had touched the summit spire, too, but here the presence of past mountaineers was less friendly. The few holds the spire offered were little more than granite glass, and I thought seriously of climbing shoeless because I had so little hope of feeling those slick edges through my hiking boots. In the end I kept my boots on because the thought of falling off barefoot seemed even worse.

I grabbed two opposing rails and sucked my hips up over a high foot nick, commanding my boot to stay put while half expecting it to blow free. Another slippery foothold got me standing and I reached high for two finger-edges, while wondering in the back of my mind just how bad the landing might really be.

I told Dawson I had found the summit spire difficult. He shrugged and looked disappointed with me. "Oh, we shimmied up it pretty easily," he sighed.

Pulling down hard on the edges, I kicked one foot high and rolled onto it, grabbing for the upper curve of the bishop's hat. Scuffing and pawing and adding my own microscopic contribution to the glassiness left by the passing generations of climbers, I scuttled up to the summit and wrapped my legs around the top point, breathing hard through a happy grin.

Joe followed me with a belay from the top. The ankle-eating rocks had supplied me with a powerful disincentive against falling; Joe seemed about equally motivated by the manila noose around his waist. He latched the fingerholds and yanked himself up over the bulge to grab the upper edge of the spire, paddling with his boots till they found the good friction at the top. We crowded in together on the summit, balanced on a pinhead of stone above a world of granite, two contented climbers with a third stretched out in the sun on a rock below.

◆

THE CORE MEMBERS of the Underhill Camp—Clyde, Eichorn, Dawson, and Underhill, with Farquhar in accompaniment—remained together for one more climb that summer, the east face of Mount Whitney. Then they scattered. Farquhar returned to the city and to Marjory. Three years later, when he asked her to marry him, she replied, "You know damn well I will!" They had their wedding in the Yosemite Valley, in the winter, surrounded by snow and granite and their friends from the mountains. Underhill had also fallen in with an accomplished climber— Miriam O'Brien, a pioneer of "manless" climbing, with plenty of hard climbs and first ascents to her credit, particularly in Europe. They spent the summer of 1932 climbing together in the Alps and after that they were inseparable. One day in the fall of 1932, several of Miriam's friends received an issue of *Appalachia* containing her article "Without Men" in the morning mail and read an announcement of her engagement to Robert L.M. Underhill later that same day in the evening paper. Laughing at the pleasant irony of her two paths and their convergence, she wrote, "Manless climbing is fun for a while, but this other arrangement is better!"

Bestor Robinson, one of the seven on the Thunderbolt climb, took his new-found knowledge of ropework to his friend and fellow Sierra Clubber Dick Leonard. Leonard thought about the systems involved, and thought they could be made better (recall the image of the "Forward Shoulder Belay"), so he organized the Cragmont Climbing Club with help from Robinson, Farquhar, and Eichorn. Meeting at outcrops in the hills above Berkeley, Leonard and his friends jumped off rocks to simulate falls, practiced dynamic belays, and studied European climbing manuals; they innovated and experimented until they felt they stood a chance against the enormous—and terrifying—cliffs in Yosemite. After a few years of systematic practice, they took their refinements, ropes, and pitons to the

Yosemite Valley, and the revolution continued. Climbers in each new decade blew the word "impossible" to pieces all over again: the Cathedral Spires were climbed in the '30s, the Lost Arrow Spire in the '40s, the faces of Half Dome and El Capitan in the '50s. These were big, technical, mechanical climbs, using hammers, bolts, and direct aid to make upward progress; the climbs took days, sometimes weeks, to complete.

Glen Dawson lived in Los Angeles, far enough away from Yosemite for a related but separate climbing community to emerge. There, the proving ground was Tahquitz, a steep-sided granite dome towering above the trees and the little town of Idyllwild. Many of the climbers who went on to make Yosemite famous first learned the craft on Tahquitz's hard cracks and insecure faces. In 1938, in the early days of the excitement when the future was again filled with possibilities, the chair of the Angeles Rock Climbing Section of the Sierra Club—one of the descendant branches of the original Cragmont Club—wrote to Underhill to let him know that he was still remembered. The letter called Underhill the "grandfather" of the Rock Climbing Section, and asked him to be an honorary member. Underhill wrote back, clearly touched: "Since your climbers have become the best in the United States the privilege of being connected with them, whether justifiably or not, is one to be hung on to."

With Dawson in Southern California and Eichorn in the Bay Area, the two young men had few opportunities to see each other during the year, but they met each summer in the Sierra to have adventures and climb mountains. They followed this pattern all through the 1930s, until marriages and the Second World War interrupted; then new patterns took shape, and the two met less often in the peaks, more frequently in the cities.

Clyde had nowhere else to be. At the end of the Underhill Camp, he returned to the Palisades and climbed mountains on both sides of the crest for a month. Then he worked his way north and climbed Bear Creek Spire and other peaks in the Rock Creek basin. In November, as the snow returned, he was still climbing high hills west of Bishop and east of the crest from which he could look in on the mountains gathering their winter white.

Clyde was probably the least affected of any of the Californians by Underhill's time in the Sierra. Afterward, when Clyde took a Sierra Club group up a peak, he might offer his flock a belay through a tricky spot, but on his own he climbed much the way he always had, rambling through the mountains, searching out interesting climbing and beautiful stone, pioneering new routes and revisiting old friends. In his later years he figured that he had climbed North Palisade more than fifty times. Competitive fires might be roaring down in the Yosemite Valley as climbers looked for the next hardest climb and the next way to one-up the previous generation, but Clyde never seemed to take too much interest, even though he was very much alive through it all. Apparently, he had no need or want for others to dictate the terms of a challenge; he looked to the mountains for that.

Nowadays, some climbers choose to climb without ropes. Soloing has acquired a fringe reputation—the radical edge of modern climbing populated by lost souls and those missing critical bits of wiring in their brains. No doubt, high-level solos are heart-stopping to contemplate. But the essential impulse of soloing is as old as climbing itself. It reaches back to the original days when the mountains called to Bolton Brown and Jim Hutchinson and Charles Michael. They could not help but take hold of the rock and chase the summit no matter what they lacked in equipment. And the desire to climb alone, on the mountains' terms, in the lonely company of the ice and stone when the human is smallest and the land at its most awesome, persisted in men like Norman Clyde and Pete Starr—one who survived the impulse and one who did not—even after the tools arrived that made climbing alone unnecessary.

◆ ◆ ◆

MATT AND JOE had one more climb planned but I was done. They set out in the early morning for Mount Sill while I gathered up my things by the lake under the glacier.

My pack was full, the straps cinched, but I couldn't leave yet. The mountains and the glacier held me in place. I sat against a rock, facing the summits, listening to the laughter of moraine rocks diving into the lake and the low breath of the wind.

I thought of a line of Clarence King's from his Sierra collection. Looking back to his childhood home in New England, he wrote, "I have been at times all but morbidly aware of the power of local attachment, finding it absurdly hard to turn the key on doors I have entered often and with pleasure." I have lived in so many houses, dorms, and apartments that I can leave one without a backward look and move into another like changing a shirt. But these mountains I cannot leave easily. When I try, my boots stick to the ground and my eyes clutch at the peaks. So I often find myself packed and ready to go but stopped by a force I have learned not to fight.

Eventually the pull loosens, at least enough so that I can get myself upright and pushed into motion. Putting on my pack and pointing myself east and away, I thought of another line, one of Muir's: "Going to the mountains is going home."

Home is no easy thing to pin down in the West, where people come and go and roots get yanked up before they go much below topsoil. The West is still a mythic place, made of epic human migrations and a landscape full of vastness and objects of wonder. It's strange and sad that the word "myth" has become almost pejorative, as if modern man has become too advanced and complex for such naive notions. After all, what are myths if not the stories that express the fundamental workings of the human mind? Calling the West "home" means embracing one or several of the western stories—or writing one's own from the raw materials still in the ground: the bones of Westerners passed, the bones of the earth poking up through the land and into the mind. I find my stories in the mountains.

ACKNOWLEDGMENTS

THIS BOOK COULD not have been written without the manuscript archives of libraries across California—archives that represent an enormous amount of time and devotion on the part of librarians and past researchers who have collected and made accessible the materials I used to recapture this era of climbing. The librarians with whom I have worked have my deep respect and gratitude for their care of materials put in their charge and for the help they have given me. I would particularly like to thank the Bancroft Library at U.C. Berkeley, where I spent many weeks, as well as the Green Library at Stanford, the Holt-Atherton Special Collections Department at the University of the Pacific, the Huntington Library, and the county libraries in Bishop and Lone Pine where I always had a place to read on storm-days.

The written documents of the era have been preserved, and the land has also been protected. All of the mountains and pathways in this book exist inside national parks, national forests, and wilderness areas. Our collective decision to set aside these places not only allows for a thriving American wilderness, but also preserves the history of adventure that is so integral to our nation's past—my thanks to all of you who support our national parks and wild spaces.

The Creative Writing Program at San Jose State University gave me a tremendous amount of support during the years I worked on this project. I would particularly like to thank Cathleen Miller for all of her time and advice, as well as John Engell and Susan Shillinglaw who provided close, attentive readings of my manuscript, and program director Alan Soldofsky.

John Daniel very generously read an early version of my book and introduced me to Jack Shoemaker at Counterpoint Press. Working with the staff at Counterpoint has been a true privilege. My editor, Roxanna Aliaga, refined my writing with remarkable insight and this book has benefited enormously from her attention.

Though I was generally alone on these climbs, I was occasionally joined by good friends; my thanks go to Evan Pearce, Bryan Palmintier, Matt Farrell, and Joe Cackler. Glen Dawson graciously shared his time and memories. Thanks also to my parents, who have been endlessly supportive of both my climbing and my writing, and particularly to my mother, Stephanie Arnold, who was the first person to teach me anything about words and continues to be one of my sharpest readers. Finally, none of this would have been possible without my wife, Ashley Laird, who is my partner in all ways on and off the rock.

NOTES

• 1 •

William Brewer's letters from his time in California are collected in *William Henry Brewer Papers, 1830–1927*, Yale University Library, New Haven, CT; the specific letters included here are from his "diary of a trip to California" letters, in series I, boxes 8 and 9, folders 211–217. A typed copy of the letters is held by the Bancroft Library, University of California, Berkeley, BANC MSS C-B 333 (hereafter cited as Bancroft). The dates of the letters quoted in this chapter are as follows:

"luxurious comforts": September 28, 1863

"mousy": June 26, 1864

"he will do well": May 29, 1864

"Ohio in spring flood": August 17, 1862

"a short year ago": March 25, 1861

"quick trip of news": November 15, 1860

"*water,* more *water*": December 7, 1860

"Glauber's salts and clay": June 4, 1861

"knife at my belt": December 7, 1860

"the work ahead of me": February 24, 1861

"southern Secessionist": July 5, 1863

"than can be described": September 14, 1862

"severely": September 14, 1862

"imagination wander": October 5, 1862

"Stars and Stripes hold jurisdiction": October 26, 1862

"exciting from its danger": June 21, 1863

"any grander than this": June 21, 1863

"grandest chain of mountains in the United States": July 5, 1863

"even if not of plenty": August 24, 1861

"filled with anxiety": June 14, 1864

"rippling of the streams": June 26, 1864

"as I did last summer": June 22, 1864

"900 pounds or more": July 7, 1864

"much abused mule": March 25, 1861

"sublimely grand": July 5, 1863

"almost inaccessible to man": July 7, 1864

"geography of the region described": July 7, 1864

Francis Farquhar describes Charles Hoffman as the "progenitor of modern American topography" in the preface to William Brewer, *Up and Down California*, edited by Francis P. Farquhar (Berkeley: University of California Press, 1974). Josiah Whitney's "mere shepherd" epithet is recorded in Shirley Sargent, "Distant Beginnings," in *Yosemite: The First 100 Years* (Santa Barbara, CA: Sequoia Communications, 1988). Clarence King's description of the Gothic appearance of the mountain and canyon appears in his "Through the Forest," in *Mountaineering in the Sierra Nevada* (Lincoln: University of Nebraska Press, 1970). His suggestion that the silhouette of Mount Brewer did not match up with the view from the Owens Valley appears in "The Ascent of Mount Tyndall" from the same work.

• 2 •

The Clarence King material in this chapter comes from two essays in his *Mountaineering in the Sierra Nevada*: "The Ascent of Mount Tyndall" and "The Descent of Mount Tyndall." William Brewer's description of the parting on the Brewer wall, and his note that King had read John Tyndall, are in "Miscellaneous Notes," *Sierra Club Bulletin* 12 (1927). Bolton Brown's criticism of King appears in his "Wandering in the High Sierra Between Mount King and Mount Williamson," part 1, *Sierra Club Bulletin* 2 (1897). William Ashburner's "confounded little 'blow hard'" line is quoted from a letter in Thurman Wilkins, *Clarence King* (Albuquerque: University of New Mexico Press, 1988), chapter 5; the book is an excellent and comprehensive biography that pointed me toward several other sources.

• 3 •

Clarence King's description of Mount Clark, of the "vulgar gold dirt," and of finding the fossil are from his "Merced Ramblings," in *Mountaineering in the Sierra Nevada*. William Gabb's criticism of King appears in the same essay. King's assessment of the best way for a young man to learn literature comes from his "Artium Magister," *North American Review* (October 1888). His fears of killing a man are from his letter to James

Gardiner, March 18, 1862, HM 27824, Huntington Library, San Marino, CA. Henry Holt's description of Yale appears in his *Sixty Years as a Publisher* (London: G. Allen & Unwin, 1924), page 34; Henry Adams' compliments to King are from *The Education of Henry Adams: An Autobiography* (Boston: Houghton Mifflin, 1918), page 313. Gardiner's letter to his mother describing their first meeting with Brewer is included in Brewer, "Northern Mines," in *Up and Down California,* footnote. The drawing of the ice minaret appears in John Tyndall, "Expedition of 1856," in *The Glaciers of the Alps* (Boston: Ticknor and Fields, 1861). John Hay's praise for King appears in his contribution to *Clarence King Memoirs: The Helmet of Mambrino* (New York: published for the King Memorial Committee of the Century Association by G. P. Putnam's Sons, 1904). King's mother's description of her house as a "veritable museum" is quoted in Wilkins, "Wind's Will," in *Clarence King.*

◆ 4 ◆

The journal became John Muir, *My First Summer in the Sierra,* in *John Muir: The Eight Wilderness-Discovery Books* (omnibus collection of eight Muir books) (Seattle: The Mountaineers, 1992), and the entry for Cathedral Peak can be found in chapter 10. Muir's knowledge of the Bible and the episode with the boat can be found in chapters 1 and 3, respectively, of his *Story of My Boyhood and Youth,* in the preceding omnibus collection. The letter to Alfred Bradley Brown (Hickory Hill, Wisconsin, 1856) is in the John Muir Papers, Holt-Atherton Special Collection, University of the Pacific, Stockton, California, as is the letter to Jeanne Carr ("The Hollow," January 21, 1866). The work of snowflakes is described in John Muir, *The Mountains of California,* in *John Muir: The Eight Wilderness-Discovery Books* (Seattle: The Mountaineers, 1992), chapter 1.

◆ 5 ◆

Muir describes his time with the artists and his climb of Mount Ritter in his "A Near View of the High Sierra," in *The Mountains of California.* He calls himself the "runt of the family" in his *Story of My Boyhood and Youth,* chapter 6. Jesus' conversation with Satan is from Luke 1:1–4; Jesus' instructions to the apostles are in Mark 6:8–9.

• **6** •

Bolton Brown's descriptions of the thunderstorm and of Lucy Brown's efforts to help him light a fire, as well as their climb of Mount Williamson, appeared in Bolton Brown, "In Rational Mountain Costume They Scaled the Dizzy Peaks on a Bridal Tour in Skyland," *San Francisco Examiner,* January 31, 1897. His account of his ascent of Mount Clarence King appears in Bolton Brown, "Wanderings in the High Sierra, Between Mt. King and Mt. Williamson Part II," *Sierra Club Bulletin* 2 (1897). Brown's concerns about segregated art classes are in his letter to David Starr Jordan, January 1900, Jordan Papers, series 1A, box 25, folder 243, Stanford University Archives, Stanford, California. The "thin, but not transparent" line appears in Bolton Brown, letter to David Starr Jordan, March 24, 1901, Jordan Papers, series 1A, box 28, folder 281, Stanford University Archives, Stanford, California. Carl Eric Linden's description of Lucy's eyes appears in Woodstock Historical Society pamphlet, August–September 1937. Ellen Elliot (Bolton Brown's sister) comments on Lucy's beauty in E. C. Elliot, *It Happened This Way* (Stanford, CA: Stanford University, 1940), page 256. Lengthy sections of Bolton Brown's manuscript "Boyhood Memories" are quoted in Clinton Adams, *Crayonstone: The Life and Work of Bolton Brown* (Albuquerque: University of New Mexico Press, 1993). Brown's descriptions of loneliness and of playing naked in the storm-swollen creek come from these passages. Francis Farquhar, in an interview with Ann and Ray Lage, describes Dr. Jordan's summary of the incident with the nude model that caused the early tension between Brown and Mrs. Stanford ("Sierra Reminiscences," volume 1, page 59, BANC MSS 75/26 c, Bancroft). The comments of Mary, Bolton Brown's sister-in-law, regarding his final feeling about his marriage to Lucy, appear in Adams, *Crayonstone,* chapter 12. An early version of Bolton Brown's drawing *Play* occupies a page of his book *The Painter's Palette* (New York: Baker & Taylor, 1913). Adams and I arrived independently at the conclusion that Lucy and Bolton are the subjects of *Play*.

· 7 ·

Joseph LeConte Sr.'s history comes from *The Autobiography of Joseph LeConte* (New York: D. Appleton and Company, 1903). Quoted material as follows: "gloomy in the extreme" (chapter 9); "one-armed pull-ups" (chapter 3).

LeConte Sr.'s descriptions of Yosemite appear in Joseph LeConte, *A Journal of Ramblings Through the High Sierra of California by the "University Excursion Party"* (San Francisco: Sierra Club, 1930). His *Journal of Ramblings* is organized in chronological order: "as the grand old half dome" (July 31, 1870); "clear blue eye" and "This is California!" (August 5, 1870).

The Bancroft Library holds the LeConte Family Papers, BANC MSS C-B 452, Bancroft (hereafter cited as LeConte Family Papers), which includes Joseph LeConte's field notebooks and a variety of family letters.

Helen Gompertz LeConte's description of Bolton Brown following Joseph LeConte to the summit of Mount Gardiner appears in her "Up and Down Bubb's Creek," *Sierra Club Bulletin* 2 (1897). Her description of Brown's arrival in their camp is in Helen Gompertz LeConte and Joseph LeConte journal, July 4, 1899, LeConte Family Papers, carton 1. Helen's witticism about hunger and loneliness appears in the same journal.

Quoted passages from Joseph LeConte, "Recollections: A Few Notes on a Happy Life," handwritten manuscript, LeConte Family Papers, carton 1, volume 47, as follows: "out in Society most of the time" (page 48); "sort of ecstasy" (page 58); "Your father is dead" (page 58); "and never fell once" (April 1949). This document also references the hike of Mount Tallac, LeConte's use of X-rays, the story of the 1906 earthquake, and LeConte's account of traveling through Europe during the onset of the First World War.

For the most egregious example (of many) of Joseph LeConte's environmental callousness, read his *Summer of Travel in the High Sierra* (Ashland, OR: L. Osborne, 1972), the published version of his 1890 journal.

Bolton Brown names North Palisade "Mount Jordan" in his "A Trip About the Headwaters of the South and Middle Fork of the King's River," *Sierra Club Bulletin* 1

(1896). Both Joseph LeConte's 1903 field notebook, in which he calls the peak "Mount Jordan," and his typed version of those notes, in which he changes the name to "North Palisade," are in the LeConte Family Papers, carton 1.

Joseph LeConte's honeymoon journal entry about the Durbrow Party is from the 1901 field journal, LeConte Family Papers, carton 1.

The following letters are in the LeConte Family Papers, box 3:

- Emma LeConte Furman's congratulatory letter to Helen Gompertz LeConte: Georgia, 1900

- Helen's post-engagement letter to Joseph: December 27, 1900

- Joseph LeConte's letter to his mother about his appetite: July 16, 1890

- Helen's letter to Joseph about becoming fat, as well as looking at the moon: September 2, 1903

- Helen's letter to "My Dearest Home People" regarding the First World War: August 25, 1914, The Hague, Holland

The picture showing Joseph LeConte Sr. reclining in the meadow is from Joseph N. LeConte, "Photographs of the Sierra Nevada," album 4, picture 11, BANC PIC 1971.071–ALB, Bancroft.

Joseph LeConte's descriptions of the reconnaissance and climb of North Palisade are from his "The Ascent of the North Palisades," *Sierra Club Bulletin* 5 (1904).

John Muir's assertion "I never left my name" is from his letter to George W. Stewart in *Mount Whitney Club Journal* 1 (1902).

The description of Joseph LeConte's final hours is in James Hutchinson, "Joseph Nisbet LeConte: Some Recollections," *Sierra Club Bulletin* 35 (1950).

◆ 8 ◆

Joseph LeConte's letter to Helen Gompertz LeConte from high on Mount Humphreys is dated July 7, 1898, and is in LeConte Family Papers, box 3. His 1904 field journal in which he honors James Hutchinson's success on Mount Humphreys is also in LeConte Family Papers, carton 1. The suggestion that Hutchinson was LeConte's "man Friday" is in James Hutchinson, "Joseph Nisbet LeConte: Some Recollections," *Sierra Club Bulletin* 35 (1950). Muir's "tired, nerve-shaken, over-civilized people" line appears in John Muir, *Our National Parks*, in *John Muir: The Eight Wilderness-Discovery Books* (omnibus collection of eight Muir books) (Seattle: The Mountaineers, 1992), chapter 1. Joseph LeConte mentions his flying machine article in *The Autobiography of Joseph LeConte* (New York: D. Appleton and Company, 1903), chapter 12. "The heavens declare the glory" is the opening line of Psalm 19. All of Hutchinson's descriptions of Mount Humphreys and the events of the climb are from his "First Ascent: Mount Humphreys," *Sierra Club Bulletin* 5 (1905). Ralph Waldo Emerson's line about horizons is from his "Beauty," in *Nature and Selected Essays* (New York: Penguin Books, 2003).

◆ 9 ◆

Stephen J. Pyne, *Grove Karl Gilbert: A Great Engine of Research* (Austin: University of Texas Press, 1980), is a fascinating biography that I found extraordinarily helpful in understanding Grove Karl Gilbert's science and placement in the scientific community. Pyne explains the idea that Gilbert formulated time as a ratio rather than an arrow (see, in particular, "Time's Ratio" section in chapter 4). Pyne had access to a wide range of Gilbert materials, some of which I have incorporated into this chapter. Gilbert's habit of "studying a great deal when not working" is from a letter by his sister, Eliza Stanley Gilbert, October 4, 1953, quoted in "The Education of a Classicist" section in chapter 1. Gilbert's criticism of Muir as a houseguest is from Gilbert's letter to Arch Gilbert, May 13, 1911, quoted in "Geophysics in the Giant Forest" section in chapter 6. John Wesley Powell's thoughts on mountains as history are from his "Biographical Notice of Archibald Robertson Marvine," quoted in "By Virtue of Its Ensemble" section in chapter 3. Ernest Clayton Andrews' comment on Gilbert's ability to see the "main principle emerging" is from Andrews' letter to Gilbert, August 21, 1918, quoted in "A New Life" section in chapter 6.

Andrews wrote an obituary for Gilbert, which appeared in the *Sierra Club Bulletin* 11 (1920). It is the source of the camp life details from their 1908 trip, including Andrews' logic puzzles and poetry, as well as Andrews' comparison of Muir and Gilbert. Andrews also tells the story of Gilbert's discovery of the Wasatch Fault here.

All the details about the climb of Mount Darwin come from two letters written by Andrews, "Notes and Correspondence," *Sierra Club Bulletin* 12 (1924), except for the following: Willard Johnson's refusal to let Andrews attempt the summit, and Andrews' disobedience, as well as Andrews' thoughts about Clarence King's storytelling, are from Ernest Clayton Andrews, letter to Francis Farquhar, May 14, 1925, Farquhar Papers, BANC MSS C-B 517 Box 1, Bancroft (hereafter cited as Farquhar Papers). Andrews reports that his knees shook in his *Golden Threads*, chapter 21, unpublished autobiography, Andrews Manuscripts, Basser Library, Australian Academy of Science, Canberra.

Anecdotes from Andrews' childhood also appear in *Golden Threads*, and his conclusions about science and satisfaction are from its foreword.

The assessment that as of 1921, the summit tower had yet to see a second ascent appears in Francis Farquhar letter to Andrews, December 12, 1923, Farquhar Papers.

Ernest Clayton Andrews, "An Excursion to the Yosemite (California), or Studies in the Formation of Alpine Cirques, 'Steps,' and Valley 'Treads,'" *Journal and Proceedings of the Royal Society of N.S. Wales* 44 (1910), includes the quoted section of Gilbert's letter to Andrews regarding the psychology of scientific observation.

Grove Karl Gilbert, "Lake Ramparts," *Sierra Club Bulletin* 6 (1907), includes the Utah anecdote about perception and his belief that preliminary training is unnecessary for the study of basic geology. Gilbert's invitation to his 1907 Sierra expedition is quoted in William Morris Davis, "Biographical Memoir of Grove Karl Gilbert, 1843–1918," *National Academy of Sciences Biographical Memoirs* 21, no. 2 (1927).

John Tyndall's visit to the bakery is in his *The Glaciers of the Alps,* chapter 1.

◆ 10 ◆

James Hutchinson's account of the Black Kaweah climb is in his article "Colby Pass and the Black Kaweah," *Sierra Club Bulletin* 11 (1921). The photograph of Duncan McDuffie is in Joseph LeConte's "Photographs of the Sierra Nevada," BANC PIC 1971.071–ALB, album III, Bancroft. The letter to McDuffie regarding the Sierra Ski Club is from Harold Bradley, September 24, 1936, "Sierra Ski Club" folder in 88/15 c, carton 6, Bancroft. My version of *Beowulf* is the 1992 Dover edition translated by R. K. Gordon and edited by Shane Weller.

◆ 11 ◆

Nicholas Clinch describes Francis Farquhar's library as a meeting place for climbers in his obituary for Farquhar in the *American Alpine Journal* 20, no. 1 (1975). Michael Sherrick describes the "torpedo sack" and the first ascent of the Northwest Face of Half Dome in "The Northwest Face of Half Dome," *Sierra Club Bulletin* 43 (November 1958). Royal Robbins describes the spirit of Yosemite in the 1960s in "Yosemite Notes," *Summit* (1970).

Farquhar recorded two oral histories, one in 1958, the other in 1974; both transcripts are held by the Bancroft. The first was done with Willa Baum (BANC FILM 3071); the second with Ann and Ray Lage ("Sierra Reminiscences," volume 1, BANC MSS 75/26 c). Most of the detail of Farquhar's early life comes from the first oral history, as does his memory of the sight of San Francisco across the bay and his recollection of the night with Will Colby. His trip to St. Helena and his certainty that he wanted to live close to Yosemite all his life come from the second oral history. The transcript of Ansel Hall's oral history, including his inoculation with the "Sierra Nevada fever" and the conversation with Farquhar regarding Hall's cabin, is included as an appendix to Farquhar's 1958 oral history.

All of Farquhar's descriptions of the climb of Middle Palisade, including the 1920 Sierra Club outing that served as his reconnaissance as well as the note found at the top of Disappointment Peak, are from his article "The First Ascent of Middle Palisade," *Sierra*

Club Bulletin 11, no. 3 (1922). Hall's homage to John Muir is in Ansel Hall, "The Educational Development of Yosemite National Park," *Sierra Club Bulletin* 11, no. 4 (1923).

The letters between Hall and Farquhar are in Farquhar Papers, box 2. The letters from Farquhar to Lilbourne Winchell are in Farquhar Papers, box 5.

◆ 12 ◆

Enid Michael's description of her husband's cool character appeared in the Out o' Doors section, *Stockton (Calif.) Record,* March 12, 1927; her description of Charles Michael climbing steep rock on Mount Starr King appeared in the same section of the paper on October 6, 1928. I am grateful to Fernando Peñalosa's compendium of Enid's writings (*The Joy of Yosemite* [Rancho Palo Verdes, CA: Quaking Aspen Books, 2004]) for pointing out these two articles. Charles's account of the climb of Michael Minaret, "First Ascent of the Minarets," can be found in the *Sierra Club Bulletin* 12 (1924).

◆ 13 ◆

There are four major sources for biographical information on Norman Clyde: Clyde Papers, BANC MSS 79/33 c, Bancroft (hereafter cited as Clyde Papers); and the introductory essays in the three published collections of Clyde's writings: *Close-Ups of the High Sierra* (Bishop, CA: Spotted Dog Press, 1997); *Norman Clyde of the Sierra Nevada: Rambles Through the Range of Light* (San Francisco: Scrimshaw Press, 1971); and *Twenty-Five Letters from Norman Clyde* (Los Angeles: Dawson's Book Shop, 1998). Occasionally, those who write about Clyde contradict each other or the historical record. One of the best sketches of Norman Clyde's character is a letter written by Smoke Blanchard and included in Clyde, *Rambles Through the Range of Light,* and Blanchard's own memoir, *Walking Up and Down in the World: Memories of a Mountain Rambler* (San Francisco: Sierra Club Books, 1985). General background for Clyde comes from a combination of these sources; specifics are as follows.

The story of the packers' gifts to Clyde's pack is told in the introduction to Clyde, *Close-Ups*. The explanation for why Clyde did not finish his thesis is expressed by Walt Wheelock, the original editor of *Close-Ups*. The material about Winnie and Norman Clyde's marriage is from a new introduction to the 1997 edition of *Close-Ups* written by Wynne Benti.

The description of Norman Clyde's "Palace Hotel" and the "Hospital" are from Smoke Blanchard's letter in Clyde, *Rambles Through the Range of Light*. Also from the letter are the description of Clyde's use of "pithy profanity" and Blanchard's own assessment that Clyde was "not just visiting" the mountains.

Clyde's quote about "going it alone" in his childhood is in the biographical section of his *Twenty-Five Letters*. His suggestion that he writes well but fails to get enough human interest in his work is from his letter to Chester Versteeg, May 15, 1935, in *Twenty-Five Letters*.

Francis Farquhar's description of his first meeting with Norman Clyde is contained in Farquhar's introduction to Clyde, *Rambles Through the Range of Light*. For the mountaineering history of Mount Whitney, read Francis Farquhar, "Mount Whitney," in *History of the Sierra Nevada* (Berkeley: University of California Press, 1965). All of Clyde's correspondence with Farquhar quoted in this chapter is in the "Correspondence" section, Norman Clyde folder, Farquhar Papers. Clyde's assertion that he had no interest in writing about himself is from his letter to Farquhar, September 1964, Norman Clyde folder, Farquhar Papers.

Norman Clyde, "The First Ascent of Mount Russell," *Sierra Club Bulletin* 12 (1927), includes all his descriptions of the climb.

Clyde's essays, most of them unpublished, are in the Clyde Papers. His thoughts about insufficient food are from "Adequate Cooking Utensils on Knapsack Trips," folder 5:30. His description of his handguns as his "most cherished possessions" is from "My Pistols and Revolvers," folder 5:47. Also in folder 5:47 are his essays "Revolvers and Pistols Are Sometimes Useful," which tells the story of the hawk, and "My Colt Woodsman," which includes his desire for something more than a popgun in the case of a holdup, as well as his story of protecting the "two defenseless women." Clyde's suggestion that "it shouldn't disturb you whether it's ten feet down or ten thousand" is from a collection of Norman Clyde quotes in folder 5:55.

· **14** ·

Norman Clyde's correspondence with Francis Farquhar, quoted in this chapter, is from the "Correspondence" section, Norman Clyde folder, Farquhar Papers, Bancroft. Clyde writes about his misgivings at the University of Southern California in a letter dated March 15, 1929. Farquhar's reply, offering his contacts in the national parks, is dated March 25, 1929. The "crisis" letter is dated October 6, 1929. The letter explaining his acceptance of Walter Starr's check is dated September 4, 1933. On October 30, 1930, Clyde writes that he is on his way, even though he doesn't know where he is going. The woodpile letters are dated November 3 and 30, 1930. Clyde writes that he has gotten down to his writing, on January 3, 1931.

Clyde's description of "most editors" is in his letter to Chester Versteeg, March 3, 1933; and the "crayfish" aspersion appears in his letter to Glen Dawson, November 30, 1937; both letters are included in Clyde, *Twenty-Five Letters*.

Clyde's description of a tumbling climber is in "Old Man of the Sierra," *Time*, June 20, 1960. Going "off on a tangent from society" is in "Grizzled Mountaineer on Top of the World," *Los Angeles Times*, September 22, 1963.

Many details come from Smoke Blanchard's letter in Clyde, *Rambles Through the Range of Light*, including these: Norman Clyde, the "gentleman"; Clyde's losing his power of speech; the description of Norman Clyde Peak out the cabin window; "*wild, aloof, dignified, difficult*"; parody of Clyde and his anvil; "at least one right and proper piece of equipment"; rubber on rock, steel on ice; Clyde's reading list in 1971. The story of Clyde's ashes is from "Norman Clyde," in Blanchard, *Walking Up and Down the World*.

For an excellent account of the search for Pete Starr's body, read William Alsup, *Missing in the Minarets* (Yosemite National Park, CA: Yosemite Association, 2001). For the story of the dedication to Winnie Clyde, read Wynne Benti's foreword in Clyde, *Close-Ups of the High Sierra* (1997 edition).

Norman Clyde's story about riding avalanches is in his "Snowslides in the Sierra Nevada," in *Rambles Through the Range of Light*. His assessment of the beauty of snow and clouds on the mountains is in his "Sierra Clouds Weave Beauty Around Peaks," *Motor Land* (April 1936). His story of the hummingbird in the snow is from his "The Humming Bird Along the Crest of the Sierra Nevada," Clyde Papers, carton 4, folder 32. His description of his Kelty pack is in his "Afoot Along Mountain Trails," Clyde Papers, carton 5, folder 32.

All the details of the first ascent of Norman Clyde Peak are from Norman Clyde, "Up the Middle Palisade," *Touring Topics* (1931).

Clyde's account of the crevasse-leaping accident is in an interview with Hervey Vogue and Bob Swift, December 21, 1967, transcript in Clyde Papers, carton 1, folder 7. Clyde's "hibernation" quote is from an interview with Hervey Vogue, December 31, 1967, transcript in Clyde Papers, carton 1, folder 10. Harold Crowe summarizes Clyde's ability to find corpses in an interview with Richard Searle, "Sierra Club Reminiscences," volume 2, BANC MSS 75/26 c, Bancroft.

Glen Dawson's description of his father's friendship with Clyde is from an interview by the author, April 1, 2008.

⋄ 15 ⋄

Francis Farquhar describes his trip to Canada in 1930, the ascent of Unicorn Peak in 1931, and the beginning of his relationship with Marjory Bridge in his oral history interview with Willa Baum, BANC FILM 3071, Bancroft. The first proper use of the roped belay in the Sierra was probably made by John Mendenhall and Max Van Patten on Laurel Mountain in 1930. Farquhar describes the Underhill Camp time in the Palisades as their "post-graduate course" in his "The Sierra Club and the High Sierra," in *History of the Sierra Nevada*. Jules Eichorn's "whizzed by" quote, referring to the proximity of the lightning, appears in this same chapter. Marjory Bridge's reply to Francis Farquhar's marriage proposal is from the Marjory Bridge Farquhar oral history transcript, BANC CPF 023, Bancroft.

Norman Clyde describes Bob Underhill as an expert rock climber in Clyde, "First Ascent of the East Face of Mount Whitney," in *Rambles Through the Range of Light*. Clyde's thoughts on the progression of mountaineering are from the same essay. He calls himself "not over-endowed with precaution" in his "Up the North Face of Mount Humphreys," in *Rambles Through the Range of Light*. His letter to Francis Farquhar about Thunderbolt Peak, July 9, 1931, is in Farquhar Papers. Clyde's description of the climb of Thunderbolt Peak is in his "The First Ascent of Thunderbolt Peak, the North Palisade," in *Rambles Through the Range of Light*.

The anecdote describing Jules Eichorn's relationship with Ansel Adams comes from Eichorn's obituary, by Cameron Burns, in *Climbing* 196 (August 2000), as does Eichorn's quote about music and the mountains. Eichorn's appreciation of Clyde's skill as a mountaineer appears in Jules Eichorn, prologue in Clyde, *Rambles Through the Range of Light*. Eichorn's description of the thunderbolt is from his recollections of the event, in "Thunderbolt," *Sierra Echo* 33, no. 6 (November–December 1989).

Bob Underhill compliments Glen Dawson and Jules Eichorn in his "Mount Whitney by the East Face," *Sierra Club Bulletin* 17 (1932). Underhill's comprehensive article on roped climbing technique appears in the *Sierra Club Bulletin* 16 (1931). Miriam Underhill describes her husband's opinion of accident victims in Miriam Underhill, "Skiing," in *Give Me the Hills* (her memoir) (Riverside, CT: Chatham Press, 1971). The same book includes the story of their engagement announcement ("Dent Blanche by the Viereselgrat") and her line about manless climbing ("Manless Climbing"). Howard Koster (Rock Climbing Section chair), letter to Bob Underhill, October 25, 1938, and Underhill's reply are in Bill Oliver, "Passing the Torch," *Sierra Echo* 52, no. 2 (April–June 2008).

Clarence King's line about home appears in "Shasta," in his *Mountaineering in the Sierra Nevada.* John Muir's line about home is in his *Our National Parks,* chapter 1.

Glen Dawson, interview by author, April 1, 2008.

Among those who care, there is debate over whether Thunderbolt Peak and Starlight Peak are separate mountains or sub-summits of North Palisade. Those who try to climb all of California's fourteeners generally include Thunderbolt and Starlight, while those attempting the highest hundred peaks in the contiguous United States do not. Criteria used in these discussions are inevitably arbitrary. By the most frequently employed rule—that a mountain should have three hundred feet of prominence— neither Thunderbolt nor Starlight would be a separate peak. Personally, I find this kind of numeric subdivision somewhat pointless and distasteful. I would rather think of a mountain in light of its uniqueness, individual character, and history. By these entirely subjective measures, Thunderbolt would certainly be its own mountain, while Starlight would probably not be.